If You Leave Me,
Can I Come with You?

If You Leave Me, Can I Come with You?

Daily Meditations
for Codependents and Al-Anons
(with a Sense of Humor)

Misti B.

Hazelden
Publishing

Hazelden Publishing
Center City, Minnesota 55012
hazelden.org/bookstore

ISBN: 978-1-61649-615-9

Library of Congress Cataloging-in-Publication Control Number:
2015024209

Editor's Notes
This book was formerly titled *If You Leave Me, Can I Come with You?
365 Humorous Daily Meditations for Al-Anons and Codependents*.

In the process of being reissued in 2021, *If You Leave Me, Can I
Come with You?* has undergone minor editing updates.

The Checklist for Maturity quoted on pp. 182–183 refers to
"A Checklist for Evaluating Our Maturity" in *Alcoholism, the Family
Disease* (Virginia Beach, VA: Al-Anon Family Groups, 2005).

25 24   2 3 4 5

Cover design: Theresa Jaeger Gedig

For Mom and Dad,
with whom the journey began.
May you be at peace.

God, grant me the serenity
to accept the things I cannot change,
courage to change the things I can,
and wisdom to know the difference.

Acknowledgments

I decided to write this book for no other reason than to keep myself from losing my mind after having bottomed out emotionally in Al-Anon. I started writing stories about recovery and reading them to my friends, who encouraged me to put them in print.

I believe it is possible to find happiness and joy on the road to recovery. And although my Al-Anon home group is rife with laughter, I've been to some meetings where, well, there's not a lot of smiling going on. I wrote these meditations for those who might feel a need for more humor—and who couldn't use more laughter?

I'd like to thank everyone who has participated in my recovery, in particular my sponsor, Corinne, and those special friends in the program who've taken my (many) calls and loved me on this journey. I owe you so much more than I'll ever be able to return.

Thank you, God, for giving me the words. You have never failed me.

In spite of myself,
Misti B.

Introduction

Al-Anon saved my life. For someone like me who tends to embellish, I promise that's not an exaggeration.

I'll spare you the gory details, because if you continue reading you'll find out soon enough, but also because people seldom read book introductions. I mean, what is there to say, really? I could cut and paste a paragraph from Charles Dickens's *A Tale of Two Cities* here and no one would even notice. But I strive to live a program of rigorous honesty, so I won't do that.

What you really want to know is: Why should you read this book?

Well . . . let's face it, we codependents and Al-Anons aren't especially known for our humor. (Go ahead, do an online search for "Al-Anon" or "codependent" and "humor" or "funny.") While I identify as an Al-Anon, I include codependents in the title because they'll definitely relate.

As the silent sufferers—the hall monitors—of the recovery community, Al-Anon and codependent lives are the stuff of country music lyrics. We've got a reputation for taking the fun out of a party and popping all the balloons afterward.

Until now.

If You Leave Me, Can I Come with You? was written to bring humor to anyone recovering from the harsh realities of addiction. It's high time we threw a party in honor of our own growth! Alcoholism and other addictions are serious problems—and yet I'm totally convinced laughter is a sign of healing.

If this book reaches just one person and gives them some relief, then I've been of service. Honestly, I'd rather it reach millions, but as a codependent Al-Anon, it's important for me to keep my expectations at a minimum.

I hope you laugh, or at the very least, smile a bit. And if you don't, please don't be mad at me. I hate it when people are mad at me.

An Important Note

For simplicity's sake, I use the term "Al-Anon" throughout this book, as it is my primary Twelve Step program, and it has provided much of the inspiration and wisdom that this book offers. However, I include codependents in my definition and descriptions because, while it's possible to be codependent without being in a relationship with an alcoholic or an addict, most Al-Anons *are* codependent, and we share many of the same behaviors and characteristics. Many codependents attend Co-Dependents Anonymous (CoDA) Twelve Step meetings, which share similar insights, principles, and practices with Al-Anon.

JANUARY

New Beginnings

Happy New Year's Day! Today is the first day of the rest of your life. It truly is the beginning of the beginning—unless you're following the Mayan calendar or something. But let's not try to cover all the bases and keep everybody happy. We all know where *that* leads. For Al-Anons, few other holidays bring this much hope, because today Al-Anons from all walks of life rally to the internal cries of "Finally! A chance to fix my life *and* everyone else's!"

The New Year provides Al-Anons the rare opportunity (and a very welcome chance) to offer unsolicited advice to others and to discuss the things we find lacking in our loved ones. We begin with the gentle, totally non-leading question: "Speaking of New Year's resolutions, do *you* have any?"

If ever there were a day for Al-Anons to cut loose and embrace their need to control *everything* and *everyone* around them, it would be today!

New Year's is the nationally designated day to turn over a new leaf. Together, we *will micromanage* the change we want to see in the world. Especially because *we* aren't hung over! Hung up, perhaps, but never, ever hung over.

In spite of myself:

Of course I'll read one hundred books
and get *him* to lose ten pounds by July.

1

Powerless

Step #1: "We admitted we were powerless over alcohol—that our lives had become unmanageable."

Early on in recovery—okay, later on as well—I thought my powerlessness would be diminished in time. As in, the more recovered I was, the less powerless I would be over people, places, and things.

There's a part of me that wants, above anything else in this entire world, to be in control. Of everything. Of myself, you, the nation, the industrial complex, and the European Union. Heck, I'd manage the whole darn solar system if I could.

There's this voice in my head that whispers things like, *Someday, you'll have it figured out, and you'll be able to manage your life. You won't need meetings, and you'll be able to lighten up on the whole "spiritual" part of things.*

In reality, I know zero about the world's economy, I barely passed astronomy in college, and when I look at the results of trying to manage life by myself, it's clear I should not be listening to that voice in my head.

Instead, I'll stop, pray, and remember that voice is wrong about this particular issue. I might even have to tell that voice to shut the heck up! And at times, I may need to use harsher language. With my voice, that is.

In spite of myself:
God, help me shut the front door on that voice!

Yells

You can't hear anyone else when you're yelling.

For instance, just the other day, I was in a yelling match with the overly tanned, juiced-up manager of my gym. As things got more heated between us, I began to lose perspective about what was happening. I could feel the other people in the weight room watching us, but they didn't seem real. And the louder we yelled, the more faint the other people became, like holographic images. It's as if our raging had sucked all the life out of the room.

Anger is my primary character defect. It has affected my life in countless ways, none of them good, and yet I still struggle with keeping my big mouth shut. In recovery, I've learned that even if someone else is freaking out, I don't have to react in the moment, or at all. I can step back and take a deep breath before responding to someone else's anger. Or, I can walk away without responding at all.

When I react to someone else's anger with anger or irritation or sarcasm, it never, ever ends well. Ultimately, it leaves a trail of hurt and an emotional hangover that lingers for days. And it makes juiced-up, macho gym managers want to punch me.

In spite of myself:

God, please help me engage my ears
before opening my mouth.

Short

When I first heard someone say "Life is short," I was six years old. I immediately began to fear my mortality. *Am I going to die soon?* I wondered. Then I started obsessing. *Am I living every moment to its fullest? Am I squeezing all the fun I can out of first grade?*

As a kid, I would worry about things like being on my deathbed and saying, "I wish I'd played harder, eaten more Atomic Fireballs, and worked less." Adorable little codependent-in-training that I was, fearful thoughts constantly consumed me: *Am I unconsciously doing something to keep myself from being happy? What else could I be doing to wrestle more satisfaction from life?*

Even today, when I hear the phrase "Life is short," I want to scream, "No, it's not! Bad days go on forever, and the only days that seem to fly by are when I'm on vacation!"

Yes, it's important for me to remember that time is precious, and to ask my Higher Power to help me live in this moment, because it's all I really have.

But enough already with the reminders that I'm not going to live forever, because warning me that life is short does nothing to help—in fact, it stresses me out. And according to a well-known government agency (yes, that one), stress related to running out of time is the number one factor in hospital visits for codependents over the age of six.

In spite of myself:

I'll live for today, but not because I'm running out of time.

Other People

"I think there's something wrong with me," I said when my turn came to share in the Al-Anon meeting. "I'm beginning to dislike other people. And when I say 'other people,' I mean *everyone*."

Since I had already put my foot in it, I continued to disclose my growing impatience with "other people." And I didn't mean just the folks close to me, but humanity in general. I had started to loathe people I hadn't even met yet! "Other people" were my problem.

When the meeting ended, I expected to be told I wasn't welcome at that meeting anymore. After all, Al-Anon was for namby-pamby types who loved too much, and there was no way in heck I'd be mistaken for one of those mousy, beaten-down enablers who loved too much! Except I did love too much—I just wasn't mousy about it.

Instead of being escorted out of the room and asked not to return, I got plenty of hugs and smiles from the group. Two people even came up to me and said, "I feel the exact same way. Other people annoy me too!"

It made me pause. If so many people felt that way about "other people" in their lives, might I be someone else's "other people"? I mean, it's bizarre to think that *I* could be labeled as other people's "other people," because I'm normally a very lovable person. Especially when people don't know me.

In spite of myself:

I'll notice whom it is I label "other people" today.

Hall Monitors

I can always identify the former hall monitor in an Al-Anon meeting. They're well organized, and they know all the rules about officer elections and other "official" Al-Anon-type things. They're big on "shushing" people who talk in meetings.

In school, they were the orderly ones with freshly pressed clothes and exceptional handwriting. I envied the way they stood quietly in line like little soldiers, and how they seemed to thrive on structure. So annoying.

I grew up in the chaos of alcoholism, and as a result, I was often sent home with notes from teachers saying I talked too much. So I accepted the fact that I'd never be hall monitor material. And while I never *really* wanted to be a hall monitor, I would have at least liked to have the chance to say "no" to the opportunity.

Because of my participation in Al-Anon, I've been forced to work with more than my fair share of hall monitors. And surprisingly, I've found some of them to be quite nice. Now, instead of ignoring them or running away from them, I'm learning to appreciate them.

Without hall monitors, meetings would be chaotic; no one would organize holiday parties or make sure the "no texting during meetings" suggestions are enforced. Truth be told, the hall monitors have begun to rub off on me. I actually "shushed" someone who was talking during a meeting last week.

In spite of myself:

I'll show some love for the hall monitors in my life today.

Motion

According to Newton's first law of motion, an object at rest tends to stay at rest, and an object in motion tends to stay in motion. When an object is moving, it will remain in motion until an outside force acts upon it.

From this point, there's a lot of really scientific-sounding theory and physics talk—information I'm not prepared to go into. My point is this: The Al-Anon brain is similar to the "object" in this example. When my brain gets going, especially if it's been fueled by any strong emotion—fear, pride, jealousy, or a juicy resentment—it's gonna keep going. And it'll continue until it's done the mental equivalent of a five-hundred-meter sprint in four seconds.

But it doesn't stop there. My brain then wants to do a hundred pull-ups, swim the English Channel, and jog up Mount Everest.

My brain isn't prepared to handle that much activity without the help of a Higher Power. It's like assuming I'm ready to compete in a triathlon because I can stroll to the mailbox. When my brain goes into overdrive, I need to slow myself down, ask for guidance from God, and consciously give my brain a break. Sometimes that includes paying close attention to a mundane task. Sometimes it means listening closely to the sounds created by the movements I make while I observe my own actions. Amazingly, when I do slow down, I'm able to hear my Higher Power and more likely to make good decisions. Unless they involve math or science. I rarely make good decisions when they come down to math or science, no matter how calm I am.

In spite of myself:
Today I will give my brain a break.

Peace Out

"If it works, don't fix it," the hipster was sharing at the meeting. Frankly, I wasn't paying much attention because I was engrossed in the tattoos on his neck and the massive gauges in his ears. But I heard the part about not fixing things that aren't broken.

Wait. Something is working, so I should leave it alone? Clearly this slacker has never toyed with the notion of work, so what could he know about the subject?

I wanted to interrupt with, "This guy's obviously an imposter. If he were a *real* Al-Anon, he wouldn't be settling for things that *just work*." Maybe I could steer him in the right direction.

"I enjoyed your share," I said sweetly when the meeting was finished. "Are you sure you wanted an Al-Anon meeting?"

"Yeah, why?" he asked, reaching for a donut.

"You might want to give working and fixing a little more . . . respect."

"I think what you mean is 'control,'" he said, wolfing down the donut. "It's not our job to fix anything or anyone else."

"I think you misunderstood the spirit in which my comment was intended," I said.

"Oh no, I understood you perfectly. Peace out," he said as he turned away.

"Peace out is right, dude!" I yelled back. Slacker boy kept on walking.

It's about time someone stood up for making the world a better place. I mean, just because things aren't broken doesn't mean they can't be improved. At least a little.

In spite of myself:

Let's give some love to fixing things that could work better!

Playing God

Today is Play God Day. There is no "official" information on the origination of this holiday, but let's not let details like that keep us from participating.

I rather enjoy playing God because I'm reasonably good at it. I know all about world cuisine, I'm familiar with classical and modern literature (Socrates, Shakespeare, and nearly *anything* Oprah recommends), and I'm an exceptional judge of character. As for style, my sorority awarded me the title "Most Likely to Make Emily Post Jealous."

But enough about me. Play God Day is the perfect way to do good for others, which is what we Al-Anons love to do, unless other people get in the way and screw things up.

To commemorate Play God Day, do something that will make a positive difference in someone else's life. It could be something simple, like visiting a family member who is ill or helping a neighbor. You can start small—for example, last year I reupholstered my sister's hideous orange tweed couch while she was at work. My friend had the exterior of her mother-in-law's house painted while she was away on vacation. I even have a friend who spent the day pretending he was a doctor, but that's not recommended.

I do recommend that you honor the fact that other people need help. They just don't know it. But don't let that hold you back because Play God Day gives you absolute permission and total authority to express the part of yourself that is all-knowing and all-powerful. But I bet you've already had plenty of practice at that.

In spite of myself:

I love playing God because I'm so good at it!

9

Probable Cause

I used to freeze up whenever I'd see a police car in the lane next to me, even if I didn't happen to be talking on the phone, texting, or applying mascara. I had no warrants or outstanding tickets, and aside from being a little vague about whether my insurance was current, I had no real reason to be afraid of law enforcement. I was just uneasy around authority figures.

The moment I'd see an officer of the law, panic would set in, and I'd start rehearsing what I was going to say when they pulled me over. Even if they didn't turn on the flashing lights, I'd start obsessing over things I hadn't done in years! Being stuck in front of a squad car at a traffic light could screw up my entire afternoon.

Now that I'm working an Al-Anon program, I realize I don't have to avoid or fear people in authority simply because they have authority. Especially if *I've done nothing wrong.*

That pervasive, low-level anxiety is not nearly as strong as it was. I know I'm doing the best I can every day and I have nothing to be ashamed of. I'm no better or worse than anyone else, and I don't have to fear someone who appears to have more power than me.

In fact, nowadays, I can look at a police officer and smile instead of cringe. Sometimes, I even wave at them. Okay, I don't wave anymore. I tried that once, and I got pulled over.

In spite of myself:
I have nothing to fear, except when I really do.

Interpretations

Al Capone's business card said he was a "used furniture dealer."

My ex-boyfriend's business card said he was a dentist. Truthfully, he was a dentist, but he was also under investigation for stealing money from his business partners. And he turned out to be engaged to another woman when he proposed marriage to me. These things he did *not* tell me.

Early on in our relationship, he told me of his passion for wanting to save the world through better dentistry.

So, when he told me he was working until midnight giving free fillings to local orphans, I believed him, probably like Al Capone's significant other believed he sold used furniture.

Alas, things aren't always what they appear to be, and there's a part of me that doesn't want to know when they aren't. Looking too deeply into "situations" can be untidy and painful, and I prefer tidy and painless. Or, as some people might say, *I'm not really fond of reality.* Although I want to believe what the business card says, I've found it's better to watch what people do over time, because the titles they give themselves don't always match up with what they do. Titles are subject to interpretation, and if I pay attention, the truth will be revealed in time. It's not always easy, because I genuinely believe people are who they say they are . . . unless they claim to be a "dentist"—that always gives me pause.

In spite of myself:
I'll remember that the titles people give themselves
are subject to interpretation.

Boundaries

Pardon me, but that thing you're stepping on? It's called a "boundary." I realize you didn't even know I had boundaries until just now, but you are hereby on notice that I am going to start setting them. Limits, that is.

I know, this might seem to be coming from out of the blue, but the truth is, you've committed quite a few boundary violations, and I think it's time to let you know. Many of your habits are like nails on a proverbial chalkboard. And, according to one of the self-help books I'm reading, it's time I told you about my feelings and about the ways in which you're a boundary violator. I mean, you wouldn't want me to hold all this in and then, BAM! One night I smother you in your sleep. Ha ha. Of course, I would never, ever do that.

I've been told that establishing these boundaries will greatly improve our relationship. And, by the way, that face you're making? It's a serious boundary violation. So you need to cut it out. Right now. And no more eye rolling.

And, if you don't mind, could you please step back a few feet? A teensy bit farther? Just a smidge more? I'm feeling crowded.

So . . . I think this boundary-setting thing is going to work out for us—I already feel better, don't you? Wait, before you answer that, can you back up just a tad?

In spite of myself:
Perhaps I'll define my boundaries with Post-it Notes
instead of police tape.

The One

I knew you were the one for me when the sheriff put you in handcuffs.

Frankly, when I met you last week, I wasn't even sure I liked you. But tonight, with the sirens blaring, the crowd gathering, and the way you staggered over to me and kissed me on the cheek, I suddenly found you very attractive. So vulnerable. So much passion and substance. Almost irresistible.

I'd never noticed that dimple in your chin. It's very sexy.

The sobbing and drooling are a bit of a turn-off, but since you whispered, "You complete me" and told me I was everything you ever needed, well, despite my better judgment and your stale whiskey breath, I really, really like you. And it's not because you're going to jail, either.

Yes, I believe this is the first time this has ever happened to you. And, absolutely, we can work on things while you're in jail, or prison, or wherever you end up. I mean, really, don't all new relationships require some work? Isn't everyone a work in progress? And, what is love without a little bit of pain?

Of course, darling, I'll be waiting for you when you get out. I have such a good feeling about the two of us. I think you just might be the one for me.

In spite of myself:

Is that feeling I'm having burning love—or searing pain?

Nile Denial

Okay, so I'm new to all this recovery stuff, but several times this past week, in various meetings, I'm sure I've heard someone say something like, "De Nile's not a river in Egypt."

Ummm . . . excuse me . . . but the Nile is a river in Egypt. It is a river, and it's a darn big one at that. What is wrong with these people? Didn't any of them show up for geography class in high school? Were they too busy getting fitted for veneers? This is L.A., after all.

Are these folks just plain stupid?

Ah, here we go again. The woman sitting two rows in front of me just said, "De Nile's not a river in Egypt."

Maybe it's the meetings I'm going to. Maybe these Al-Anon types aren't into maps. Perhaps they teleport themselves around town. Or maybe they don't have access to history books or a world atlas. I have no idea, but the propagation of this fallacy about the Nile, the longest river on the planet, is driving me bonkers!

Maybe it's time I check out some meetings on the other side of town. Because if I hear that Nile cliché one more time, I'm going to have to politely offer the group a quick geography lesson.

Better yet, I'll just carry a globe with me to meetings.

In spite of myself:

What? You're telling me the saying is "De Nile's not
just a river in Egypt?" Oh. Well, then . . . never mind.

Don't . . . Do It!

Despite what the Nike ads say, "Just do it" is not the best advice for an Al-Anon. "Just doing" *anything* can be a slippery slope. Whenever I start making major decisions without getting direction from my Higher Power and feedback from people I love and trust, things go downhill pretty fast. I can't ever "*just do it.*"

I've written a letter to the executives at Nike, to see if they would consider changing their campaign from "Just do it" to something more thoughtful, like, "Don't . . . just do it," or "Just do it, but wait twenty-four hours first." Even better, "Just do it, but consider the consequences."

In the meantime, I've put a Post-it Note with the word "DON'T" over the picture of the tennis superstar that's taped up on my refrigerator. It's a reminder for me to stop and think before I "just" call, text, stalk someone online, or quit my job without a backup plan. And a reminder that you don't get six-pack abs by standing in front of a refrigerator.

I haven't heard from any executives at Nike, but I feel certain that I will. Maybe I'll see a new Nike ad featuring my clever idea in a magazine or on a billboard somewhere soon. Not to worry—I'm just grateful that a major advertiser can be the recipient of the inspiration I've experienced in recovery.

In spite of myself:
Today, I *won't* . . . just do it.

Puzzled

I was listening to a woman explain the experience of recovery by analogy. She said that each of our lives is like a puzzle piece. As we recover and change, we don't always fit into the old puzzle in the same way we used to.

"So, if I change and I don't fit the old puzzle anymore, and the other pieces of the puzzle don't change, then what?" I asked her.

"Then," she said, "sometimes we have to find another puzzle to fit into, metaphorically speaking."

That really burned me.

"But I don't want to find another puzzle! I want things to fit into the puzzle I have, the one with the pieces spread out all around me, *metaphorically speaking*," I snapped.

"Just because we don't like something doesn't mean it isn't so," she replied, smiling. "It may take time, but believe me, you *will* find the puzzle where you fit perfectly."

I wanted to say, "Look, lady, I've spent thousands of hours, and tens of thousands of dollars on my particular puzzle, and I have no inclination to go out and find a new one. I'd prefer the puzzle I have just work around the 'new' me." But I didn't. I've learned that my sharp wit is not always well received in these so-called "teachable moments."

Yes, a good analogy can go a long way, but I'm a pretty simple person, so I've decided to steer clear of people who offer wisdom in the form of analogies, allegories, or puzzles. Mostly because I don't understand them, and I have no clue how to integrate them into real life. Non-metaphorically speaking, that is.

In spite of myself:

God will find the place I fit best, no matter how puzzled I am.

Trains

If a train doesn't stop at your station, then it isn't your train.
—Marianne Williamson

I used to spend a lot of time chasing trains. It was painful, running after trains that hadn't stopped at my station. Hopping on and off of moving locomotives is exhausting. And it's hard on the knees.

I no longer chase after moving trains. Yes, there have been a few I've been tempted by, trains I was 100 percent convinced were going to stop to pick me up—but they didn't. I've also stood by, heartbroken as the perfect Pullman entered the station, slowed down for a moment, and then kept chugging down the tracks, leaving me in the dust. The shame of throwing myself on the tracks for something that wasn't mine has led to some messy, dramatic scenes.

Al-Anon has taught me to trust that, despite my protestations, there's a Higher Power in charge of the train schedule, and the schedule rarely, if ever, gets posted ahead of time. I can get all aggravated about it, or I can buy a hot pretzel and peruse the selection of Kenny G CDs in the gift store while I'm waiting at the station.

No one said waiting for the right train would be easy. In fact, it can be torturous at times. But if it isn't stopping at my station, then it's not my train. I refuse to jump onto moving locomotives anymore. Especially if they aren't going to slow down for me. A complete stop would be preferred, of course.

In spite of myself:
I'll resist the urge to chase trains—
or *anything* that's moving—today.

New Glasses

There's a book based on a talk given by a man named Chuck, about how recovery is like getting a new pair of glasses. He suggests that as we heal, our perspective changes and we look at the world differently. When we pick up a "new pair of glasses," we see the world with more love and compassion.

When I put my glasses on, they tend to home in on what's wrong with everything in sight and how much work it's going to take for me to fix it.

While "seeing the world through the eyes of compassion" sounds like lyrics to a groovy easy-listening song, I'm an Al-Anon, and I need to rely on my Higher Power from the moment I wake up if I want to see the world with that kind of loving perspective.

I call it an exceptional day if I can maintain a loving attitude throughout breakfast. Sometimes, I'm all out of love before I've even gotten out of bed. On those days, I say, "God, here are my glasses. I'll let you look through them today." This generally works out really well because I wear contact lenses.

In spite of myself:

God, you can have my glasses *and* my contact lenses—today.

Almost Famous

Marco and I had been best friends since middle school. We'd seen each other through the trauma of musical auditions, horrible breakups, and even more painful breakouts.

Aside from offering each other misguided advice about dating, we talked about little other than ourselves and our jobs. Our relationship was delicately held together, tightly bound by a frayed cord and a chance that one of us would become famous, or die in a fiery crash on Mulholland.

In truth, if I were in a fiery crash, I wouldn't think of calling Marco. He wouldn't pick up the phone if it would interfere with his beauty sleep.

When I found Al-Anon, most of my relationships were like the one I had with Marco—shallow and not so stable. I'd become fixated on success and winning, and my true friends were rare, mostly because I wasn't willing to be authentic. I only wanted to be known for my accomplishments—that's all I thought I had to offer my friends.

I'm not totally over the need to win (some defects die hard), but my friendships today are beautiful and precious. They aren't based on any of us becoming rich or famous, or a fear that one of us may die soon in a fiery crash. They're built on mutual trust and acceptance, kindness, generosity of spirit, and knowing that we can count on each other when things get rough.

While I still do my best to schedule my crises during daylight hours, I don't have to anymore because I can always count on my Al-Anon pals to pick up the phone, even if it is "after hours."

In spite of myself:

I love Al-Anon because I can have a crisis any time I need to!

Icons

On the wall in the therapist's office there is a large poster displaying mood icons representing different emotions: Happy. Sad. Silly. Confused.

When I came into recovery, the only emotions I felt were definitely *not* on that poster: Enraged. Postal. Homicidal.

To say I was perturbed and filled with resentment would be putting it mildly. Life hadn't worked out the way I planned, and I was stuck in a loop of unproductive emotions ranging between angry and really, really pissed off. When I started working the Twelve Steps, my life got better, and I began to experience a spectrum of emotions I'd never acknowledged before (i.e., joy, elation, appreciation). In fact, today, I'm able to identify feelings I'm having at the moment I'm having them, which brings me great freedom! And I enjoy being able to share those feelings with others. For instance, just the other day, I noticed my friend's new shoes were unflattering, so I said (in my nicest indoor voice), "Boy, those shoes are unfortunate looking, but I still love you." Frankly, her emotion was not one of appreciation.

Later, when we were at the movies and I was laughing hysterically, my friend "shushed" me. While I didn't like being "shushed," I tried to remember that not everyone is able to experience their emotions in the moment as I do now.

My poor friend. Maybe I should offer her some of my mood icons.

In spite of myself:

I'll be more patient with frowny-faces.
And people with unfortunate shoes.

Hear Me?

A well-known commercial features a bespectacled guy wandering around different locations with a cell phone held to his ear, asking, "Can you hear me now?" over and over.

I used to feel like that guy: sort of lost, disconnected, and unheard by others. My solution? Repeat the same words over and over, louder each time.

I finally figured something out.

If people aren't listening to me, it's probably because *they don't want to.* Talking louder is not the solution. The truth is, most of us—myself included—are self-absorbed. We're all great at talking, but few of us are truly skilled at listening.

We all want the same thing: to be heard by people who "get" us. When I take the time to listen to *others,* chances are, *they'll* take time to listen to *me.* And if I'm feeling like someone isn't listening to me, it could be because they aren't feeling *heard by me.* Either that, or they don't have a decent cell phone connection. In which case, they should probably consider switching phone companies. I can always help them with that. But only if they *really want* my help.

In spite of myself:

If I'm not feeling heard by others, maybe I should listen better.

Thinking Problem

From the brain of an Al-Anon:

Yes, sometimes I think too much, but I don't consider it a problem. I'm absolutely in control of my thinking. I can stop whenever I want to. I just don't want to.

Some people say my thinking gets in the way at times, but it's not like it's interfering with my relationships or my job or anything.

Except for that time I was late for work because I was obsessed with finding a cure for cancer. And the week I missed because I was organizing an intervention for my boyfriend. Come to think of it, my supervisor did seem distant when he passed by me in the hallway at lunch today. Is he thinking about letting me go? Maybe I should update my résumé.

True, the other day, a friend told me to stop analyzing so much. But for goodness' sake, what else should one be doing with her head?

I suppose I could learn to relax more. Maybe I could give meditation a shot. I would, but it's clear I've got to start looking for a new job now, because this one is obviously on the skids, like everything else in my horrible, rotten life.

After all I've done for that ungrateful company I work for, you'd think they'd treat me better than this! I can't wait to see the look on their faces when I tell them I'm leaving.

In spite of myself:
The words "controlled" and "thinking"
don't necessarily go together for an Al-Anon.

Teachers

"When the student is ready, the teacher will appear."

I've heard that saying most of my life, both in and out of the rooms of recovery. While I agree with it in theory, my experience has been that the teachers I've wanted have rarely appeared on time. They're often late, or, in many cases, hung over. Or gross. Or spiteful and angry because they didn't want to be *my* teacher.

Whenever I did encounter the rare but oft-prayed-for "hot teacher," he seldom returned my infatuation. I'd waste entire semesters fantasizing about me and said teacher cruising along the Mediterranean coastline on his minty green Vespa. As if a straight, hot teacher would ever be caught on a minty green Vespa!

The bottom line: *My* teachers have hardly ever appeared when I was ready for them, and I was never entirely sure I wanted the lessons they were offering me. More often than not, I've had to repeat the boring courses, and there have been times when I wasn't even sure what the point of the lesson was until it was too late.

Alas, not every saying works for everyone.

In spite of myself:

God, can you just wake me when the lesson's over?

Great Caesar

I was brand new to Al-Anon and had been out of work for over a year. I'd applied for every kind of job imaginable—coffee barista, waitress, door-to-door window installation sales, real estate—but had gotten no offers. Desperation set in.

When a friend recommended me for a job at an upscale restaurant, I was there, filling out an application, within the hour. It had been years since my last restaurant job, and I'd forgotten the name of my previous boss. All I could remember was that he was an Italian we called Caesar who screamed a lot, and I could never understand him. I couldn't remember anything else, so I punted.

"You worked for . . . Julius Caesar?" The manager eyed me suspiciously as he pored over my application.

"Yes!" I answered. "What are the chances of that?"

"Slim to none," he replied cautiously.

It was obvious I was lying, but I was so embarrassed and afraid that I continued with the ruse. I went on and on about what a great leader my Julius Caesar was, and how he'd been the best boss ever. It never occurred to me to just tell the truth about having forgotten my boss's name.

Fear makes me do some absurd things. It limits my options and turns me into an accidental time traveler.

Not surprisingly, I didn't get the job. But when I returned home, I did some research on old Jules—it turns out he spoke primarily in iambic pentameter, and he's the main reason our calendars are all screwed up. And no matter what historians say, I still believe he was a superior salad maker.

In spite of myself:
God, help me not cave in to fear. It limits my options.

Detachment Issues

"Detachment" is a word I hear thrown around a lot these days. Detach from difficult people. Detach from difficult situations. It's such a cold word. So heartless and devoid of love. So . . . lackluster.

As if being in a relationship and being detached were even a possibility! As if allowing someone to experience the consequences of their actions were even close to being humane.

Ask any *normal* person and they'll tell you what relationships are about: bonding, joining together, becoming one, "completing each other," merging, forsaking all others, and a myriad of other things that might include enmeshment, smothering, and a lack of appropriate physical space.

But let's suppose our forefathers had decided to practice "detachment" and refused to sign the Bill of Rights, or the U.S. Constitution? If the guys in that group hadn't stuck together, or had quibbled about "needing space," or time to "process their feelings" when Thomas Jefferson was crafting the Declaration of Independence, we might still be speaking proper English and eating bangers and mash.

Just because some people think "detaching" is a sign of mental health doesn't mean I have to agree with them, and it doesn't mean I have to do it. Detach, that is. Because I won't. Unless I'm asked to.

In spite of myself:

Letting go is highly overrated, but I'll give it a try today.

Crisis

"Don't create a crisis."

I never *create* the crises. *They* seem to find *me*.

I equate my ability to attract crises with the story about the group of ski instructors who died on a mountain after falling into a snow cave and being overcome by toxic fumes.

The ski instructors had been sent to rescue their friend, who'd fallen into a crevasse covered by a heavy snowfall. One by one, the skiers approached the massive hole in an attempt to pull their friend out, but the carbon dioxide and gases blowing from an underground volcano overwhelmed them. Despite their athleticism and expertise, they couldn't conquer the sulfur springs. Every single one of them collapsed into the huge mountain hole and died from asphyxiation.

I am a bit like those skiers, except I am still alive and I'm not even close to a mountain right now. Yet I can easily be engulfed by conditions that seem to pull me in and take me down. It always starts out the same way—with me offering to lend someone a helping hand—and suddenly there's turmoil. Pure pandemonium. Craziness. Oxygen loss. A team of paramedics. And that's often before I've even left the house. Working a program of recovery has helped me to discern between lending a hand and contributing to a crisis.

Contributing to a crisis, maybe. But creating a crisis? Moi? Never. Hardly ever. So seldom these days, it isn't even funny.

In spite of myself:
Sometimes a well-intentioned rescue operation
is actually a crisis in disguise.

Compare and Despair

Even though I've been playing the "compare and despair" game since I was a youngster, it's rarely been fun. I've *never* won a prize, and I rarely feel good when it's over—mainly because most of my comparisons are between me and:

1. Billionaire business superstars
2. Supermodels
3. Dead artists

Obviously, I can't do much about the size of my body frame or about financial assets I don't currently have. And artists are always more appreciated when they're six feet under. Even if they aren't that talented, creative people seem to gain popularity once they're gone—especially if their death is tragic or premature.

I've learned it's impossible for me to remain right-sized or remotely peaceful when I'm comparing myself to others. The "compare and despair" game is one I'll never win, and it can lead Al-Anons like me to despondency.

For now I have decided not to play the comparison game, and I especially refuse to play games with billionaires, supermodels, and dead artists. Even if they ask me to. Instead, I'll say no. Because I can never, ever be rich, thin, or dead enough to win at that game.

In spite of myself:

For today, no compare, no despair.

Appreciation

I've been reflecting on something my Al-Anon sponsor told me last week. She suggested I spend more time appreciating the things I have instead of focusing on the things I'm missing out on. (Insert scowl here.)

This kind of appreciation isn't easy for me because I'm more comfortable being depressed about what I'm lacking than praising what I have. I am *trying* to warm up to the concept, though.

After giving it some thought, I've decided the best way for me to take this whole appreciation thing out for a spin is to think about it like a vintage Chanel scarf. Like it's something I can throw on whenever the mood strikes, or when I'm late for work and there's no time to shampoo my hair.

Today, I am going to practice being more appreciative of everything I have, whether it's big or small. If it's good, I'm going to give it a big round of applause. For instance, I have all ten of my fingers and both of my feet. So in honor of my hands and feet, I'm going to give myself a manicure and a pedicure. Then I'm going to take out the pair of shoes I bought yesterday and put them on the feet I'm so damn grateful for. It might not be very spiritual, but it's a start.

What about you? What will you appreciate and be grateful for today? Name five things, right now!

In spite of myself:
C'mon, name five things you're grateful for!

R-E-L-I-E-F

Acceptance may bring relief, but most of the time, I'd rather just swallow a few Rolaids.

Recovery tells me that when I can accept that things are exactly as they should be in this moment, I will experience relief—and that has been true for me. Still, a lot of the time, I'd prefer to close the curtains and go to bed—and wake up to a brand-new life, free from struggle, pain, or discomfort.

Until I can accept and trust that my Higher Power has a plan for me, serenity is next to impossible and I'm not at peace. So even though at times I don't feel like I have much of a choice in the matter, I really do. I can keep ramming my head against the wall and refuse to accept that what's happening is exactly as it's supposed to be, or I can accept that things are going down in the way God wants them to.

Sometimes I go with ramming my head against the wall, and other times I go with acceptance. Yes, acceptance may take longer than chewing a Rolaids tablet, but acceptance and prayer are the only things that bring me peace and long-term relief.

In spite of myself:

How do you spell relief? A-C-C-E-P-T-A-N-C-E.

Plagiarizer

I want to plagiarize so badly, it's killing me. I just read something that was so interesting and funny, it made me want to steal it and claim it as my own. But I didn't. So be forewarned: Today's meditation will be sparse. And unfunny.

Because frankly, my little chickens, I am fresh out of ideas.

The Al-Anon part of me that wants to look good and doesn't want to admit I have nothing pithy to say today knows it would be easier for me to rip off someone else's idea and pass it off as my own. But I can't because my need to be recovered outweighs my need to plagiarize.

The truth is, I won't always be here for you, readily dispensing nuggets of gold, fulfilling your intellectual and spiritual hunger. So, perhaps now is the time for you to take on my role of "infinitely wise meditation guru."

Give it a shot: Think of something having to do with recovery that makes you smile or even laugh aloud. Write it down and carry it with you today, and read it as often as you need to throughout the day. It can be anything that encourages or inspires you—but please, no plagiarizing.

In spite of myself:
Insert pithy yet profound spiritual thought here.

Fixer-Uppers

I used to think relationships were like houses—much more gratifying when they required strenuous work. I could never figure out why *anyone* would buy a new home when they could buy a fixer-upper.

For years before the movie *Under the Tuscan Sun* came out, I fantasized about buying an old, rustic Italian farmhouse and fixing it up. I pictured myself refinishing hardwood floors, fixing leaky roofs, and speaking fluent Italian to workmen. Mostly, my fantasies included the cute workmen and roaming the Italian countryside, not replacing toilets or retrofitting copper pipes.

The truth is, a fixer-upper takes effort and a lot of hard labor. There are walls to tear down, roofs to patch. And after you've put a ton of time into it, something inevitably goes wrong—you find out the city requires a permit, or you get slapped with a lien. It never, ever goes smoothly, unless you're in a movie.

That's how it used to be with all my relationships. If things were move-in ready, I didn't want them. My passion was for people and things that needed lots of repairing.

Because of Al-Anon, I don't feel that way anymore. I'll take relationships that require *some* work, but I no longer seek out the ones that require a ground-floor remodel.

If it isn't broken, I don't need to fix it. In fact, today I try to take a thing or a person "as is," and I'm much happier.

I do still think about those Italian workmen from time to time, though.

In spite of myself:

Today I will not fix anything,
especially if it involves a copper pipe.

FEBRUARY

Picker

Six months into the production of the feature film I had written and was directing, I learned my investor was under investigation for securities fraud. He'd been accused of masterminding a Ponzi scheme and stealing hundreds of millions of dollars from investors.

It's a long story, meant for something other than a meditation book—but suffice it to say, I have a history of finding people whom other folks might consider to be surrounded by a few *red flags*. As I've heard people in meetings say, "My picker might be broken."

In Al-Anon, I've learned to be more selective about the people I develop relationships with. I take my time before getting involved in new relationships, whether they be personal or business, and I don't accept everyone at face value. It's not like I run credit checks on acquaintances or anything, but I'm definitely more discerning. And I seek input from trusted friends when I start to question things about someone in my life. For example, I've decided that the next time I'm considering doing business with someone and an official from the government stops by to investigate them while we're in a meeting, that will give me pause, and I will definitely give the person more scrutiny. Unless he's really good-looking. And single. And tall. Then all bets are off.

Now that I have some time in recovery, I know better than to jump into business or personal relationships with everyone who will have me. No matter how good-looking, persuasive—or tall—they are.

In spite of myself:
Thanks to Al-Anon, even I have standards now!

HALT

I've heard it said that when we allow ourselves to get overly hungry, angry, lonely, or tired, we experience a change in body chemistry. When that happens, we run the risk of putting ourselves in physical and emotional danger. In Al-Anon, this is known as HALT (hungry, angry, lonely, tired).

While I'm not really down with saying things like "HALT" out loud—unless I'm being stampeded by a herd of elephants— I get the gist. As corny as HALT may sound, it's important for people like me who aren't used to acknowledging and taking care of our own needs. It's also a valuable and necessary tool in my toolbox—another corny but helpful nugget of hard-earned recovery wisdom.

Al-Anon has taught me that *it's up to me* to make sure my basic needs are taken care of, and I risk putting others in danger if I don't do so, because, believe me, I can be hell on wheels when I get too *anything* in the HALT acronym. When I'm hungry, I need to eat. When I'm lonely, I need to reach out to others. When I'm tired, I need to rest.

And when I'm angry? In my case, it's better that I cover my mouth with masking tape until the urge to express my anger subsides. That's not an official Al-Anon saying, that's just something I've learned.

In spite of myself:
HALT, in the name of love!

Restoration

Step #2: "Came to believe that a Power greater than ourselves could restore us to sanity."

When I came into Al-Anon, I had a hard time believing this Step had much value for me. First, I despised the word "insane" and refused to identify myself in that way. Those other folks were insane. I pretty much had my act together.

Second, I genuinely believed that I could, with a bit of help, restore *myself* to normalcy. That is, if I could figure out what normal was. Once I'd done that, I reasoned, then I'd go back to my old life as I knew it. Same me, just more *normal*, and happier. And thinner, if I could swing it.

I worked very hard during the first few months in recovery to prove to myself that the "alcoholism" thing was just another one of life's hurdles, and I had the mental and physical reserves to "get over it" and get back to real life.

But in spite of that hard work, I came to realize that I needed a Higher Power to restore me. I, in and of myself, could not restore myself.

I finally accepted that I wasn't in the self-restoration game, and I began to turn things over to my Higher Power. And even though I'm not even sure what the self-restoration game is, I know I'm *not* in it. But God is, and I'm extremely grateful for that.

In spite of myself:

Thank God I don't have to pretend to be
in the self-restoration game anymore.

Gratitude

I was new to Al-Anon and so depressed that I hadn't gotten out of bed for days. Finally, I called my sponsor. Instead of consoling me, she suggested I take a shower, go for a walk, and write out a gratitude list. I took a shower and then sat staring at a piece of paper for hours. It was sundown before I had the list completed.

"Okay, my gratitude list is done," I told my sponsor over the phone.

"Great, sweetie," she replied. "Read it to me."

"Okay . . . Diet Pepsi . . . and . . . Altoids."

She was silent for a moment. "Well, that was a start. Anything else you're grateful for?"

"I can't say I'm grateful for being alive, but I'm grateful for the giant willow tree behind my apartment," I continued. "And I'm grateful I don't have alopecia. I've also been told I have pretty nice nail beds."

"That's fantastic," she said. "Call me when you get fifty things on your list."

I thought fifty was excessive, but I agreed to try. Later that week, when I'd completed the list, I decided to celebrate. I went to the store and bought a Diet Pepsi and a box of Altoids. I also bought a bottle of nail polish and painted my pretty nice nails. And I came up with five more things I was grateful for.

In spite of myself:

Write down ten things you're grateful for. C'mon! Give it a try.

Leaky Boats

Imagine you're on a sinking boat and there are no life preservers. What is the first thing you should do?

Stop imagining!

We Al-Anons love creating imaginary scenarios that will never happen. My favorite pastimes included rehearsing conversations with people I would never meet (politicians, dead relatives, exes, TV show hosts) and anticipating problems that would never befall me.

I'm a drama queen with an overly active imagination, and sometimes the only way for me to get grounded is to reach out to someone I trust—my sponsor, a friend in the program—someone who has their head on straight.

When I'm in the midst of one of my epic flights of imagination and it starts going downhill, I can pick up the phone and ask for help. It's amazing how my inner turmoil melts at the sound of a caring voice on the other end of the line.

Except when I call someone and they don't pick up and I'm forced to leave a message. Or when voice mail cuts me off before I've completed my scenario of impending doom.

Aside from the occasional technological glitches, conversation just flows with an Al-Anon on the phone. They're always eager to lend a hand and help me out of the boat. Which is great because imaginary sinking boats can be just as terrifying as real ones.

In spite of myself:
Sometimes my imagination is better off
doing absolutely nothing.

Politicking

I'd arrived early for my interview with the infamous political powerhouse who was looking for someone to do marketing for her company. Wearing a powder-blue Dior suit, she waltzed into the library of her mansion to meet me. She was surprisingly small, but confident. I was so intimidated I could barely speak.

"So, darrrlink, did you reeead my latest book?" she asked in a Mediterranean accent, looking me up and down like a naval sergeant.

"Yes, I took some notes on it. I appreciate your approach to corporate responsibility, and . . . well, I don't remember what I wrote. The notes are in my car, I can go get them . . ."

"No, no! No notes!" she said, cutting me off. "Talk to meeee about me. Vhaaat can you tell meeeee about me?"

"I know . . . that you write books. I can't remember which ones. I, ummm, like your hair." When I'm more worried about what you're thinking about me than anything else, I get tongue-tied, I don't listen, and generally I act like an idiot.

"Darrrlink, you don't seem to be able to articulate your thoughts verrry well," she said as her assistant ushered me to the door. "I don't think you're the right fit for me."

What struck me most about the legendary powerhouse—aside from her flawless skin—was the fact that she only wanted to know more about *herself.* I figure a woman like that already knows a lot about herself. Why did she need *me* to remind her?

In spite of myself:
If I'm focused on what *you're thinking about me*,
I'm not focused on *you.*

(E-mail me if you'd like to tell me what you think of this meditation.)

Stalkarazzi

I have this "friend" who fears she's not living the life she was supposed to have. Last week she spent hours online looking up old flames and the sorority sisters who irritated her most in college. It turns out all of them are living extraordinary lives. She immediately sank into a depression.

When my "friend" called her sponsor after wallowing for several days, the sponsor zoned in like an LAPD officer with a radar gun.

"Have you been stalking people online?"

"No. Sort of. But only for a moment. Only long enough to see my college crush. The guy who took me to my sorority pledge ceremony now has a gorgeous wife, two beautiful kids, and a super successful business. He's training for a triathlon." She paused.

"I've really screwed up my life, haven't I?" my "friend" finally asked in despair.

"I don't know," the sponsor said, "but I do know that few people post pictures of themselves when they've just been dumped and they're lying on the floor in a fetal position, crying. My advice is that you stay off the computer for the next few days, and spend time doing things you enjoy."

My "friend" knew her sponsor was right, but she also thinks it has to do with the fact that her sponsor doesn't know how to use Twitter or Instagram. At least, that's what my "friend" told me.

In spite of myself:

I'll stay away from technology if it makes me feel like life isn't exactly as it should be.

Loofah

One of the best things about Al-Anon is that we get to share the deepest, most intimate parts of ourselves with other people in meetings.

It's like the beginning phases of a new relationship, when you're able to say whatever you feel because you're not afraid you'll get dumped. What's even better is, in Al-Anon meetings, there's no pressure to *be adorable.* You don't have to put on cologne or pretend that you don't burp or talk to yourself when you're alone.

Opening up and being authentic without fearing the judgment of others is so totally healing. And cleansing—like having a bubble bath and taking a loofah to your soul, and then wrapping yourself up in one of those big, fluffy bathrobes from a five-star hotel. And then being able to order anything you want from room service and not having to pay for it!

There's something magnificent about disclosing those hidden, vulnerable, even painful secrets and knowing people will embrace and care for you. In Al-Anon, it's usually when you've shared your most embarrassing stories and fears that you experience the most love and support.

And even after all the crying, they still invite you to keep coming back!

In spite of myself:

I'll give my soul a spa treatment by attending a meeting today.

Service

Sometimes my family looks at me like I'm wearing a yellow jockey cap and a tangerine-striped polyester shirt with a name tag that reads, "Welcome to Carl's Jr." I have to resist the urge to shout, "Would you like to try our new cheesy ranch onion rings with that?"

I'm kind of like the surly teenager at the drive-thru—so *totally* over everything and not in the mood to be of service. To anyone, for anything.

I've learned in Al-Anon that being of service is a lot like exercise. I don't always want to do it, but I always feel invigorated and refreshed after I've done it. It's rewarding. And when I have truly helped or done something for someone else, I usually feel as good as—if not better than—the person I've helped.

When I'm of service to others, even if it's for my not-so-appreciative family, my life gets better. Infinitely better.

As my sponsor says, "We do right *because* it's right."

While I'm generally with her on that, I do have a few exceptions—namely, any service that requires me to wear a yellow jockey cap and *anything* made of 100 percent polyester. Polyester and service never, ever belong together.

In spite of myself:
How can I help you today? No, really!

Sanity

Step #2: "Came to believe that a Power greater than ourselves could restore us to sanity."

I don't always know when I'm acting insanely. Sure, there are times when I get *signs*. But who hasn't gotten a few dirty looks, or doors slammed in their face? Who hasn't had a few restraining orders sent their way?

It's not always obvious to me when my version of insanity has taken over and is showing.

I'm an Al-Anon, and I am a master of disguise. I look normal. I have a job and a family. I pay my taxes (mostly) and try to blend into the crowd. It's only when people engage with me that they catch on to the depths of my crazy.

My insanity is usually revealed in my casual references to what I do for others, how gracious and long-suffering I am, how I care more than the rest of humanity, and how hard I try compared to *those . . . other people in those "other programs."*

Speaking of *those other people in those "other programs,"* I am eternally grateful to have had so many of them in my life because they remind me to be grateful. After all, I could have ended up like them: insufferable, impatient, arrogant, and completely unaware of the depths of my craziness. Thank goodness, I didn't.

In spite of myself:
At least *my* insanity is tolerable. Right?

Al-Anon and On

I don't enjoy listening to other Al-Anons complain. Part of the reason is most of them don't do it very well.

It's my humble opinion that if you're going to complain, there are a few unwritten yet universal rules about the nature of your complaints. Ways to make your grievances reasonably more interesting, if you will.

For instance, before going into great detail about any particular problem, I recommend considering the following questions: Is my complaint somewhat entertaining? Is it topical? Is there any way I can exaggerate the facts, or add a bit in the way of humor? Do I know when to pause, or when to pick up the pace when criticizing someone? Have I tried to "bury the lead," so the receiver won't notice I'm blaming them?

Would it help to toss in something about "what I'm learning" or taking responsibility for "my part," so my grumblings will be more palatable?

If we Al-Anons gave thought to the delivery of our complaints, we might find a larger audience for our stories of affliction and woe. Complaining is truly an art form; yet it, like any other skill, is improved with practice. So let's do our part to get better at it. Practice makes perfect. But you already knew that— you're an Al-Anon!

In spite of myself:

If it's interesting, is it still considered complaining?

Qualify What?

"My qualifier told me she was coming straight home from work, but I found her at the bar—again!" said the uneasy looking young man before he burst into tears.

"His qualifier?" I whispered to a woman seated next to me. "That can't possibly be her name! What the heck is a qualifier?"

"A qualifier is the *reason* we come to Al-Anon," the woman said in an overtly patronizing manner.

"I thought *I* was the reason I came to Al-Anon," I said under my breath, although I liked the idea of having a qualifier. Anything to get me off the hook!

When I tried using the term in a conversation with my sponsor, she informed me, "There's really no such thing as a qualifier. You don't need any help, dear. You qualify all by your little old self."

For me, using the word "qualifier" keeps the focus off of my behavior and makes it seem as if someone else is causing me to act like a whack job. And while I *love* having excuses for acting like a whack job, it's generally just a way to rationalize my own controlling, obsessive behavior.

I'm qualified on my very own to be a member of Al-Anon. Just ask anyone who really knows me. They'll tell you. On second thought, don't ask them.

In spite of myself:

I qualify for Al-Anon every day,
even when I'm all by my lonesome.

Done

"You're *still* going to those meetings?" my friend asked impatiently. "You broke up with the alcoholic, and life is so much better now. Aren't you done with Al-Anon?"

The first time someone said that to me, I paused. *Is she right? Am I done with recovery?* I'd done a lot of Twelve Step work, and my relationships were going well. Life was good. Actually, life was great!

Maybe I am finished with Al-Anon, I thought to myself one night after leaving a meeting. *I think I've got things squared away; maybe I don't need Al-Anon anymore.* The next morning, I got up and went to work. I had a few meetings about a new project, and then I stopped by the DMV at lunch. After work, I dropped some clothes off at the dry cleaners and hit the grocery store. And I remembered the reason why I go to Al-Anon meetings: I have a problem with other people—not all of them, but many of them. In fact, lots of them.

In Al-Anon, I've learned that my reaction to other people is what creates the majority of my problems. The solution I get in Al-Anon—through meetings, Step work, and literature—is a spiritual connection to a Higher Power and a better way of living. Surrender is a continual action I must take, and the daily reprieve I require. I need the constant reminder that I don't have to do life alone anymore. No matter how "recovered" I may feel, I'm never done with recovery.

Yep, I'll keep coming back.

In spite of myself:
The next time I think I don't need Al-Anon,
I'll just open my door and go outside.

V-Day

I could be romanticizing things slightly, but Valentine's Day was so much more fun when I was a kid. In the old days, everyone gave each other cards and chocolates, and at the very least, the homeroom teacher would evenly dole out boxed paper hearts and store-bought cupcakes so no one felt left out.

My best Valentine's Day was when I was in fifth grade. Everyone got handwritten cards, fistfuls of chocolate kisses, and pastel-colored candies that tasted like cardboard. And, as if life couldn't get any better, Mike F. told his friend to tell my friend he liked me and wanted to hold my hand at lunchtime. Then Diane, the class bully, found out that Mike F. liked me and threatened to beat me up at recess.

Okay, it wasn't the best Valentine's, but it *was* memorable. And very dramatic. I *love* dramatic.

Recovery is a little like Valentine's Day. It all depends on my perspective. I can wait for love and cardboard-tasting candy hearts to come my way, or I can give them to others first. Even though it seems contrary, life is so much better when I pass along joy and generosity instead of waiting for them to come to me. Besides, being kind to others without expecting anything back makes me feel good. And it lessens the likelihood that someone will want to punch me at recess.

In spite of myself:

Today I will pass around love to others, and expect no punches.

Reservations

A friend of mine has a tiny sterling silver chair that she keeps on her desk at the office. She says it's to remind her to save a place for God at work.

Now that I'm developing a relationship with my Higher Power, I thought it would be kind of nice to take God out to dinner. So, last Saturday night, I called this trendy new restaurant I'd been dying to check out.

"Hi, I'd like to make a reservation for two at eight," I said. "The name? God . . . and uh, me."

Click. She hung up. I tried calling again with the same results. I tried again. She stopped answering the phone.

It's not as if I was throwing God's name around to see if I'd get a nicer table. I was just practicing being in a relationship with God. Besides, everybody has to eat, right?

I learned a valuable lesson about thinking before I share too much about my relationship with my Higher Power. Unless someone asks me, it's probably better to keep it to myself. That might be why my friend who has that tiny silver chair doesn't talk about it with her office pals, unless they ask her about it and she's comfortable sharing with them.

Not everyone needs or wants to know that I'm saving a place for God, and that's just fine.

This is another reason I love Al-Anon. We all get to choose who we want in the seat next to us.

In spite of myself:

I can save a place for God
no matter what anyone else thinks about it.

Lost

Yesterday, I heard someone in an Al-Anon meeting say, "I can't be afraid of losing something I wasn't supposed to have." It sounded profound when he said it, but when I thought about it later, I was just . . . confused.

I live in a constant state of fear about losing things: my memory, my motor skills, my Marc Jacobs sunglasses, the PIN for my debit card. Is that guy saying I'm not supposed to have any of those things?

And what about the things I lose but I'm positive I need? For instance, I was out running on the beach one time last year and the ignition key to my car fell out of my pocket. I spent hours searching in the sand, but I never found the key. Does it mean those keys weren't meant for me? Was I not supposed to have that car anymore? If not, is it a sign that I should have a better car? Or should I be riding a bike?

There are things people in meetings say that provide me with deep insights long after the meeting is over. Then there are people who say things that make me doubt my own sanity. I guess that's why they say, "Take what you like and leave the rest." "They" being the wise people, not the people who say things that cause me to doubt my sanity. Which makes me wonder: If I lose my sanity, was I simply not meant to have it?

In spite of myself:
I will take what I like and leave the rest.

Let Go

Before I'd ever attended a Twelve Step meeting, my friend Brian and I had this ritual. Whenever one of us would get all worked up about something—which was quite often—we'd hold out our hands and tighten our fists as hard as we could. Then we'd open our fists and chant in unison, "Let go and let God."

It started out as a joke, a punch in the face to the whole self-help movement. I tried it a few times when I was alone and stressed out by life. I closed my fist, but my problems were still there when I opened it again. It didn't work, and it wasn't funny. Imagine my surprise years later when I went to an Al-Anon meeting and heard people using the phrase, "Let go and let God," in a pure, non-sarcastic, non-cynical way. It was meant as a prayer.

Recently, I was in a really stressful situation and I tried tightening my fist while chanting, "Let go and let God," and I meant it as a prayer, a decision to let go of control and allow my Higher Power to work things out. I felt so much better when I opened up my fist, knowing I now had a Higher Power to hand that big ball of stress over to.

No joke, it feels really good when I release my fist, let go, and let God.

In spite of myself:
Go ahead, make a fist and then let it all go.

Nothin' Is Nothin'

Brad was a former Marine who drove a crimson-red Corvette. He managed the new home sales division where I was a Realtor. He was short on time and shorter on tolerance for people. All people. Especially Realtors. Seemingly every day, arguments would break out between Realtors who would accuse each other of stealing one another's clients. These fights would inevitably occur before the home had been sold.

I was sitting in Brad's office one morning quarreling with another Realtor about a commission. Things were getting pretty intense between us until Brad stepped in.

"Have you people got a contract in your hands? A signed contract, a deal?" Brad demanded.

"No, sir," we confessed, in unison.

"Get outta my office! There's nothin' to talk about till you people got a buyer and a signed contract!" Brad shrieked.

"A hundred percent of nothin' is nothin'," he said, pointing toward the door.

It took a while for me to comprehend Brad's math, but it finally clicked. One hundred percent of nothing is nothing. We were fighting about things that hadn't happened and might not *ever* happen. The deals were all in our heads. None of them were real.

I often repeat that phrase to myself when I start worrying about things that *might* happen. If they haven't happened, there's simply nothing to worry about. Or, as Brad would say, "a hundred percent of nothin' is nothin'." Even *I* can understand that math.

In spite of myself:
A hundred percent of nothing means
there's nothing to worry about.

Attagirl!

When I came into Al-Anon, I was majorly pissed off at the alcoholics in my life. It seemed to me that they had all the fun and took no responsibility for their actions. And if and when they decided to clean up their acts, they'd get an "attaboy" and a big fat pat on the back. *What about me?* I thought. *When do I get a pat on the back or a standing ovation for going to Al-Anon?* When I'd tell folks I'm going to Al-Anon, they'd look at me quizzically and say, "So glad you've stopped . . . what is it you've stopped doing?"

"No one understands me," I growled to my sponsor. "An alcoholic stops drinking, and they get a bunch of high fives and a parade. When do I get a pat on the back and an 'attaboy'?"

"A lot of people don't understand Al-Anon," my sponsor replied. "So get over the need for an 'attaboy.' Besides, if someone said 'attaboy,' that would be strange. You're a girl."

In Al-Anon, there's no substance to put down. It's a mental obsession and a mistaken belief that I can control people, places, and things outside of myself. The antidote is a spiritual connection with God, a community that supports me, and Steps to show me how to live life on life's terms.

I'm looking forward to the day when I no longer need an "attagirl" from anyone outside myself. Till then, I'll be proud of my achievements, even when nobody throws me a parade.

In spite of myself:

My recovery matters, even if no one else is watching.

Someone

My solution to the problem of alcoholism had been to Be Someone. I was addicted to anything having to do with the "Top 10 Things Successful People Do." I read every biography of successful leaders, and in my opinion, the worst crime I could possibly commit was to be mediocre.

When I came into Al-Anon, I'd lost my mojo and I wanted it back. I thought if I could pull myself together, I'd be okay. So when my sponsor insinuated that a career was just one aspect of life, not the purpose for being or a reflection of my value, I ignored her. When she told me that hardship might serve a bigger purpose, I figured she was cute, but misguided. And when she told me her greatest satisfaction came from small things in life and suggested I savor the good times instead of rushing through them, I almost threw up. I wanted to hate her, but I couldn't because she was living the life she described. And she was pretty happy. Happier than me.

"Nothing's more important than how you treat yourself, the people around you, and your connection to your Higher Power," she said.

It took a long time for me to see that my purpose wasn't to Be Someone.

Today, I find success in the small things: laughing with friends, talking to God, listening to music—building a life that sustains me and makes me happy. Strangely enough, now I kind of feel like Someone.

In spite of myself:

I might not Be Someone, and that's just fine with me.

Expiration

I hate throwing things away. Anything. I once carried a container of fine French laundry powder with me from California to Colorado, and from Colorado to Arizona, then back to California. I traveled 1,800 miles with a bottle of fine laundry powder because I couldn't let it go. *What if there's an earthquake, or even a nuclear blast?* I thought. *A girl should never be without immediate access to a French launderette powder.*

There are things I don't believe in discarding—especially if they are nowhere close to their expiration date. For a long time, I also applied that thinking to people and relationships.

In Al-Anon, I've learned that if I'm desperately attached to anything or anyone, even though all the signs are saying the effective date has passed, it could be a sign of trouble. Not everything lasts forever, even relationships, and some things I simply have to let go of.

As for the French launderette powder, yesterday I used it to wash my beloved vintage cashmere sweater. Then I threw the rest of it away. Six years after I purchased it, two years past its expiration date, I finally tossed that laundry powder in the trash.

Don't tell me recovery doesn't work!

In spite of myself:

I don't have to wait until something has expired to let it go.

Surviving Robots

I was listening to a radio show, and the host was telling a story about his son who was away at college. The son told his father he had decided to major in snowplowing. "I figure it is the one career that can't be outsourced to China," the son said.

"But snowplowing can be outsourced to robots," the show host retorted. "People need to think about their careers fifteen, twenty years in advance and plan accordingly. The robots are on their way."

I immediately called a friend, in terror. "Call when you can. I don't think I'll survive the robots." How in heck can I plan my life fifteen years out when I don't even know what I want to have for lunch? How can I plan my entire future when I'm just now learning to take life one day at a time?

I took out my smartphone and began researching "robot-proof" careers. I scoured the web for several hours, and I came up with a list that included midwife, counselor, doctor, organic farmer, and robotic engineer. Then, exhausted by the prospect of choosing between spending the next decade in medical training or under the supervision of a titanium-based probe, I took a nap.

When I awoke, I decided to let God worry about the robots. I've got enough to think about now, with applying to medical school and learning more about organic farming.

In spite of myself:
Today, I'll let God worry about the robots.

Just Today

My first two years in Al-Anon, I was in a constant state of terror. What potential disaster was waiting on the other side of the door? How would I make it through the next crisis? Why wouldn't people just listen to me?! I was a total wreck.

"It's just Tuesday, sweetie," was the response I often heard from my sponsor. I mean, she would only say that when it *was* Tuesday. She wouldn't say, "It's just Tuesday" if it was, say, Wednesday. If it was Wednesday, she'd say, "It's just Wednesday." Or "It's just Thursday," if it was Thursday.

At first I thought it was a bit condescending. Of course I knew what day of the week it was. What the heck? I was stressed out, not mentally incompetent!

"It's just Tuesday, sweetie," she'd say over and over. "Let's just do *Tuesday.*"

I finally started to get it. I could only do what was in front of me. The past was over; the future was unknown. I could only tackle the next thing before me, and I could handle it with my Higher Power's help.

As time went on, and my life began to improve, I was able to remind myself that it was just Tuesday, or Wednesday, or whatever. I didn't have to figure out the solutions to all of my problems in one day. I could just do one day at a time.

I still keep a calendar handy, in case I need a reminder. For instance, if it's Tuesday, and my head is in Thursday, I'll politely remind myself to look at the calendar.

In spite of myself:
It's just today. I know because I checked my calendar.

Dung

There's a story about a little girl whose father drives her to a farm on her birthday. When she opens the door to the barn, the entire place is covered in horse dung. The little girl jumps up and down, screaming with joy.

"What are you so excited about, honey?" her father asks.

She replies: "Because, Daddy, with all this poop, there must be a pony in here somewhere!"

I'm a lot like that little girl. My true nature sees the wonderful possibilities in a less-than-stellar situation, which might include a new pony. Ultimately, though, my "adult" brain takes over and convinces me everything's gone to crap.

My head and my heart are constantly at war. Is my life a bunch of horse manure—or am I about to find the pony? Do I dare believe that my Higher Power has something marvelous waiting for me behind the next barn door?

No matter what's going on around me, I can remain hopeful. I like to think of Al-Anon as God's reminder for me to keep my focus on the pony, instead of the manure.

In spite of myself:

My true nature trusts there's a pony.

Take You There

A famous gospel song talks about a place where there "ain't nobody cryin', ain't nobody worryin'. . . ."

The song talks about a world where anxiety and struggle don't exist, a place where freedom and happiness without fear abound. I've met a few people who seem to have that kind of peace. And although I can't prove it, I'm fairly certain they were on some type of prescription medication—or living off of a massive trust fund.

I personally have had stress-free moments of being at complete peace and total acceptance, but I sure as heck haven't been able to stay in that state. Not even when it involved pain medication.

While I can appreciate the fact that the writer of that gospel song has offered to take me to that special place, I can't be sure if I'm all that interested in an absolutely worry-free place. I might not be ready for that kind of calm. What would I do with all of my free time? Who would I talk to? Who would I try to improve?

After giving it some thought, I concluded I'm not that interested in the songwriter's offer because hanging around exceptionally happy people creates an exceptional amount of anxiety for me. But I guess I don't have to worry about going to that place right now. At least, I don't think I do.

In spite of myself:
When it comes to serenity, I'll let God take me there.

God Convos

I have an acquaintance who claims to be an intuitive healer. When I first met her, she was just a normal person like me, but several years later, she changed her name and added the word "healer" to the bottom of her business cards.

This acquaintance recently decided to write a book about conversations she's begun having with God now that she's a healer. The book focuses on the questions she poses to God and the answers she receives while channeling. The questions she asks God are spiritual and rather selfless. She asks God things like, "When will there be world peace?" And God replies with things like, "World peace will come when all beings are united."

When she asked God why so many bad things happened to people, he told her that she "should focus not on what is wrong, but rather on how she could be the light she wants to see." I don't remember all of God's responses to her questions because I tend to get bored. Her God talks slowly and is very, very wordy.

Unlike me, she's enlightened, because she didn't ask God anything about her own life, her weight, or her income. Not one thing about where all the good men have gone.

Which is probably why she's become a healer in just a few years and why I'm still me. Except now I have a connection to a Higher Power of my own because of recovery.

I'll try to ask God a few enlightened questions today, but they'll probably be less about world peace and more about where all the good men have gone.

In spite of myself:
I can talk to God, even if I don't have a special title
on my business card.

Shakes

There once was a time in my life when, if I was feeling hurt or rejected by someone, I would shrug my shoulders, throw my hands up in the air, and say, "I don't give two shakes what so-and-so thinks about me."

It wasn't true. I did give two shakes.

I was a glutton for approval, and I cared a *lot* about what other people thought of me. And today, I believe that people who say things like "I don't give two shakes what you think about me" are big liars.

Now I tell the truth—in meetings, at least—about my tendency to lie and manipulate in order to get people's approval. In fact, when it comes to love, lying and manipulation are just the tip of the iceberg. One might say the things I've done to get approval would cause a Marine to blush.

While Al-Anon has taught me to love myself more, I *do* still care what you think about me. A lot. But I'm working on having *my* opinion of me be more important than *yours*. In fact, someday, your opinion of me won't matter. Wait, that's not true, *your* opinion matters to me. I really like *you* and I really want *you* to like me. Which, I *think* you do. Don't you? Like me, that is?

In spite of myself:

Whose opinion is it, anyway—yours or mine?

Queen Knowledge

I have a friend (actually she's a family member) whom I call Queen Knowledge. And I don't call her that behind her back; I say it right in front of her, and she doesn't mind it at all. She likes being called Queen Knowledge because she knows that she knows a lot.

It used to be that people who know a lot more than me were intimidating, and I would react by pretending to know things I didn't. I've even caught myself saying, "I know," about things I had absolutely no flipping clue about. I acted like a know-it-all.

Pretending to know things I didn't was hard. It stressed me out because I lived in fear that I might be called out to explain something I didn't know. It was stressful, and I don't like being stressed out. It's hard on my nails and my skin.

Al-Anon taught me how to say, "I don't know" when I don't, and not feel bad about it. It's kind of fun. Sometimes I say, "I don't know," even when I *do know,* because it's liberating. I especially love saying, "I don't know" when I'm on the phone with Queen Knowledge, because she'll take it as a cue to tell me everything she knows about whatever subject we're discussing, and I can pretend to listen while I play sudoku.

In spite of myself:
I will try saying "I don't know" a few times today.

Leaps

If you're reading today's entry, you're experiencing a leap year, which means there will be 366 days this year. The purpose of leap year is to keep the numbering of the days in line with the earth's positioning, since one rotation of the planet isn't exactly twenty-four hours. If we didn't account for this continual slippage of time, the seasons would shift about a quarter of a day every year, and after a hundred years, the seasons would be off by twenty-five days.

"What has this got to do with recovery?" you may ask.

"Quite a bit," I shall answer.

Codependents are often chided and berated for our scheming, controlling ways, yet leap year proves there *are* times when overt manipulation is necessary. While this is no excuse for us to "revel in our defects," as they say, or to tell everyone we meet what to do and how to do it, it *is* absolutely fine to honor the control freaks who figured out the calendar slippage thing hundreds of years ago. Without those meddling Romans (Julius Caesar and Pope Gregory XIII), we would be celebrating Christmas in July.

Now, I'm no chronologist, but I will tell you one thing: I *don't* need more proof that leaving stuff alone ensures that slippage will occur and everything will eventually fall apart. And I'll tell you another thing: I'd never want to celebrate Christmas in July. Having to spend an extended amount time with my relatives when it's a hundred degrees outside is beyond insane.

In spite of myself:
Today I'll give a silent nod to the positive benefits of control.

MARCH

Billboards

I appreciate obvious signs, or, as my sponsor likes to call them, billboards from God. Which is another way of saying auspicious messages from my Higher Power, hints that everything is going to be okay. Or warnings that things are about to go off the rails.

I can count on one finger the number of billboards I've received from God.

As Step #3 in Al-Anon reminds me, we "made a decision to turn our will and our lives over to the care of God." Since I had given up control over other people, places, and things, I was hoping that God might consider giving me neon signs, light beams, warnings—at the very least a heads-up—about what was coming.

Not so. Turning my life and will over meant that I had to accept what came to me without knowing it ahead of time.

I had to be in acceptance of what is. There are no promises that I'll be given a heads-up about *anything*. There are some who say, "If you know what the future holds, you'll have no free will." To those people I say, "Shut up! If I knew what the future holds, it'd make planning my life a whole lot easier."

As I continue to daily turn my will over to and trust my Higher Power more, I am less apprehensive about the future and needing to know what it is. That being said, I am also open to receiving a billboard from God.

In spite of myself:
No billboards or neon signs required today.
I'll just turn it over to God.

Question What?

I have never trusted people who answer a question with a question. Maybe I'm too skeptical, but when someone answers my question with a question, I assume they're hiding something.

For example, I once asked my ex-boyfriend, "Are you seeing other people?"

"I see a lot of people in the course of a day!" he barked. "Don't you trust me? Do you think it's time for you to take a look at your trust issues?"

The fact that he answered my question with another question piqued my curiosity, to say the least. I won't go into the grisly details, but I will say things would've gone better if he'd simply answered the question.

When I asked, "Are you seeing other people?" he could have said, "Actually, I am seeing someone else. And I won't confuse you with some random question that'll make you think you're crazy. I'm a cheat, and I lied about going to Yale."

With that, I could've made a decision, which, now that I'm in recovery, might not have included bodily injury.

As you might have guessed, things didn't work out for us. But I learned that I *can* trust myself. And while people who answer a question with a question aren't always lying, I can trust my instincts and act on them. Especially when they don't include physical force.

The moral of the story: People who answer a question with a question aren't *always* lying. But usually they are. I can trust my instincts.

In spite of myself:

It's okay to question an answer that's a question.

Door Number?

They often say that when one door closes, another door opens. You know what? I think *they're* wrong.

I don't want to sound ungrateful or anything, but what if I want what's behind that first door? You know, the one that closed on me?

I know, I know, people who understand these types of things have told me that behind the open door something really wonderful awaits. But I'd rather keep what's behind the door that closed, and I'm wondering, why can't we just . . . kick the closed door open?

I mean, what if that first door closing was an accident? It wouldn't surprise me if a breeze picked up and, *whoosh!*, slammed it shut, causing me to miss out on what was supposed to be mine!

Look, I certainly don't want to go fooling around with my Higher Power's will, screwing up providence, or futzing with "what's meant to be," but I do have a hairpin and a credit card, and *MacGyver* was once one of my favorite TV shows, so . . . you get my drift.

All I need is four minutes, a credit card, and a hairpin.

In spite of myself:
When a door closes, might it have
simply been a strong breeze?

Stripes

When I was told I'd been selected to write for the high school newspaper, I was pretty smug and self-righteous—until I found out that the only reason I was chosen was because I showed up.

And then I met Zora. Zora, one of my fellow crack journalists, was infamous for writing headlines that had absolutely nothing to do with the story she'd written. One article I remember in particular was titled "Men in Vertical Stripes."

"Ummm . . . what's with this headline, Zora?" I asked snarkily. "What do men in stripes have to do with soccer?" I remember thinking, *How's this chick gonna make it? Not only does she not have both oars in the water, the only oar she has is broken!*

"It's pretty obvious," Zora replied, rolling her eyes at me. "The soccer referees wear vertical striped shirts." Then she clicked her high heels and stormed off. I often wondered what had happened to poor, clueless Zora, who couldn't extract a headline from a story if her life depended on it. I often wondered how a girl with a broken oar would fare in the world—a cruel, merciless ocean filled with sharks.

I found Zora's profile online recently. She's a TV journalist and married to a fabulously handsome, successful man. They have four children, and they own homes in Spain and New York, as well as a bevy of horses. She's as happy as a clam. In a vertical striped shirt, no doubt.

In spite of myself:

I rarely know the whole story, so I won't judge by the headline.

Lifesavers

I can't deny it. If I'd known the real purpose of Al-Anon was about saving myself as opposed to other people, I might've done things differently. For instance, before I found Al-Anon, I was in the business of saving lives, and I was good at it. Reasonably good. Astonishingly good.

And then I found Al-Anon and was told it wasn't my job to save other people. It made me wonder: *If I'd been given the chance to don my cape and tights, and make that final run into the metaphorical burning building, could I have liberated more people? Could I have spared more lives and made the world a better place?*

I'm not complaining; it's just that for all the death-defying acts of courage I've engaged in, not to mention the endless nagging, wheedling, and stalking I've done, I would've expected better results. It's slightly disheartening to have spent so much of my life trying to rescue other people only to find out it's not really what I'm here for. Sigh. I guess I have to accept that, as far as lifesavers go, I was . . . am . . . just okay.

I no longer play the role of superstar or hero—I'm just slightly less controlling and manipulative than I used to be, and these days I rarely rush into burning buildings. Although, I will admit, I do look pretty cute in my cape and tights.

In spite of myself:
I think I'll let God wear the cape today.

Strange Humors

Today is Michelangelo di Lodovico Buonarroti Simoni's birthday.

Legend has it Pope Julius II ordered Michelangelo to redecorate the plaster ceiling in the Sistine Chapel. But Michelangelo thought the work was beneath him. Michelangelo did not want the job of plasterer.

"The Pope wants to prevent me from sculpting, an art at which I am perfect," Michelangelo said, because he was sure Raphael, his rival, had put the idea into the pope's head. "The pope wants me to paint in fresco, so everyone will see that I paint worse than Raphael."

So, hotheaded Michelangelo began the job of plastering and continued to "expand the scope." Finally, he got exactly what he wanted: not just a plastering job, but to paint the ceiling of the Sistine Chapel.

"He is full of strange humors," Pope Julius said of Michelangelo, "but that is to be expected in a man of genius."

Michelangelo was a perfectionist who complained when he didn't get special treatment, felt gravely misunderstood, and wasn't above giving the head of the Catholic Church a dressing down if necessary. . . . Sounds vaguely familiar—geniuses who are greatly misunderstood and underappreciated. Seems like there might be a program for people like that.

In spite of myself:
Happy birthday, Michelangelo, honorary Al-Anon!

Jackpots

I'd been asked to speak at an Al-Anon meeting on the topic "Miracles of the Program." I told one of my friends about how excited I was to speak. I love miracles! Especially when people end up happy and in love, with a gorgeous home and a fantastic car! Or, if it's my miracle, when it's wrapped in a beautiful blue Tiffany box.

"Those aren't miracles, sweetie," she said, laughing. "Those are *jackpots*. Miracles don't always equal fun."

Yes, I seek enlightenment, spiritual growth, and maturity as much as the next guy, but what's wrong with wanting my miracles to be fun? Aren't miracles supposed to be easy? Miracles that require me to do tasks don't hold interest for me. Miracles that occur as a result of great patience or a sustained effort on my part are even *less* interesting.

As I was speaking at the meeting that night, it occurred to me that, while I prefer miracles that involve a spectacle and theatrics, or at least a winning lotto ticket, the sweetest miracle in my life has been the *direct result* of my commitment to Al-Anon and a growing relationship with God.

My biggest miracle has been that of a changed heart.

I'll take the miracle of a changed heart over a beautiful blue Tiffany box or a winning Powerball number. Most days, that is.

In spite of myself:

True miracles rarely include Powerball numbers.

Half-Arsed

People in recovery often talk about "half measures availing us nothing." Before I found Al-Anon, I was a big believer in half-arsed measures.

Everyone has a dream, I told myself. *It takes a lot of work to make dreams happen. It requires focus—weekends working while everyone else is out at parties, having fun. Let's face it, it's just not worth it to give something a hundred percent. How many people have wasted years of their lives in pursuit of an Oscar, or run for public office and never achieved their dream?*

When you do everything half-arsed, you never have to fear you've wasted your life giving it your all and failed.

Thanks to Al-Anon, I don't do life half-arsed anymore. Because of recovery and a renewed connection to my Higher Power, I am able to commit to at least trying my best, and to be of service to others. My best, at times, may just mean smiling at someone and not leaving work early when I know I can get away with it. Or, my best might be just refraining from being a jerk to someone else. My best may not be one hundred percent, and that's okay. But I can guarantee, I never settle for doing anything half-arsed anymore. It's simply not very nice.

In spite of myself:
Half-arsed measures avail me nothing,
but if I am willing, I will change.

Control

I was invited to Al-Anon by a friend of mine. Actually, I wasn't really invited; it was more like I was *told* to go. As in, "There's a meeting on Third Street. Good luck, and don't ever call me again."

You see, by the time I'd gotten into recovery, I had exasperated enough of my loved ones that no one said, "Really? You think you need some help? You're kidding!"

Most of my friends and family members responded with, "Thank God. You're a wreck." Or, "It's about time, sister!"

I was slightly offended by their responses. I wasn't a horrible person. It's not like I had buried bodies under my floorboards. I was just a tiny bit dramatic and a little . . . controlling.

"A little controlling?" my cousin snorted. "The nuns at my Catholic school were a little controlling. You, my dear, are very . . ."

"Okay, okay, I get it," I interrupted. "I'm a control freak. So stop calling me if you don't want me around."

"I want you around," she replied. "It's just that I want you around in a less controlling way."

"Fine!" I screamed, as I headed off to my first meeting.

Because of Al-Anon, I've gone from "very" controlling to "slightly" controlling. And while I, myself, am capable of distinguishing the difference between *a little* control and *a lot* of control, some people aren't. The great thing is, I no longer feel the need to explain the difference to people who will *never* get it.

In spite of myself:

Today I'm setting myself, and my dial, on "control-light."

Passive-Aggressive Playbook

I've always admired passive-aggressive people because, although they make everyone else around them absolutely miserable, they are truly skillful when it comes to avoiding conflict.

I used to have no idea how to resolve *anything* without conflict, so I decided to take a page from the relatively unknown, incredibly useful Passive-Aggressive Al-Anon Playbook.

For instance, I tried an experiment with the alcoholic in my life. I'd say yes when I meant no to see if he'd do what I wanted. I'd "forget" to complete tasks I had promised to do, all while appearing to be friendly and super cooperative. I'd withhold my opinion when I was asked for it, and I'd agree to doing things I had no intention of participating in. Because it worked so well, I started trying this approach with friends and colleagues at work. But before long, the real me came out: the critical know-it-all, the one who couldn't keep an opinion to herself if her life depended on it. And before long, I began to do something that a dyed-in-the-wool passive-aggressive Al-Anon would *never* do: I told people to "shove off."

While I fantasize about life being easier if I were passive-aggressive, deep down I know I'll never pull it off. It's simply not in my character to pretend people aren't irritating me.

The good part about this story is that, since I found Al-Anon, I have noticed that people, in general, are a heck of a lot less irritating than they were before I came into the program. I must be rubbing off on them.

In spite of myself:
I'll put the playbook down today.

Happy Talk

Numerous scientific experiments, carried out by some very smart people who do experiments, have proven that human beings are poor predictors of what will make them happy over the long term.

In fact, 90 percent of the people surveyed in one of those experiments were more disappointed after having received the very thing they claimed to have wanted. Does that sound familiar, oh, friend of mine *who was sure that landing that promotion was all she wanted?* Or, other friend of mine *who promised that once he got a girlfriend he'd never ask for anything again?*

When it comes to wanting, our imaginations can be slippery, and yet the strange part is that we still continue to want certain things, believing they are critical to our happiness. I'm sure there's some very specific evidence about this—propagation of the species and that sort of stuff—but for me, the takeaway is: Be careful what you wish for because you just might get it.

Or, in the words of my wise, old grandfather, "If you've got a bed and food in your belly, you have all you need. So pull yourself together!" Or, in the words of my grandmother, "Be thankful for what you don't have, because one thing's certain, once you get what you want, you'll be belly-achin' about it soon enough."

No matter what I have, what I lack, or how difficult things may be, I have decided to be happy today.

In spite of myself:

Today I will be happy, no matter how hard it is.

Caring

My version of "caring" before coming to Al-Anon was losing myself in other people. "Caring" involved a lot of worrying about those people: what they were doing, how they were doing it, and how I might help them do it better.

When I ran out of people to "care" about, I started "caring" about world issues, like war and poverty, and why so many world leaders say "nu-cu-lar" instead of "nu-cle-ar."

Now that I'm working an Al-Anon program, "caring" rarely involves obsessing over or trying to change others. These days, "caring" is more about being there for others, whether it's listening to them or laughing with them, or simply enjoying a cup of coffee together. My new version of caring doesn't involve following people around in my car, reading their e-mails, or teaching them how to dress better. Or trying to solve their problems.

Caring also no longer includes screaming matches with people who don't agree with me.

Someday, I might be so caring that I'm mistaken for a saint, but for now, it's enough that I do my best to let those close to me know they're loved and appreciated. Minus the screaming, the stalking, and the reading of e-mails.

I've also backed off from obsessing about world issues, especially those I can't do anything about. Unless it involves the mispronunciation of the word "nuclear." I can't be held responsible for the fallout on that one.

In spite of myself:
Caring and controlling: not the same thing.

Conspiracies

Several years ago, a UK magazine found that 25 percent of the people it surveyed did not believe Neil Armstrong actually landed on the moon. These people were convinced the moon landing was an elaborate scheme of epic proportions between Hollywood and the U.S. government.

It got me thinking: What kinds of people are stubborn enough to insist the hundreds of moon-landing reports and photos, and all those written accounts, were made up? Do they think the lunar landing was a massive conspiracy that the entire world participated in? Wouldn't it have been easier and cheaper to just go to the moon than to waste all that time and money faking it?

Seriously, what kinds of holdouts believe they're right despite all the evidence to the contrary? What sorts of people think they are right and *the rest of the entire world is wrong?* Who is so obnoxious to think they have it all figured out, but the rest of the world is just outright stupid? What kind of a person secretly believes they could do things better than God, at times?

Who? I'll tell you who. Me. Without Al-Anon.

In spite of myself:
God, help me not hide behind misguided theories.

The Hokey Pokey

Recently, I saw a bumper sticker that read, "What if the Hokey Pokey really is what it's all about?"

I've spent a lot of time pondering the meaning of life, so when I came to the conclusion that it may just boil down to the Hokey Pokey, I actually felt a lot better. That bumper sticker got me thinking: All the worry and stress I put on myself—perfectionism, obsession with self-improvement, the need to control—and what if it all boils down to putting my right foot in and my right foot out and my right foot in and shaking it all about?

After all, I did a mean Hokey Pokey when I went to the roller skating rink in grade school. I went roller skating every weekend and lived for the moment when they played "The Hokey Pokey" song. And that really was what life was all about—those moments of freedom and joy, being blissfully uninhibited and jumping around on a pair of roller skates.

Maybe the point is to stop with all the worrying about what other people are doing or thinking and to enjoy life, lighten up a bit, and let go—throw on your roller skates, eat Cherry Garcia ice cream, and hug random people you see on the street. Though I'm not really sure how to do those things while on roller skates.

In truth, nobody really has any idea of what it's "all about," but I'm guessing the Hokey Pokey and putting "your whole self in" to whatever you're doing might be a darn good place to start.

In spite of myself:
Today, I'm going to shake it all about.

Breathe

Someone said, "Life isn't measured by the amount of breaths you take, but by the amount of times your breath's been taken away."

Before I came into Al-Anon, my breath was taken away almost daily—because I was frequently in a state of shock about how stupidly people behaved. I know, I know, everyone is doing the best they can, blah, blah, blah. But let's get real—in most instances, the bar has been set pretty darn low. At least, that's how I used to think. I was fairly cynical and judgmental. I was certain that I knew how to do things *the "right" way*, and life would be better if other people would follow my lead.

Even after some time in recovery, there are still moments when I have to restrain myself because I want to scream to my colleagues and friends, as well as my family members, "Really? This is the best you people can do? Because if it is, you seriously need to look at the meaning of the term 'best'!"

In Al-Anon, I'm learning to take a deep breath and say a little prayer before I shout anything out loud.

These days, if I am forced to shout, I try to refrain from saying anything about "redefining the term 'best,'" because I don't know what someone else's best is. I can make a few suggestions. That is, if people ask.

In spite of myself:
I don't always know what *the "best"* is.

Words

Lord, give us the wisdom to utter words that are gentle and tender,
for tomorrow we may have to eat them.
—MORRIS UDALL

I was so inspired after I read this prayer the first time, I vowed never to utter another word unless it was gentle or tender or kind.

Within ten minutes I regretted making that promise. Because if I'd been forced to eat my words, they would've tasted like a liver and sausage milkshake. In truth, I thought I was gentle and tender, but I had a tendency to be thoughtless and harsh with my words.

In recovery, it's gotten easier for me to tame my tongue and to keep my mouth closed when I want to give someone a "piece of my mind." I have to stay conscious, as my words can easily harm others. It's a struggle. I may have good intentions, but I don't always know if my comments have come off as insensitive, instead of the way I'd intended them. I still need my Higher Power's help to keep my words kind and gentle, especially when emotions are high or I'm feeling really frustrated.

Today, I'm much more careful about offering my unedited opinion about any situation. When I'm tempted to correct someone else, I have to consider how my words are going to taste when they come back up again. And again.

In spite of myself:
If I have to eat my words, I'd like them to be tasty.

Counseling

My friend was frustrated about her nonexistent love life, so her therapist suggested she begin talking to God as if *he* were her fiancé. Sort of taking God to premarital counseling, if you will.

So, I thought *I'd* try taking my Higher Power to counseling. I started talking to God as if he were my last boyfriend. I gave him a list of the many things that bothered me, including his unwillingness to work on our relationship, and, more specifically, how I had to make most of the effort to keep things "fresh" between us. I told him I didn't feel he was available when I needed him. I got no response. I told him I might have to leave if things didn't improve. Nothing.

Then I told God I didn't think he understood me or really cared about my feelings. Silence. I tried again, and demanded that he tell me what the future held for us. Nada.

Wow, this really is like my last relationship, I thought. I finally told God that if he wasn't going to communicate with me, it might be good to spend time apart. Still nothing.

The next day I got a phone call out of the blue. It was an old friend calling to say he loved me. I didn't answer the phone because I was still upset with God. Why can't *my Higher Power* ever say those kinds of things to me?

In spite of myself:

Silence doesn't mean God doesn't hear me.

Lemons

When I was in fourth grade, my teacher talked about how, if one lemon threw itself over a ledge, the other lemons would follow, without question. One lemon after another, until one by one, they all disappeared into the sea below.

I couldn't understand why lemons would do that. It seemed so sad, all those depressed little lemons.

"It's the lemon's nature," my teacher explained. Apparently, lemons are migratory beings, and when their population becomes too great, some jump off cliffs in search of new habitats.

"Lemons are a lot like humans," my teacher then said. "When we go along unquestioningly with popular opinion and follow others without thinking for ourselves, we risk our own happiness and suffer the consequences."

I decided then and there that I would never allow myself to act like a lemon, or be swayed by groupthink. Over time, it became more difficult to remain true to that inner voice. And yet, whenever I was in trouble, I'd harken back to that mental picture of hundreds of bright little lemons heaving themselves off rocky cliffs.

Years later, when I finally realized the teacher was talking about lemmings, not lemons, I began to question his decision to present such dark subject matter to a bunch of fourth graders. And when I learned that lemmings don't actually choose to jump off cliffs, I also started to seriously doubt the quality of my grade school education.

In spite of myself:
When life gives me lemons,
I won't let them throw themselves off a ledge.

Trademarkable

My boss had decided to hire one of those expensive Ivy League business coaches. After a few months of working with said coach, my boss came to the conclusion that many of his own ideas were so brilliant they deserved a trademark.

When my boss wasn't out golfing or skiing, he would often send me e-mails about his latest brainstorm. One morning he called me at home from the road.

"Did you read the e-mail I just sent you?" he asked impatiently.

"You mean the idea for the Thai Me Up restaurant chain campaign?" I replied in a 6:00 a.m. stupor.

"Shhhh!" he interrupted. "Don't repeat *a thing to anyone* until I've called my attorney and gotten the idea registered. And I'd like you to start keeping a list of all the brilliant things I say, in case they're trademarkable."

"Brilliant, sir," I said. Someone yelled, "Fore!" in the background.

I wanted to ask my boss if he'd thought of trademarking the term "jackass," but I didn't. Recovery has taught me not to react in the moment to *anything*. It's critical that I keep some of my thoughts to myself. Especially the first ones that come to mind. Especially if they're trademarkable.

In spite of myself:

God, help me know which thoughts to keep to myself today.

Flip

I often struggle with knowing the difference between my will and God's will. Life can be very confusing, and there are times when I can't find the answers to my questions. Some are important questions, such as: How much should I contribute to my money market account? Is nondairy the solution to permanent weight loss? Do Uggs work with skinny jeans?

Recently, I started carrying a silver dollar to help me when I have a big decision to make but I don't have clarity about what to do. I'll pose my question to the silver dollar and throw the coin up in the air to get the answer. Heads is generally God's will; tails is mine.

Sometimes it takes a few coin tosses before I'm sure of the answer. There are times when I have to go a few rounds—three out of four, five out of seven . . . just to make sure.

I'll admit, I could be more scientific about my decision-making process, but I try to steer clear of anything that involves statistics or the law of averages, two things I know nothing about.

I also stay away from kooky, bizarre things, like the Magic 8-Ball or the pendulum. Who honestly thinks they're going to get an answer from a silly rock tied to the bottom of a piece of string? Really!

I much prefer things that are reliable. And what could be more reliable than silver? Aside from gold, that is.

In spite of myself:

Today I'll rely on good sense
and my Higher Power for direction.

Dear Sir

I received an e-mail this morning that was supposedly from a friend of mine. The e-mail said something like:

> I am being held against my will in a small Chinese village against my will. Please remit funds equivalent to $55,000 dollars American to account now. I have with certainty knowledge that individuals are to be absolved. Shortly of any wrongdoing for my being withheld. But you must remit funds now or I will not last long. Please reply to my email in urgency. Much of your support is appreciated.

I don't believe my friend wrote that e-mail because he's a much better writer than that. Plus, he's never even left the country. Also, I saw him last night at Yogurt Mania.

Unfortunately, I often hear stories about people who do fall for these e-mail scams and end up losing their life savings. I guess people believe what they want to, even when it doesn't make sense. Even when it goes against their better judgment.

I decided to respond to the person who wrote that e-mail. I told them I didn't appreciate them taking the easy way out by bilking people out of money. I suggested that they find a more honorable way to earn a living, like the rest of us do. I also attached information on a "work from home" ad I saw online.

In spite of myself:

Is there any area of my life where I'm taking the easy way out?

Deeper Thoughts

Research says the average person has 40,000 thoughts per day. I've heard it said that Al-Anons have *the same* four thoughts, 10,000 times per day.

The only thoughts I had when I came into Al-Anon were:

1. What are you thinking about?
2. What are you thinking about me?
3. What the hell is wrong with you?
4. Why doesn't anyone listen to me?

Now that I've been in recovery a while, my thoughts are less centered around other people and what they are doing or thinking. I'm more aware of my own feelings, and I spend a lot less time worrying about other people.

That isn't to say that the above questions still don't come up every once in a while. For instance, Question #3 still comes up— almost daily—but I spend considerably less time on Questions #1 and #2. Unless I've just met someone, and I really like him.

Today, I have a broader range of thoughts. I just can't remember any of them at this particular moment. I would, however, like to know the answer to the following question: What are the four thoughts the other Al-Anons have 10,000 times per day?

In spite of myself:

Am I thinking my thoughts, or are my thoughts thinking me?

Inside Job

"It's an inside job," is what many people say about recovery. The work is hard and intensive and highly personal. It requires a commitment to the truth and rigorous honesty. And, truth be told, I'd rather it be an outside job.

I live in a city where I can find more help for fixing my outsides quicker than you can say "Botox party." People who can get "outside help" are a dime a dozen in my town. Which isn't to say I'll refuse to get that kind of "outside help" when the time comes, but that's another subject, entirely.

Fixing my outsides is a heck of a lot easier than fixing my insides. Thankfully, I don't have to do the inside "fixing." As long as I stay willing and open, my Higher Power is in charge of making lasting changes to my character. Of course, I have to take contrary action, but God is ultimately in charge of the resulting changes in me.

As long as I show up and keep working the Twelve Steps, I will get better and more recovered.

Unfortunately, as time passes, gravity affects me, and I also get more wrinkled. And believe me, when that time comes, I'll take all the "outside" help I can get. But I'll always trust God for the "inside" help.

In spite of myself:
*I'd prefer a good old-fashioned nip and tuck
to a lot of hard work.*

Faces

I once had a friend who could read people's faces. She said the amount of space between a person's eyelids and brows directly relates to their ability to be open and intimate.

I cried after she read my face because, according to her theory and my facial symmetry, it takes too much time for me to open up. I want to be one of those people who are naturally trusting and approachable. But, alas, I was born with high brows and arches, so I'm destined for misery and isolation—it's all there in the space above my eyelids.

My friend also said she could determine a person's need for attention by the thickness of their lips. According to her analysis, I tend to give more attention to others than I demand. Luckily, my lips didn't give me away on that one, because I really *want* more attention given to me than I want to *give* to others. In true Al-Anon fashion, I allow people to think it's all about them, but it's really all about me.

This friend and I had a falling out a few years after she read my face. She said she didn't feel our friendship could progress because my face didn't work for her. I told her that was fine with me because I didn't like the way her ears were positioned on her head. It signified to me that she had a problem with loyalty.

In spite of myself:
Is my face giving me away?

Slogans

I once worked for a clothing company and part of my job was to write slogans to go on T-shirts. They didn't choose me because I was talented. They just didn't want to pay licensing fees to a famous artist, so they had me write knock-off versions of her corny, sappy cards.

I'll admit I enjoyed seeing my words printed on T-shirts in retail superstores. Slogans printed over floral designs with sayings, like: "A dream is a heart your wish makes," "Your footprints are forever on my soul," and "You have my heart . . . inside out."

I thought I was rather clever. Actually, I thought I was somewhat of a virtuoso and this ragtag company was lucky to have someone with my level of talent working with them.

As part of my Step work in Al-Anon, I've had to look at my attitude and how it affects all areas of my life. When it comes to my career, I discovered I was a perfectionist and *slightly* full of myself.

Recovery has taught me to be genuinely grateful, aware that I'm no better or worse than anyone else. I am a "worker among workers," and my spiritual job is to be of service to others and to God. It's no longer all about me and ego gratification. Although, I must admit, I do still have a few clever ideas. In fact, I've already thought of a few of the punny names I'd come up with should I ever get a gig working for a nail polish company. My first color: "The Twelve Shades of Recoberry."

In spite of myself:
What's your shade of recovery?

R.E.S.P.onsibility

Recovery is a bit like being on house arrest, only without the ankle bracelet and the probation officer. Even though I don't have a prison record and I retain the right to vote, I need to keep recovery and my connection to God first in my life, or I'll slip back to my old ways of being selfish, arrogant, and a bit of a drag.

Recovery's hard work. Going to meetings, putting up with annoying people, apologizing for mistakes I may or *may not* have made, being responsible for my own life, staying out of other people's business. It can be exhausting. Sometimes, like yesterday, I feel like screaming, "Hey, can't I take it easy for a day? For once in my life, can I *not* do the right thing?"

Then there are the times when I actually do scream those words and I skip a few meetings and stop praying. But eventually I find myself *wanting* recovery and *missing* my Al-Anon meetings.

"Recovery *is* a lot of hard work," my sponsor tells me. "But what else are you gonna do?"

She's right. Recovery may be hard, but un-recovery is even harder. Getting what I want right now feels good, but it seldom results in long-term peace for me. Ultimately, I'd rather be doing the things that lead to lasting happiness, peace, and a connection to my Higher Power. Things that don't lead to house arrests or ankle bracelets.

In spite of myself:
Recovery rarely leads to ankle bracelets.

Keeping Score

I'm not great with lists—except when it comes to keeping track of all the injustices that have been done to me. With those, I am astoundingly accurate.

It's not like I have a scorecard of injustices on a shelf in my bedroom, next to the jewelry drawer. I don't. Anymore. I threw it away. Yes, there have been plenty of times when I've been tempted to retrieve that list, but I don't.

Actually, I burned the list, so it can't be retrieved. For a long time, I kept a copy of the list on my laptop. I dragged it into the trash, but it doesn't take a rocket scientist to realize that all computers have a secure trash, so if I wanted to, I could retrieve the list from my hard drive, if I really wanted it.

Anyway, that's not the kind of person I want to be: one who knows where she keeps the list of wrongs done to her by others.

No, I want to be the person who doesn't even know what a scorecard of injustices looks like, or where it might be stored in a laptop trash can or on a shelf next to a jewelry drawer. I'd rather be the one who doesn't even remember the last time she was wronged. For now, I'll settle for throwing the list away after I've written it.

In spite of myself:
God, help me forget where I keep my lists.

Members Only

Tradition #3 in the Big Book of Alcoholics Anonymous says it's up to individuals to decide if they qualify for membership in a Twelve Step program. It's very different from those trendy New York nightclubs where you have to prove you're hot enough to make it past the velvet rope.

Part of the allure of those posh clubs is the potential for being accepted. The potential for rejection from some fully tattooed, muscle-headed bouncer dressed in black can be anxiety provoking.

There's a high that comes from getting the nod of approval and being granted entry when other people are being turned away. It feeds the ego and implies you're "special," a part of the in crowd. The downside is that once you're in, you have to deal with the other "special" jerks that have also been granted access.

In Al-Anon, no one gives me the once-over. No one can grant me entry or banish me from a meeting because I'm not "special" enough. Which is a great relief, because I'd rather not have to forgo dinner so I can afford to get my hair blown out so I'll look good enough to get into a meeting.

No velvet ropes, no lines, or being judged by our hair or our clothes. In Al-Anon, we're all good enough.

In spite of myself:

There are no velvet ropes to get past in Al-Anon.

Ode to You

I love you, even though you aren't the easiest person in the world to be around. And no matter what other people say about your selfish and narcissistic tendencies, I find you interesting and fun—especially when you aren't yelling at me.

I'm an Al-Anon, which means that easy-breezy love, as portrayed on those online dating commercials, holds no interest at all for me. I want love to push me beyond my limits, leaving me bereft of sense and unable to think clearly. I want love to test my capacity for pain and sorrow because I believe that intensity is a sign of passion.

Admittedly, there have been times when I've thought about dropping you off in the middle of the desert with no cell phone or water—but I couldn't do that. I'd miss you way too much! The way you fold your arms over your chest when you don't get what you want. The way you second-guess everyone, including the GPS. It's your unbridled confidence, your arrogance and surety, that's so sexy! It makes me want to kiss you—or, alternately, smother you in your sleep.

I have a tendency to pick people who are challenging, but out of all my relationships, you're one of the easiest. And I mean that in the kindest way possible! Thanks for being you. I wouldn't change a thing about you . . . not too many things about you.

In spite of myself:
Easy-breezy love: Who needs it? Not me!

Good Fortune

I recently got a fortune cookie that read, "You shall have every-thing you desire in this lifetime, providing you do not, under any circumstances, read a fortune cookie."

While it made me laugh, a small part of me wondered: *What if it's a sign? What if this is proof I'm karmically cursed?*

The truth is that it was just some smartass who writes fortune cookies for a living having some fun at work. But for someone like me, who is both superstitious and neurotic (a very charming combination), the fortune felt very personal.

After calling a few friends to make sure it wasn't a sign from God that my life was heading in a downward spiral, I decided to rewrite the fortune for myself.

The fortune now reads, "You shall have everything you desire in this lifetime, providing you ignore stupid fortune cookies." I still keep the fortune in my wallet as a reminder that fortune cookies don't speak for my Higher Power, and they are not the most accurate predictors of my chances for happiness. At least, I don't think they are. I mean, I really hope they aren't.

In spite of myself:

I shall have everything I desire in this lifetime—
including fortune cookies!

Seriously?

Yesterday was one of those days when I wanted to scream at my Higher Power, "Are you serious with this week? You've got to be kidding! What the hell is wrong with people?"

I remember looking at the calendar, specifically, last Tuesday and thinking, *When did the Mayans predict the ending of the world? Because if it isn't this week, then it's this month for sure. The world has gone completely insane!*

I'm normally an optimistic type, but there are times when I wonder if everyone around me is either unconscious or just really, really stupid. So I took an aspirin and went to bed because sometimes I can't deal with humanity, and when I get overwhelmed with life, I generally find that taking a nap helps.

I've also learned that when I'm feeling like people are insane and I'd be relieved if the world were coming to an end, the last thing I should do is consult the Mayan calendar. In fact, when I'm feeling this way, the solution is to take a deep breath, say a prayer, read some Al-Anon literature, and get to a meeting. Oh, and stay unarmed.

In spite of myself:

A bad day doesn't mean I'm insane,
or that anyone else is, either. Seriously.

APRIL

Should've

There's nothing that makes me want to go postal more than any sentence that begins with, "You should have." And unfortunately I've had my share of people telling me, "You should have" throughout my lifetime. Even over the past twenty-four hours.

People who use this phrase usually do so during times of great distress, like after you've lost a job, or found out your ex has been siphoning funds from his employer, or chosen to have elective surgery and it didn't go so well. "You should have" is not useful, especially when the comment has *anything* to do with money you've already spent or a binding contract you've already signed.

"You should've known better" is what the person really means. Or, "You should have been smarter than you are," or, "You should be smarter than you are." The truth is, no one can know what they don't know, and it never helps to remind someone they've just made a huge mistake.

"Should haves" are simply not recommended. Ever. In fact, the next time someone begins a sentence with "You should have," I give you permission to thump that person on the head and then say, "I'm sorry, I should not have done that."

So then, I guess "should haves" *can* be helpful at times. But I was wrong about the thumping part. Please forgive me. I stand corrected. Violence is never recommended. I should have given that statement more thought before making it.

In spite of myself:
No "shoulds" and no thumps for anyone today.
Just plenty of love.

Lies, Lies, Lies

One of my favorite lines comes from an episode of *Seinfeld:*

GARY: The truth is, George, I'm living a lie.
GEORGE: Just one? I'm living, like, twenty.

When I came into Al-Anon, I was living a lot of lies. Nothing criminal—it's not like there were severed body parts stuffed under the cushions of my couch, or like I was selling crowns from cadavers out of my trunk—so I was able to rationalize them with, *What's the big deal? Isn't everyone living a lie or two?*

When I read Step #4—"Made a searching and fearless moral inventory of ourselves"—I figured it would be a piece of cake. I didn't have much to hide.

I didn't know that a searching and fearless inventory would reveal the lies I told myself, unveiling layers of rage and pain, jealousy and self-righteousness. I rarely shared my true feelings about anything, especially if it meant being vulnerable. I'd become a master at deceiving myself and others. There were lies I'd buried and forgotten about. I also had to look at the ways I'd been keeping the truth from myself. While doing my Step #4 work, I discovered how those seemingly pint-sized lies were wearing away at my serenity. And my soul.

Today, I aim for rigorous honesty in all of my relationships, including with myself and especially with God. And while I'm not perfect, I'm doing much better than I used to. It feels fantastic to not be living, like, twenty lies anymore.

In spite of myself:

A searching and fearless moral inventory
may turn up a few surprises.

Retail Therapy

I once worked for a high-end retailer. The thing I hated most about it was women who would try on roomfuls of designer clothes and toss them on the floor, inside out, and leave without buying anything.

I had to keep in check the part of me that was tempted to follow them out of the store and yell, "Do I look like your mother? Get back in there and pick those damn clothes up off the floor!" Sometimes the darker part won the argument, and I'd make snarky remarks loud enough for them to hear.

Slowly by slowly (my version of "*slowly but surely*"), I began to practice the tools of Al-Anon. You know, the tools that remind me not to make a big deal out of everything. The tools that tell me to pray for the very people I resent, even when I don't mean it.

I spent a lot of time just praying for the willingness to pray for those women. Eventually, there came a time when my thoughts changed from the insincere and cynical, *How can I be of service to this totally inconsiderate, self-absorbed, entitled idiot who thinks the world is her laundry hamper?*" to a genuine, *How can I be of service to God and this person?* End of sentence. Period.

That change of heart took time. I was fascinated to find that my serenity had become more important than following women around the store to lecture them about how to behave in public. For the most part. There were a few times when it *was* important to give them such feedback.

In spite of myself:
Slowly by slowly, I'll practice the tools of Al-Anon.

Searching and Fearless?

Step #4: "Made a searching and fearless moral inventory of ourselves."

Unlike many Al-Anons, I have no qualms about completing a moral inventory. I do inventories almost constantly, and I've discovered I have the rare talent of being able to do inventories for other people: friends, family members, colleagues, and—when appropriate—complete strangers.

I believe in giving back whenever I can, and I think it's important to take my hard-earned wisdom and share it with those who are less fortunate. I come across so many people on a daily basis who could benefit from an internal house cleaning—or at the very least, an attitude adjustment. There are even a few folks I'd like to offer grooming and etiquette tips to, and others who are in dire need of complete makeovers.

But all in good time!

I'm actually looking forward to doing my own personal inventory when I can get around to it, because I am all about fearlessness and searching . . . all about the moral and the humble. These are things I strive to do and be each and every day. With an emphasis on the moral and the humble.

In spite of myself:

I vow to always make myself available to offer others
tips on their Fourth Step work.

Wanting

Much of the time I do not want what I have.

Insatiability is one of my biggest character defects. Even before Al-Anon, I was never one for the "want what you already have" concept, and counting my blessings is something I rarely do because I'm generally too busy counting the things I *don't* have.

I've discovered that the antidote for my insatiability is to remember my blessings, whether they are love, abundance, or time, and to then share those blessings with the people around me. If I have extra time, I try to share them with someone who needs my help. If I have financial abundance, I share what I can with others, and when I feel full in my relationships, I try to show more kindness and appreciation for the ones I love.

I don't do these things because I'm so noble; I do them because I know they lead to serenity. When I give my time, my creativity, or my love to others, I'm reminded of how blessed I am. It also helps me appreciate the things I already have.

On average, I'd say that when I give my time and blessings to others, 95 percent of the time I feel better. That's pretty good, 95 percent, is it not?

Wanting what I have takes effort on my part. It's not easy, but it gets easier with time. Usually. There are times when it gets harder with time, but let's not go there right now.

In spite of myself:

Today I will want what I have.

Panic

I had called my friend for the third time that afternoon, panicked. "I'm worried, Scott. I think I've forgotten how to love."

He asked me if I'd been to an Al-Anon meeting lately.

"Why?" I asked huffily. "What if I have forgotten what it feels like to love? What if my opportunities for love are over? This is a real crisis. Meetings don't solve everything, you know."

"Ummm . . . okay, a meeting is just a suggestion," Scott said. He mumbled something about a pot boiling over and hung up the phone.

Exasperated, I went to my home group meeting that evening, where I was greeted with smiles and hugs. It's a joyful Al-Anon group, where I feel completely safe. And loved. When I came home and checked my phone later that night, there was a message from my friend.

"I hope you're feeling better," Scott chirped, "and you've overcome your crisis."

Crisis? What on earth is he talking about? I'm not having a crisis!

I decided I'd call Scott first thing in the morning to make sure he was okay. Sometimes he can be dramatic and over the top. I wish I could get him to an Al-Anon meeting, but all in good time, as they say. All in good time.

In spite of myself:

I often forget what the crisis is
when I'm feeling loved and supported.

Challenges

There are many people in the business world who annoy me, but the ones I find the most irritating are those who use the word "challenge" instead of "problem," the office brownnoser who won't take lunch, and the folks who use phrases like "You're a rock star!" "Let's think outside the box," or "Give it 110 percent."

I'm pretty sure there's a difference between a "challenge" and a "problem." A challenge is something I choose to participate in: climbing the Rocky Mountains or completing the *New York Times* crossword puzzle. They're difficult, but things I choose to take on. A problem, however, is something that is foisted on me against my will: getting pulled over and ticketed by a police officer or being laid off from my job.

I don't want problems. Ever. But I will take on a challenge, especially if it includes traveling to exotic places or involves jewelry.

What does any of this have to do with recovery, you may ask? I'm not entirely sure, but as a point of clarification for those folks who are in recovery, a "problem" is not a "challenge," and human beings cannot give 110 percent. The science just isn't there to prove it.

Finally, unless a person has a top-100 hit song and is posting pictures of themselves partially naked online, they are *not even close* to being a rock star.

In spite of myself:

I can't choose my problems,
but I can choose how I'll respond to them today.

Who Moved My Ruler?

I put down the ruler after measuring the final column on the spreadsheet. Then I called my sponsor, again, to discuss the Fourth Step inventory I'd written and was going to read to her.

"If you want my inventory on an Excel spreadsheet, do the width and height need to be equal? Or, will a Microsoft Word document suffice? And, how many copies should I bring with me?"

"No spreadsheets, no margins," she interrupted. "I get the feeling you're trying to get an 'A' on your inventory."

Me? Trying to earn points, in recovery? Me? Trying to get a good grade? How rude, I thought as I hung up the phone abruptly.

Later that day, I reconsidered my sponsor's highly inappropriate comment. She was right. I wanted my searching and fearless moral inventory to "look good," or at least be better than anyone else's she'd read.

"For the love of God!" I screamed aloud. "Is there any area of my life that isn't affected by my constant need for perfection and moral superiority?"

"No, not really," the walls of the empty room echoed back to me. "Your perfectionistic, overachieving tendencies go wherever *you* go."

Feeling defeated and depressed, I threw my ruler into the trash bin and went to bed. But I fished it out the next morning because it just might come in handy someday. Rulers are highly undervalued in our society.

In spite of myself:
When a ruler makes its way into my inventory,
perfectionism may have taken hold.

Boxing Gloves

I was reading the comments section of one of my favorite blogs. Some of the remarks were rude and inflammatory, and others were unreadable. One of the commentators used no punctuation whatsoever. The guy simply couldn't be bothered to use complete sentences. Instead, he used one-letter responses combined with numbers and acronyms. I was so angered by his bad grammar and poor spelling, I couldn't follow anything he was saying. That's how I respond when people get on my nerves. I forget that they're probably law-abiding human beings, who have families, jobs (in this case, that might be debatable), and friends.

I was growing more and more aggravated by this guy when someone else jumped into the conversation and posted: "Dude, seriously, are you typing with boxing gloves on, or what?"

It was hilarious. It made me LOL so hard I was literally ROFL. So Gr8. But it also reminded me of myself. Whenever I get really passionate or hypercritical about other people's faults, I lose perspective. I judge the people I love—and those I don't— harshly. I forget that they're real people with whom I just happen to disagree. They're not purposefully trying to ruin my day.

With help from God and Al-Anon, I've learned to allow people to be exactly who they are. Even if they don't know how to use full sentences or make intelligent comments. Or if they use hackneyed, overwrought acronyms and abbreviations.

In spite of myself:

I'll take the boxing gloves off before I start judging others.

What Ifs

Once upon a time, there was a princess whose favorite pastime was sitting on her throne in her castle and pondering the question, "What if?"

What if other people in her life never changed?

What if she never got another great job?

What if she never loved again?

What if there was an earthquake and she hadn't stockpiled enough canned goods or silver?

Then one day, the princess decided to write down all of her "what ifs" on a piece of paper. It took her three years to finish the list. Afterward, she took a very, very, very long nap.

When she awakened, months later, the princess looked at the list and had a long, hearty laugh, because she realized that most of the "what ifs" that had been causing her great sorrow were entirely out of her control and would probably never happen.

The princess immediately put the list of "what ifs" into a small wooden box. She said a prayer of surrender and turned all of the worries in that box over to God. The princess hasn't opened that God box since the day she placed her list into it.

Of course, it's only been a day since she turned her worries over, but the princess feels fairly certain she won't open her God box again. Not today, anyway.

In spite of myself:
What if I forgot I even had a list of "what ifs"?

Blossomin' Bud

There's a quote attributed to Anaïs Nin that reads, "And the day came when the risk to remain tight in a bud was more painful than the risk it took to blossom." It may not have been Nin, but a poet named Elizabeth Appell.

When I first heard that quote, I didn't quite understand it. Obviously, I want to blossom—who doesn't? In fact, for a long time, I wanted to *be* Blossom, the girl from that old sitcom. She was so adorable! And fun.

Regardless of who said it, the quote makes it sound as if blossoming and getting unstuck is a breeze. It's not. The only time it's easy to get unstuck is when someone else is making all the effort. Getting unstuck requires a lot, and taking such risks when you're all uptight and constricted is a whole different ballgame.

My own "blossoming" was not graceful, like a lovely red rose flourishing in stop-motion in a Jane Austen movie montage. I had to make compromises. I had to stretch myself, move in new directions, and take a lot of contrary action.

And once I started blossoming, I couldn't stop. I had to stay open, keep growing. It was very uncomfortable, and it hurt. But in the end, it was worth it.

If I could, I'd probably amend that Anaïs Nin quote to this: "Blossoming may be risky, but sitting on your bud hurts more."

In spite of myself:
God, help me get off my bud today.

Examinations

They say the unexamined life is not worth living. And as an Al-Anon, I couldn't agree more.

I examine life all the time. My life, your life, his life, her life. Their life together. Her life, should she wise up and dump him. His life, if he were to adopt a Rhodesian ridgeback, marry me, and move to Uruguay.

It is much easier for me to examine the lives of other people than my own. I can see where the people I care about have gone wrong. I know their blind spots, their obsequiousness; I can identify their predisposition to self-sabotage, and I know what aspects of their personality need improvement. But when it comes to my own life, I rarely have enough perspective to see things clearly.

That's why I love having a sponsor and friends in recovery. They can see where I need more support, areas where I'm holding on too tightly, or situations where I need to take contrary action.

They offer me solutions that include less navel-gazing and more surrender to my Higher Power. These solutions usually don't . . . in fact, *never* include an examination of *anyone else.*

In spite of myself:
Obsequious: sycophantic, submissive, fawning.

Bookends

"Bookending," in recovery, is calling someone before and after you do something that is risky or anxiety provoking, for support.

Prior to Al-Anon, I had my own adaptation of "bookending." It went as follows: I'd call a few friends and ask them how I should handle a certain problem. Inevitably, I'd get a few very different answers, which would do nothing but confuse me more. So I'd go with the answer that sounded the easiest. If things didn't work out, I'd be mad at my friends. *Who the hell were they to tell me how to run my life?*

Today, I use the Al-Anon version of "bookending." It starts with a call to a buddy in the program. Usually we begin with a prayer, and together we discuss my options, weighing the possible outcomes and consequences of each decision. It rarely involves my Al-Anon buddy giving advice.

Once I've reasoned things out, made my decision, and gotten feedback, then I take the next indicated action. If need be, I check back in with my buddy, and then I move on with the rest of my day. I let God work out the results.

This new, saner approach to "bookending" was hard for me to do at first. Mainly because there was no one to blame if things didn't turn out the way I'd planned. That was when I *really* started to miss my old friends.

In spite of myself:
The bookend was patented in 1877.

Gettin' All Recovery

I was arguing with an Al-Anon friend of mine. One of us is always running late for our plans, and it was making the other one upset.

So the friend who was troubled asked the other one, "Have you talked to your sponsor about how to handle the character defect of being late all the time?"

"For goodness' sake!" the other friend shouted. "My character defects are none of your business!"

"Well, I'm just saying," the friend replied sweetly. "Only out of concern for your recovery."

"Don't go 'gettin' all recovery' on me just because you don't like it when I'm late," the friend snapped. "Suggesting that I call my sponsor, recommending an inventory—you're using recovery to try to control me."

My friend was right. I *was* using recovery language to manipulate her. Ironically, the very next day, one of my Al-Anon friends suggested I do an inventory on my *chronic tardiness*! I couldn't believe it. What a control freak! Besides, who in the twenty-first century uses the word "tardy"? At least *I* had the good sense not to use the word "tardy" with my friend.

In spite of myself:

Am I "gettin' all recovery" with someone in my life?

Honest

"Honesty" is highly overrated in our culture. I don't know if it's the result of being deluged with technology twenty-four hours a day or the swift pace of life now, but it seems everyone—Al-Anons included—feels the need to give an "honest" opinion about *everything*: religion, politics, child-rearing, fashion, entertainment, gluten-free products . . . I mean, everything!

Perhaps it's time we Al-Anons considered withholding our "honest" opinion. You know, by saying things like, "Wow, you look great today," or, "I like what you had to say at the sales meeting," even if it is a bit of a stretch.

Am I suggesting we lie to each another? No. I just think we might apply the recovery slogan "Act as if" in a way that serves the population. It could be that my best friend doesn't want my critical opinion of her new sweetheart, or whether she should allow her toddler to drink Mountain Dew. Most people would probably rather just get a hug or a kiss on the cheek instead of my insightful, penetrating viewpoints about their brother's narcissistic tendencies.

The kind of "Acting as if" I'm talking about assumes that my friends are doing their best and the problems of the world aren't mine to solve. It assumes that God is in charge and life is exactly as it should be.

While honesty makes for a good life, I would also rate "Acting as if," peace, and happiness very highly.

In spite of myself:

My honest opinion: Things are gonna be just fine today!

Autonomy

The meeting was about Al-Anon's Fourth Tradition: "Each group should be autonomous, except in matters affecting another group or Al-Anon or AA as a whole."

At first, this Tradition sounded boring, like reading the directions for a TV remote, or a prenuptial agreement, or any of the other various and sundry contracts I've signed and not bothered to read. When I finally sat down and studied the Fourth Tradition, I found out how important it is to my recovery.

I've heard it called "self-governance with responsibility." While each group is independent, it must remain considerate of the whole. This gives each group the freedom to decide the topics and content of the meetings. The group decides when and where the meeting will be held, and if it will be open or closed. Every Al-Anon group can change the format and has the authority to spend the money it receives as it deems appropriate.

Each group does its own thing within the overall guidelines of the Al-Anon program, being careful not to make a meeting about any particular philosophy, religion, political viewpoint, or hidden agenda. That means I don't have to worry that the sweet old lady who's just given me her phone number is going to offer her opinion on global warming or con me into being part of some bogus Tupperware scam.

This is what keeps the rooms of recovery safe. It also gives me the opportunity to practice governing myself responsibly—which, at some point, will include actually reading the directions for my TV remote.

In spite of myself:
I will try to govern myself responsibly today.

Time Out

I told my Higher Power that I needed some space. It wasn't a huge deal, but as with *any* relationship, things had gotten a bit tense between us; we weren't spending quality time together and things just didn't *feel right*.

In my opinion, my Higher Power had been distant and slightly uncommunicative, and my needs weren't being met. I'd been pretty clear about what I wanted, and I wasn't getting it.

I was pissed off at God, and I said so. Miraculously, he didn't smite me or cause me to be infested with boils. So I told him that if things didn't change, I would have to move on. I poured out my heart and told him exactly how I felt, and what I got back was . . . nothing. Absolutely nothing.

No calls, no e-mails. No tweets. No online pokes or friend requests. I figured I'd give it more time and things would turn around. He'd realize what he was missing out on and beg me to come back.

It was a very dark few weeks.

Then I got a call from two friends in program, seemingly out of the blue, just to tell me they were thinking of me. One friend even said, "I just felt my Higher Power telling me to let you know that you are loved."

I wanted to think this was God's way of reaching out to me, but I couldn't be sure. Things between me and my Higher Power are better now, but there are times when I wish our relationship were as easy for me as it seems to be for my friends.

In spite of myself:
I'll try to keep the lines of communication
with God open today.

Sponsee

The newcomer approached me at the end of an Al-Anon meeting. We chatted for a while, and I gave her my number. After a month or so, she asked me if I'd sponsor her.

My mouth said, "Sure, I'd love to!" but my head said, *What the heck is wrong with you? I'm a complete wreck. I can't help you!* I called my sponsor, thinking she'd support me in waiting until I was "normal" before I began sponsoring others.

"That's a fantastic idea. You'll be a great sponsor to a newcomer," she said.

"You must be confused," I whimpered. "It's me, the spastic one with the blonde hair. Don't you remember me?"

"Just be willing to listen and care," she said. "Work the Twelve Steps, and share your experience, strength, and hope." Sponsoring is a big deal, and I didn't want to screw it up, so I crafted a PowerPoint presentation on how to be a great sponsor. I tried to find that perfect balance between Buddha and Tony Robbins, but with a girly, feminine flair. Just as I was starting to feel good about being the perfect sponsor, my sponsee called. She was taking a break from Al-Anon and would no longer need my help.

"Do you think I did something wrong?" I asked my sponsor.

"It happens, honey. People find their way. Just stay willing to be of service to others."

Later that year, when another woman asked me to sponsor her, I decided to try it without PowerPoint and let God be in charge. I still have no idea what I'm doing, but my sponsee seems to think it's working.

In spite of myself:
God, help me remember that I can't screw it up.

Mr. Emmy

I once worked in advertising for an Emmy Award–winning director who had masterminded several groundbreaking TV commercials. Part of my job was to keep Mr. Emmy inspired. Apparently, I'm the kind of Al-Anon that is skilled at reading other people's emotions.

This talent of mine was discovered one morning when I came to work and found Mr. Emmy in the parking lot pitching creative ideas to a homeless man. He was supposed to be in a new business pitch meeting. Because I was able to convince Mr. Emmy that he was needed in the meeting, he impressed the client and we landed a huge account. My boss promptly promoted me to head cheerleader.

It's not like it was a difficult job. Mr. Emmy was pretty easy to read—any Al-Anon worth their salt could figure him out. I could tell he was feeling restless when he'd organize his model car collection. I knew he wasn't feeling tall enough when he drove his Ferrari to work.

There were times when it was painful watching Mr. Emmy—when he'd wander around the office with his sunglasses on, clenching the award he'd won for directing a dancing tequila bottle. On those days, I knew he was struggling with his mortality, and I knew exactly what to do, which included: (1) reminding him that advertising did not deserve someone as gifted as he was, and (2) asking him if I could watch his award-winning commercial. Again.

In spite of myself:

I might be the sanest one here,
but it doesn't mean I should be running the show.

Lifting

I recently joined a new gym. Sometimes, instead of feeling like a healthy way to work out, it feels like a cult. People are driven by a fanatical loyalty. All of the weight-lifting exercise regimens have their own names, and people wear the gym's branded T-shirts like a badge of courage. I love their workouts, but the people can be annoying.

It reminds me of my early days in recovery, when I went to an Al-Anon convention. The first day into it, I pulled my sponsor aside.

"These Twelve Steppers are weird," I whispered to her.

"You're right, we are weird," my sponsor giggled.

"It's a cult!" I continued.

"Yes, it could be," she affirmed gently. "Except no one tells you what to believe, you don't have to give anyone money, and you choose a God of your own understanding. No one sets the pace for you, and you're free to come and go as you please."

Her candor inspired me. I knew she was right. Even though it seems kind of weird at first, recovery is entirely up to the individual. There are no rules in Al-Anon, only suggestions. The rest is entirely up to me.

I don't have to do anything I don't want to, or wear a T-shirt to feel a part of the fellowship. No one cares who or what I choose as my Higher Power or expects me to believe what they believe. And the best part? I've never once been asked how much I can bench press at an Al-Anon meeting.

In spite of myself:
I'll exercise my right to believe what works for me.

Copilots

I've often heard people in recovery say, "God is my copilot." My sponsor has a different take on that slogan.

"If you're in a plane and God is the copilot," she said, "you're in deep trouble."

Huh? I told her I didn't get her point.

"If you're flying a plane and God is sitting next to you, why would *you* want to be in charge of the plane?"

Good point. I needed to give that some thought.

I think if God showed up on my plane, I'd probably say, "Hey, God, thanks for stopping by! Would you like some coffee, tea, or juice? No? Okay. Well then, let me be honest. I've never flown a plane before, but it's not rocket science, is it? I mean, I can drive a car, right? I'll just flip this switch, turn on those lights, push that lever, and we'll be on our way! Why don't you relax a little, get some shut-eye? If I need your help, I'll give you a nudge. If that should happen, of course, feel free to pull out that control panel over there and take over. Although I doubt that'll be necessary."

That's what separates people like me from the wise souls in recovery. You know, the people who can out-slogan a slogan and always know the perfect thing to say? Definitely not me.

I am, however, going to do my very best to allow God to be my pilot today. I guess I should read up on what a copilot actually does.

In spite of myself:
Today I'll let the pilot with the most experience fly my plane.

Closeouts

I'd heard rumors about what people in Al-Anon called "doing a Fourth Step." I didn't know much, just that it had something to do with an inventory.

Since "Inventory Close-Out Sale" is one of the most lovely phrases in the English language, I figured I'd get a jump-start on the inventory process and do one of my own.

I made a list of my winter scarves, gloves, and sweaters. I separated them by color schemes, labeled them, and stored them in secure yet breathable plastic containers. I did the same thing for the rest of my winter wardrobe. Those Al-Anons were right. It was hard work, but it felt really good.

"It's not that kind of inventory, sweetie," my friend in the program told me.

Boy, she wasn't kidding! When I finally got to my Fourth Step inventory in Al-Anon, I was shocked! My sponsor said nothing about my wardrobe. My inventory was about admitting my shortcomings and looking at my attitudes and behaviors, and ways that I'd harmed others and myself.

It was much different from organizing my closet.

Now I do a daily inventory, which includes looking at areas of my life that need work and asking God to help me make those changes.

It always improves my emotional state.

Inventories aren't easy. They take willingness, honesty, humility, and contrary action on my part. Sometimes I'd rather just be cleaning out those messy closets and kitchen drawers.

In spite of myself:
I'll take an inventory today, and leave the shoes out of it.

Take a Chance

Today is National Take a Chance Day, the perfect day for you to try out something new. What will *you* take a chance on? Will it be love? Joining a gym? Will it include buying a lottery ticket or a truckload of lollipops? Will it be moving to a different country? Shaving off all of your hair?

Balance, people, balance.

While today was created to encourage risk taking, it's important to try something that will make you feel good about yourself and said accomplishment. You don't have to go overboard, because, as you're surely aware, Al-Anons tend to overdo things.

Try to manage your expectations.

Today you have the freedom to try anything you want to, without having to do it perfectly. Now would be the time to throw in the cliché "Nothing ventured, nothing gained"—but I've decided not to, because Al-Anons know how to make gains, even when they haven't ventured anywhere. For example, once I won a trip to Cancun while I was sick at home, in my pajamas.

So, go on, take a chance, knowing that you can achieve anything—in moderation—that you want to. Except winning the lottery. It's National Take a Chance Day, so everyone will probably play today. Your odds of winning are very slim.

In spite of myself:
Why not take a chance on you today?

Under Pressure

They say the oak grows stronger in contrary winds and diamonds are made under pressure. Both have to endure a lot of adversity in order to . . . *become.*

I'm a delicate sort. Much like a pansy or a rose, a dainty flower that thrives when pampered and treated ever so gently. No harsh winds. And as for gemstones, I like to think of myself as the more humble sapphire or red ruby, as opposed to a showy diamond.

None of that is true. If I were a flower, I'd be of the complex, intense variety—an iris or an orchid—and if I have a choice, I prefer diamonds, and the bigger, the better. However, I have absolutely zero desire to be blown about by a contrary wind; nor do I wish to be strengthened by facing adversity, thank you very much.

Yes, pain may be a part of life, but if less pain means I'll become the metaphorical willow instead of an oak, that's okay by me. If less pressure means I'll end up like a cubic zirconium, the kind they sell at Costco, instead of a Tiffany-quality canary-yellow diamond, then I'll settle for less.

Unfortunately, I've never been able to opt out of adversity. Which is why I'm grateful for Al-Anon, because I can *always* find a meeting where people are kind and gentle when the winds of life grow contrary. Al-Anons accept me as I am—complex, intense, and not always eager to grow.

I may not be able to avoid pain or adversity, but I can find a soft place to land in Al-Anon. And I can always count on them having good snacks.

In spite of myself:
No harsh winds today. Just a light, gentle Al-Anon touch.

Silent Asides

The speaker ended the share by saying, "They did the best they could." Afterward, I nearly lost it. "Oh, no you don't," I hissed. "You're not letting them off that easy! What a bunch of horse doo-doo!" Okay, I didn't say it aloud, but boy, did I want to!

I didn't believe *they* did the best they could. If *they* had done the best they could, I'd be calmer, more successful, and thinner. I wouldn't have found it necessary to spend thousands of dollars on various and sundry therapeutic initiatives.

A short time later, I found myself in a meeting saying, "They did the best they could." I mentally ended the sentence with, *And it sure as hell wasn't good enough.* Since I didn't say it aloud, I figured it was no one's business. It was *my* silent aside.

Eventually my sponsor called me out on these "silent asides" (it turns out she could sense my *real* feelings) and suggested I do some Step work on them. Eventually, I could say, "They did the best they could," and really mean it. No "silent asides" or hidden judgments. What's more, I only had a *few* fleeting thoughts about how much better *I* would have done things.

In spite of myself:
Am I harboring any "silent asides"?

Allowing

When I first came into Al-Anon, I was set on doing recovery "right" and getting through the Twelve Steps as quickly as possible. One day, a well-respected friend of mine in the program asked me, "Do you think flowers toil and struggle? Do you think trees push themselves to grow taller?"

Since we were standing in a church basement and not a garden, I had to close my eyes. I tried to conjure up the image of a rhododendron I'd just planted.

"No," I responded. "I guess they don't."

"Right. The same is true for recovery. Straining does not speed spiritual growth."

I didn't want to tell her I had no idea what she was talking about because she was smiling so sweetly and I was freezing in that basement. I just didn't get her point. Why wouldn't working harder bring me more spiritual growth?

"Don't force things," she said, placing her hand gently over mine. "Stop trying so hard." I stood there for a few moments after she walked away. It felt like one of those pivotal scenes in a film. You know, when the main character has this profound revelation and everything falls into place.

Unfortunately, my friend's wisdom was lost on me. All I could think about was my new rhododendron. I had forgotten to water it. Again.

In spite of myself:

I'll allow things to go, and grow, as they will today.

Missed Boats

Sometimes I worry about missing the boat. Literally, as in being late for boats or appointments. And figuratively, as in, "I've missed the boat. This cannot be my life!"

As a child, I remember the Bible verse about the lilies of the field and how they—and the birds—never worried because they trusted God and they were taken care of.

That used to soothe me until I realized the reason lilies don't worry is because they don't have the ability to think! Also, birds are seldom forced to endure credit checks. And neither has to worry about paying late fees to the IRS.

This tendency to worry about missing the boat really messes with my head, and it never results in peace. When I find myself overwhelmed with worry, missed boats, and wondering what the future holds, I sit myself down and I say a prayer like this: "Okay, God, I am not a flower; neither am I a two-legged, winged bird. I'm a living human being who doesn't trust all this rhythm of the universe malarkey, and I'm scared. I need to be reminded that I haven't missed any boats, and I'm where I should be."

Then I go on with my day. Does the worry return? Yes, it does, sometimes within minutes. But repeating that prayer helps. When it doesn't, I'll go out for a walk in nature. Spending time listening to the birds and reveling in the beauty of the flowers calms me down and helps me connect with my Higher Power. Sometimes I even forget about the boats I've missed.

In spite of myself:

I haven't missed the boat. I'm exactly where I should be.

Unattraction

"If you keep your vibrations up, you'll be powerful enough to attract everything you desire in life," trills the woman who claims to interpret voices from "infinite spirits."

I spent hours upon hours listening to her Law of Attraction CDs before I made the connection that the more I tried to raise my vibrations, the worse my life got.

Still, I decided to give the "Law" one last shot. The channeler was coming to my town in her Airstream travel trailer to host another "Power of Positive Intentions" seminar.

"Oh, no, you don't," a friend of mine said. "You're not spending another dime. You've spent thousands of dollars on that 'attraction' stuff, and it hasn't worked!"

"I know, I feel like the poster girl for the Law of *Un*attraction," I whined. "The more *I* try, the *worse* it gets."

"I think it's time you faced the fact that you're not God, and you're not in control of the universe," she replied softly.

"Well, that was pretty un-positive," I said, as I hung up the phone.

I can do negativity on my own. I don't need her doing it for me, I thought as I promptly took every book, positive affirmation, motivational poster, and *anything* else that was remotely positive and burned it in the kitchen sink. I may not be in control of the universe, but, by golly, I don't have to listen to people who bring my vibes down.

In spite of myself:

I am not in control of the universe.

Flashback

There are times I'm so busy worrying about what other people are doing that I forget I have a life of my very own.

I've lost large blocks of time as a result of what I call a "worry blackout," and I've spent days recovering from emotional hangovers caused by fixating on people I love. *Where are they? Why haven't they called me back? Are they getting enough vitamin D?*

Some of my best memories don't even include me.

It's majorly depressing when you flash back on your life and, instead of reviewing your own history, you see other people's memories: European cruises *they* took, improvements *they* made on *their* bathrooms, new hobbies *they* discovered, or puppies *they* adopted.

Al-Anon has shown me that I need to leave other people's memories, plans, dreams, worries, and lives alone. God has given me a life of my own to enjoy, and I'm responsible for living it. If I want enjoyment from life, it's up to me to go out and make it happen. When I focus on making myself happy and pursuing my dreams, what other people do, or don't do, isn't nearly as important.

All this talk about dreams makes me want to go online and sign up for that Alaskan cruise, or at least remodel my bathroom, so I can experience more of my own cool flashbacks. A puppy is definitely going to be at the top of my list.

In spite of myself:
When my flashbacks consist of other people's memories,
I could be in trouble.

Default Playlists

When my situation feels hopeless, and I can't figure a way out, I have two default responses: shut down or isolate.

When I'm in shutdown mode, I close the door, pull the shades, and spend my days listening to morose eighties songs by The Smiths.

When I withdraw, I close the door, pull the shades, and spend my days listening to morose eighties songs by The Smiths.

Not surprisingly, these versions of the same response net the same results. Nothing.

Al-Anon has taught me to reach out instead of shutting down or withdrawing into a dark, musically induced vortex. Learning to have uncomfortable feelings without spiraling into self-pity and despair is a new response for me.

When I choose to acknowledge how I feel by writing about it, and praying for guidance or going to a meeting, things eventually turn around. I save myself from heartache when I don't respond to sadness by dropping out.

The change isn't automatic, but I don't stay in the morass nearly as long as I used to.

Deciding not to hit the "Play" button on certain music playlists when I'm tempted to indulge in sadness and self-pity is the first step to feeling better. Today I save The Smiths for times when I'm on top of the world.

In spite of myself:
Who's on my playlist right now?

MAY

Rapid Globalization

I'm a "rapid globalist," which has nothing to do with creating a healthy connection to the earth or other life-forms. It's my way of quickly assessing people and drawing swift conclusions.

Whenever I find people's behavior deplorable, I quickly globalize their behavior and make them completely useless in every other aspect of their rotten lives. *That guy is the biggest jerk. . . . She is the dumbest human being ever. . . .* You get the point.

It takes work on my part to remember that, while some people may be callous or disrespectful, no one is *all* bad, *all* wrong, or all *anything*. They're people with flaws doing the best they can. And although I wish they'd work on doing things better, I never know what someone else may be going through at any point in time.

Like me, people do dumb things, but throwing them into a category based on a single behavior leads to misunderstanding and, ultimately, a lot of hurt.

I've decided to use the term "rapid globalization" to remind myself not to make snap decisions about someone's character based on how I feel. No one is *all* bad or *all* good.

While this realization won't lower emissions or greenhouse gases, it makes my world cleaner and brighter. And since I wouldn't be caught dead in a Smart car, that will have to do.

In spite of myself:
Today I'll emit good things into my environment!

Step #5

Step #5: "Admitted to God, to ourselves, and to another human being the exact nature of our wrongs."

Step #5 in Al-Anon allows us to tell the truth about ourselves. We examine our distorted beliefs, broken promises, grudges, and long-held resentments. We also take responsibility for the ways we have harmed others and ourselves.

We may have screwed up seven ways till Sunday when it comes to relationships, jobs, family, even the law. No matter what we've done, when we're totally honest and willing to reveal our secrets to another Al-Anon, the burden is lifted. The acceptance and love we get when we are transparent allows us the chance to feel our humanity and receive the grace of a Higher Power. It's the beginning of freedom.

No matter what we've done or what has happened, we always feel better when sharing it with God and with another Al-Anon. I've never heard of anyone who didn't feel a deep sense of liberation as a result of completing the Fifth Step.

And no matter what you've done, you can be sure that someone else has done it too. Okay, I did hear the *one* story about a guy who was running a kidney brokering service out of his pickup truck, but no one's ever been able to substantiate it.

In spite of myself:
I can always tell the truth to myself and to God.

What It Is

"It is what it is." I've heard that phrase recited in and out of the program, and I have one question: What the heck does it mean?

I don't get it. I don't say it, and I don't want to hear it—because really, it's kind of insulting. When did I ever dispute what "it" was? Did I ever say, "Hey, this is not what it is," or, "It is what it's not"? No, I did not. Not out loud, anyway.

The next time I hear this thoughtless, useless phrase, I'm going to say, "Thank you for the insight, Master/Mistress of the Obvious, but please put a sock in it."

At the risk of sounding like a restless, irritable, and discontented Al-Anon, I think it's time to say good-bye to this predictable, pointless phrase. I would like to request everyone stop using it immediately because *IT HAS NO MEANING!* It's like admitting, "I'm saying absolutely nothing!"

So, as of this moment, I'm officially putting this absurd expression to rest. There is, however, one version of this idiom that I will accept. It's from Darrell B., the coolest guy in my middle school, who was famous for saying, "To what it is and to what it shall be."

At least *that* makes *some* sense.

In spite of myself:
To what it is and to what it shall be.

Holding On

By letting go, it all gets done.
The world is won by those who let it go.
—Tao Te Ching

I tried that this week. I let it all go. Slept in late and ate French fries. I cleaned my house, but that was about it. I didn't try to change *any aspect* of my life. I didn't try to become a better person (one of my favorites), and I decided to stop attending the self-improvement group I've been going to for the past year.

I didn't read one thing about improving my health or my brain, and I didn't look for a better job. I did, however, add a few extra Al-Anon meetings to my schedule.

Just like the Tao Te Ching guy suggested, I said, "To heck with it all. I'm not fixing one thing about myself. I'm stepping off the self-help train."

I told God I was taking a break from navel-gazing, and if anything needed to get done, he would have to handle it. I went out and bought a mini Zen garden and spent all my spare time raking the gravel in the travel-sized kit it came in.

At the end of the week, I received two new job offers, and the herbs I planted in my garden a year ago finally sprouted. I'm considering giving this whole "letting go" thing a try again soon.

In spite of myself:

Life is prettier when I don't hold on.

Right

I was reading a story about conflict management in business. The mediator said that when things get tense, someone should use the phrase "You *are* right."

As in, definitively, absolutely. No weaseling out of it.

The mediator suggested that, after saying, "You *are* right," you find something the person *is* right about. The point is to find the grain of truth in something that person is saying. As in, "You are right . . . I did leave the door unlocked." Period, end of sentence. Not, "I did leave the door unlocked, but you always leave towels on the floor" or, "I did leave the door unlocked, but you're incredibly stupid and ineffective at your job." According to the mediator, when we admit the other person is right about what *we* did wrong—and we don't call attention to what *they* did wrong— it will diffuse even the most difficult situations. Being willing to lose the argument is key to conflict resolution. Because, most of the time, we're at least a *little* wrong.

The Al-Anon version of this is, "You *could* be right." I prefer the Al-Anon version, which, for someone like me—who is right quite often—is much easier to say.

I'm going to practice it right now. You. Could. Be. Right. Now *that* I can do. It's true. Someone other than me "could" be right. It has been known to happen.

In spite of myself:
Today I'll try, "You could be right."

Rope Burns

The relationship expert was saying that although a tug-of-war may be a blast at picnics, it could be deadly for a relationship. She said that trying to drag your partner over to your side of the line in a tug-of-war leads to hurt feelings and broken trust.

"You have to let go of the rope," she said.

At first, I wanted to shout, "No, you should never, ever let go of the rope during a tug-of-war! Someone can get hurt!"

But I was watching TV, so the relationship expert wouldn't have been able to hear me. Moreover, she was speaking metaphorically. In metaphor land, no one suffers from rope burns. It's a good thing she was a relationship expert instead of a tug-of-war expert.

For an Al-Anon, letting go of a conflict that is brewing might mean putting "it"—resentment, anger, sadness—down. If both sides are struggling, one side can end the struggle by simply dropping the rope. Letting go of the tug-of-war.

Doing life this way takes courage and strength, and in the real world, it can leave you with some rope burns. To me, just not picking up the rope and playing tug-of-war seems to be the best solution. I've always preferred eating watermelon and hamburgers to playing games at picnics, anyway.

In spite of myself:
Drop the rope, already!

The Best

One of my friends in Al-Anon has a license plate frame that reads, "The Best Is Yet to Come." She's a cheery, hopeful type of person, so this motto suits her. She truly believes the best is yet to come.

And I believe it, too. At times. But if I had my druthers, I would move the timeline for the best happening up a bit—to, like, today. Preferably within the next ten minutes.

I've seldom been accused of being patient or long-suffering. In fact, I've *never* been accused of being either of those things. If it ain't happening *right now*, in the way I want it, my automatic response is generally, *How can we make this happen right now, and in the way I want it?*

That goes for just about everything: job vacations, new shoes, even . . . snacks.

I can't lie. I think the world would be better if we could all move beyond this "better later" stuff. If it's the best, then why wait? I'll take mine now. Later might not even come, or I might be doing the laundry when it does. Besides, if it's the best, but it's going to take a long time, I'll take slightly less than the best. Heck, I'll settle for so-so, if I can take it home with me right now!

In spite of myself:

Hey, best, can you hurry it up?

The Life

The speaker at the Al-Anon meeting opened with, "I don't have the life I wanted, but I want the life I have."

I get that, sort of. Granted, the life I have today is not at all what I expected when I was younger. I thought when I grew up and found the right job and got my own place, every day would be a great hair day. I'd have the perfect relationship, and eventually I'd be able to tan without burning first.

My life *is* totally different than what I'd imagined it would be, and despite what my feelings tell me at times, it *is* what I want. I can't imagine how my life would have turned out if I didn't have the love and support I've gotten in the program of Al-Anon.

Recovery has shown me how to establish a deep, daily connection with a kind, loving Higher Power. Even though I still have bad days, I wouldn't want to miss any of the experiences that life has presented to me. Aside from the identity theft part. I wouldn't want to relive the identity theft. It's a pain in the you-know-what to get your credit back on track after your identity has been stolen.

So while my life might not be what I had *imagined* it would be, today I have a really good life and it's exactly what I want. Most days. Sans the identity theft. But I already said that, didn't I? I implore you to make sure no one *ever* steals your identity.

In spite of myself:
Thank God I want the life I have today.

Lookin' Good

Some Al-Anon meetings are like social networking sites. A lot of seemingly happy people living exceptional, enviable lives, eating at trendy restaurants, and traveling in style. Well-dressed, tan, always saying the right things, and with an entourage of ultra-hip friends.

In truth, I have no idea what's going on behind the scenes with people, or what happens after the meetings. Not everyone tells the truth about what's going on with them in meetings. Some people think "looking good" is more important than sharing their shame or their struggles. Like a social networking site, there are people who aren't interested in being transparent.

"Looking good" often wins because, well, it looks . . . good! And, the reality is, even when people in meetings share their difficulties or talk about their emotional malaise, I don't remember it. I only remember their cute outfits, or how ultra-white their teeth are, or the fact that their husband dotes on them.

With my limited viewpoint, it's easy to believe that everyone else is having an easier, cooler, more gratifying life than I am.

I have to remind myself that the snapshots of other people online and in real life are but a sliver of their reality. Even if they do have perfect teeth and doting husbands.

In spite of myself:

Is it just me, or is everyone *else* having a fantastic life?

Un-basic Instincts

I used to call myself an "intuitive" person. I could read (judge) people immediately, and I instinctively knew how to handle situations. At least, I thought so. When I came into the program, I found out my initial instincts were often wrong. My tendency to make snap judgments about life and immediately act on those decisions had caused me a lot of grief.

"Stop trusting your intuition so much. You're wrong a lot of the time," a friend of mine said.

"Wait a minute," I flared. "I'm a Scorpio, born under the sign of the dragon. We're famous for our keen instincts!"

"Like the keen decision you made to buy that fixer-upper by a freeway? Or the time you moved to a new state, sight unseen?"

While I hated her for saying that, I knew my friend was right. My instincts were not spot-on. My decisions were based on my best thinking—a dysfunctional stew of fear, ego, and anxiety. And my choices never included the consideration of a Higher Power.

Today, my choices are based on meditation, prayer, and the support of trusted friends. I do still pay attention to my intuition—but I don't automatically assume it's right.

Yes, my intuition is right a lot of the time, but I no longer assume it will be. Even though it is. A lot of the time.

In spite of myself:
God, help me remember I wasn't born
under the sign of omniscience.

Understanding

Life can only be understood backwards;
but it must be lived forwards.
—Søren Kierkegaard

"Understood" might be a tad bit loose, in terms of verbiage. I'll admit, I have no desire to understand life backwards. It's been hard enough to comprehend forwards.

Perhaps it's because I'm slow, but there are some things I'll never comprehend. Why some people live and others die, why there are tsunamis, why I can't ever remember the rules of football, and why I always forget the password to my checking account. Regrettably, there are things I'll never grasp, be they studied backwards or forwards.

I think Kierkegaard's point is that the meaning of experiences isn't always clear until some time has passed.

Alas, this is where faith begins and where I get . . . pissed off. I want to understand why things are the way they are *now*. I want answers. I don't want to wait years to understand why things happened. Thus, I am no longer a big fan of Kierkegaard. I enjoyed his work much more when I was in college, when I pretended to understand it.

Before you accuse me of being shallow or lazy, may I remind you I have a master's in philosophy from Yale, I sit on the board of the Aspen Institute, and I studied physics at MIT? Of course, none of that is true, but then again, someday it might be.

In spite of myself:

Today I'll just live my life forwards, with God's help.

Special Prayer

People in recovery often talk about the fourteen-day resentment prayer—where you pray that the person you're angry with be given all the things you desire for yourself. I've tried it, and believe me, it does work!

If you're struggling with a resentment, consider this special version of the fourteen-day prayer, written by a woman about her ex. I've changed a few details. Feel free to amend it as you wish.

Dear God,

If a brand-new, shiny semi doesn't run over my ex-husband today, bashing his head, mutilating his limbs, and squishing his liver into the pavement . . . if someone doesn't break into his new house with the new girlfriend, start a fire, and steal all of his expensive hair products . . . then I want the absolute best for him. Please, let that derelict find happiness and maintain his healthy body so that he can finally get a real job and earn a decent living. And, God, may his children be a blessing to him and make him proud. May he have a good home, and please grant him at least a little respect and honor in his community. May he be well and do well—at least better than he used to! And may I someday mean the nicer parts of this prayer, and not just the bad parts. Amen.

In spite of myself:
A few words can make a difference in prayer!

Skills

I realized early on in life that I would be well suited for creative work, where I could go out to extravagant lunches, brainstorm about creative ideas, and get facials in the middle of the afternoon. And be paid generously.

Luckily, I've held those kinds of positions throughout my career, so when I quit one of those jobs several years ago (I got tired of hanging out with artistic jerks who were more self-absorbed than me), I decided to start working with a career coach.

After subjecting me to a battery of ridiculous personality tests, she confirmed that I was meant for creative work. The only other jobs I was equipped to do were shoe sales or private investigation.

It appeared the creative skills I'd spent my life honing didn't translate into the real world. That was when I began to worry that my life was over.

Then a friend reminded me that the Big Book says that God is our employer, and that being all powerful, he provides what we need if we keep close to him.

Although that reminder didn't answer all of my questions, it made me feel better and laid some of my fears to rest. Whatever it is, I'll be okay. I'm not in charge, God is, and I don't know what that means for my future. It might include shoe sales. Or it might involve me hiding in an unmarked car outside an apartment building, binoculars in hand.

I don't know what God has in store for me, but I'm open to whatever. Especially if it's easy and I'm highly paid!

In spite of myself:
God is my employer, and he always lets me take a lunch break.

Haters

"Today is May fourteenth, and it's my first anniversary," my friend announced with great pride. "On this day one year ago, I officially stopped hating people."

"Wow!" I said. "You can do that? Just wake up one day and decide to stop hating people?"

"Of course," she said gleefully. "I did it. So can you!"

When I first came into Al-Anon, I would have said I didn't hate anyone. But when I started working the Twelve Steps, I recognized that I did, indeed, hate people. It's not like I wanted to harm them (granted, I wouldn't have minded if there had been an unfortunate runaway forklift accident). But I definitely had it in for a few people.

I decided to take my friend's lead and stop hating. And you know what? It didn't work. I couldn't just stop hating on my own. I needed the help of a Higher Power. Only through an inventory was I able to release the hurts that were causing me to hate others. It took a while for me to move from hatred to understanding and acceptance of a few of those people.

Maybe my adorable friend has been able to will herself to stop hating, but I can't do it without the help of God and the program of Al-Anon. And while I may not be up all night casting voodoo spells on wax dolls, if I let resentments fester, it won't be long before I am concocting dark plans for people I don't like. Plans that just might include runaway forklifts. And they don't live *anywhere near* a farm.

In spite of myself:
God, help me not even go there today.

Misunderstanding

The Fifth Tradition in Al-Anon talks about "encouraging and understanding our alcoholic relatives." For the first few years in the program, I totally ignored this Tradition.

Encouraging *them*? Are you kidding? How about I simply refrain from putting a hit out on them? Understanding *them*? Maybe they should try understanding *me* for once.

You could say I was resentful when I found Al-Anon. I'd spent enough time focusing on the alcoholic; I figured it was high time *I got some attention,* thank you very much!

Slowly by slowly, I came to the conclusion that fixing—or alternately, throwing the alcoholic in front of a rabid coyote—didn't qualify as genuine understanding. And reading aloud from the Big Book as I followed that "someone" around the house probably didn't qualify as genuine encouragement.

Criticism and insensitivity are just two of my many unhelpful reactions to alcoholism. Encouragement and understanding require thought, a lot of prayer and patience, and consistent action on my part.

While I don't do any of those perfectly, I've made progress, and my life is much better. In fact, I can't remember the last time I even flirted with a reaction to an alcoholic that included a rabid coyote or a blunt instrument.

In spite of myself:
Understanding and encouraging make things better,
and rarely get me arrested.

Attention!

Listen up! It seems as if everyone in the Western Hemisphere has been diagnosed with attention-deficit disorder. If you are one of the few people who *haven't* been diagnosed with it, will you stop ruining it for those of us who actually have it?

Every day at least *someone* I know claims to have ADD, and I don't buy it. My friends have even started to use it as an excuse for oversleeping, or when they forget a birthday, or miss an appointment.

Some people use ADD as an excuse because they simply don't feel like following along in a conversation. To which I say, "Come on, people, can't we just power through this? I mean, for goodness' sake, it's just a conversation, not a lifetime commitment!"

So, for the love of Higher Power, can we all make a collective effort to complete a thought, show up to the meeting on time, or write down the date of the darn birthday?

Now I would like to offer this piece of advice: Whatever it is you've gotta do, do it. Society *cannot* continue to put a black mark on the term ADD by using it to justify a lack of interest in or commitment to something. Even if it's just a phone call, a plan, or, God forbid, a complete sentence, let's buckle down and finish it, people!

Much appreciated. And yes, I have taken my medication today.

In spite of myself:

God help me commit to following through on things today, even if I don't feel like it.

The Tapestry

A woman in my Al-Anon meeting said that life in recovery was analogous to creating a tapestry. "When I look at the front of the tapestry, I see rich, beautiful images woven together to create this lovely, gorgeous landscape. But when I look at the backside of the tapestry, I see a bunch of bulging, tied-off knots and broken cross-stitches," she said. "It's like my life. I can't see what seemingly arbitrary stitches God is weaving together to create the picture. The side I'm looking at appears to be a complete mess, but the other side tells the complete story. God sees the larger landscape."

I'm not a knitter or a quilter, and I've never for one millisecond had enough patience to try looming (or whatever it's called). In fact, I avoid anything involving a pin or a needle. I also have no idea what my Higher Power is creating out of my life, but I believe it's good and that it will all make sense someday. At least, I think it will. I hope my life tapestry is more than just a bunch of kooky stitches that turn out to be a knitted mohair toilet roll cover.

Maybe I'll call that woman from the Al-Anon meeting and ask her to look at my tapestry, because all I see when I look at it is a cluster of discordant knots and frayed yarn. Although I suppose frayed yarn is better than frayed knots.

In spite of myself:
Knowing that God's in charge of my tapestry
kind of takes the pressure off.

Instincts

A reporter once e-mailed me after I'd posted a story about a recent breakup. She wanted to interview me.

"The story about your ex-boyfriend, the con artist, is one of the worst I've ever heard," she confessed. "He could be part of one of those *20/20* investigations. Would you be willing to talk about what happened for an article I'm writing?"

"Sure," I replied. "I think the sole purpose of my life is to serve as a reminder for others . . . of what not to do."

During the interview with the reporter, I purged my soul about how blind I'd been to the warning signs, the red flags, in the relationship. Once again, I was reminded that, for an Al-Anon like me, my first instinct is to override my wiser instincts. When it comes to love, sometimes I need to do the opposite of what my gut tells me to do.

Then it occurred to me that this reporter was going to take all the tips I was offering, as well as my hard-won heartache, for *her* article, and undoubtedly take all the credit.

Wait a minute! my gut screamed. *I'm no expert on relationships, but you, Miss Reporter, shouldn't reap the rewards of my hardearned distress and sorrow. Just because I don't take my own advice doesn't mean it isn't valuable.*

Instead, I said nothing and finished the interview. I've learned not to do the first thing my gut tells me to do. Plus, I didn't want to be identified as a woman who ignores her wiser instincts.

In spite of myself:
God, show me which instinct to trust today.

Rewards

A Chinese proverb suggests that one should never "hit a dog with a meat bun."

A meat bun is steamed dough stuffed with pork and vegetables, and sometimes quail eggs. And it's yummy. Now, let's say there's a mangy stray mutt in your neighborhood that you want to get rid of—which, of course, would *never* happen. (I know, *you're* an animal lover and would *never* engage in the following behavior, but play along for a moment.) If your goal was to punish the dog, you wouldn't lob a meat bun at him. Not only would the mutt *not* go away, he'd probably love the meat bun and you'd never get rid of him! It's the wrong approach to the problem, and it doesn't work.

This proverb reminds me that my best thinking gets me in trouble.

When I rely on self-will to solve my problems, or refuse to bring my Higher Power into the mix, I jump to faulty conclusions and take actions that *do not* lead to long-term happiness. My solutions are often as effective as throwing a meat bun at a stray dog—I take the wrong approach and I end up with not-so-stellar results.

So, instead of hurling a meat bun at a dog, myself, or anyone else—or at my problems today—I'll simply ask God for guidance. Then, I'll hit that all-you-can-eat Chinese buffet down the street and order a meat bun with pork. And lots of soy sauce. For under ten bucks, no less!

In spite of myself:
Am I hurling meat buns at my problems?

Defect

I think my Higher Power has a character defect. It's called "procrastination."

I know, who do I think I am, suggesting that my Higher Power has a flaw? I say it with the utmost and greatest respect, for I understand all about defects of character. I have a few of my own. But procrastination is *not* one of them.

For example, I've repeatedly made requests to my Higher Power, asking for more information, details, if you will, about things, and I still haven't gotten any cooperation. As it goes, I've also proposed that my Higher Power consider written communication, but I've not received it. It is slightly disappointing, this defect, as I am fairly consistent in giving people time frames on projects or appointments, and I would appreciate the same from my Higher Power.

This "procrastination situation" between my Higher Power and me is, as they say, "fluid." We're working on it. And I must say, there are times when I get impatient and it takes great restraint for me not to blurt out, "Why, for your sakes, won't you tell me what's going on here?"

Actually, I *have* blurted that out, more often than I'd like to admit, but no one's perfect. After all, I do have a few defects of my own, though, as previously mentioned, procrastination is *not* one of them.

In spite of myself:

God, I'll trust your time frame, even though it isn't easy.

Cluckers

There's a woman in one of my Al-Anon meetings who has a habit of sitting in the front row and giving feedback to the speakers, *while they're speaking.* This is done in the form of sighs, eyebrow lifts, and tongue clucking.

One time, after I'd finished speaking, I received feedback from "the Clucker," as I call her, through another member. She had a list of things that I could do to improve my share. At first, I was upset and I wanted to send her some of my own feedback. But my sponsor reminded me that Tradition Twelve tells us to "place principles above personalities."

"But I haven't finished my Steps yet," I pleaded with my sponsor. "Why do I have to practice all that Tradition stuff now?"

My sponsor's answer was simply, "Because."

I didn't quite feel that was a legitimate explanation, but I went along with it.

"The Twelve Traditions remind us to make the big picture of recovery and love the priorities. Let the personalities, no matter how weird, be what they are," she said. Then she told me that the goal was to take the Traditions into all aspects of my life.

I thought my sponsor was being nitpicky and no fun, until I began to see the Clucker as just another member of my Al-Anon family, which, like my own family, is very bizarre. And even though she's weird, the Clucker still has her place in the Al-Anon family.

In spite of myself:
Even the cluckers get love in Al-Anon.

Yay for A's!

Last week, a friend of mine in Al-Anon told me I needed to slow down. She said I was "too Type A"—trying too hard to make things happen on my timetable instead of God's.

Why do the morally superior Type Bs feel the need to tell us Type As we're wrong all the time? Maybe, instead of telling us to relax more, they could relax *less*! Look, I get it. "Relaxing" is important, and I *do* do it. Almost daily. Nearly every week. Monthly. When I can remember.

I took her lead, and signed up for a mindfulness meditation class. There were eight of us in a room, and the teacher had us take off our shoes, sit down on the floor . . . close our eyes, and just breathe in and out for forty-five minutes. No talking or thinking, just breathing. I made it through the entire exercise, and I thought, *I can do this. In fact, I will spend more time relaxing on a daily basis!*

But then I thought about it a little more. *If I start meditating, I might become one of those Type Bs—a little too relaxed and morally superior.*

The truth is, without us Type As, who'd open the stock market? Who would drive a taxi, or go to medical school? Who'd go postal? That's right. Nobody. So, Type Bs, let's give some respect to the Type As of the world!

Besides, if my Type B friend is so relaxed and together, why isn't she the one writing today's meditation?

In spite of myself:
God, thank you for the Type As and Type Bs.
But mostly the A's.

Make the Whistle

My cousin loves the rodeo. Primarily, my cousin loves the rodeo because of the cowboys. She *loves* her cowboys. So the last time I went to visit, she took me to a rodeo—the kind with dirt, bulls, dust, and tobacco-chewing menfolk in snug jeans.

What I immediately noticed was the fact that if a cowboy can ride a bull for a whole eight seconds, he's "made the whistle." How a whistle became associated with riding bulls, I never found out, and I didn't think to ask because I was admiring the cowboys. However, I do remember being surprised by how hard it is for a cowboy to stay on a bull for eight seconds.

I'm not saying I'd do any better, but all that energy, effort, and preparation for a mere *eight seconds*? That's an awful lot of work for an experience that nearly always ends with somebody being thrown onto the ground and possibly trampled to death. I'm an Al-Anon. I like knowing I'm going to get something valuable if I'm risking my ass. I'm not spending time on a moving target without any guarantees.

I'd rather sit in the stands, where I can play armchair bull-rider and blow my own whistle. And make fun of the rodeo clowns. And enjoy the cute cowboys.

In spite of myself:

I'll "make the whistle" in my own life, not on a bull.

Why Ask Why?

Being a naturally curious person, I'm constantly asking questions of myself. Before I came into Al-Anon, my questions were fairly self-centered, and they often revolved around things over which I had no control. A typical conversation in my head would go as follows.

Did Alice notice I was late for work today? I wonder if she'll tell our supervisor. Is she smiling at me because she just ratted me out, or is she happy to see me? I wonder if John in the legal department likes me. I can't tell. Do I care if he likes me? No. I mean, yes. Does it matter in the scheme of life? No. Well, maybe. Will I die if John in legal doesn't like me? No. I'm taller than him anyway, and I'll never be able to wear heels if we go out. What am I thinking? I can't date another employee. Besides, I'm taller than him. Do my arms look chubby in this shirt? Is that why I haven't been promoted? Because my arms are too chubby?

Now that I have a measure of emotional sobriety and serenity, I've learned to ask myself questions that are less self-centered and more about how I can contribute to the world and other people.

Most of the time.

Are the questions I ask myself totally different? Mostly. Are they more mature and thoughtful? Absolutely. Do they include other people more often? Of course. Are there times when I ask myself questions I already know the answer to? Yes, but not always. Do I still ask questions about things over which I have no control? Yes. No. I mean, I don't know. I'm not sure I can answer that.

In spite of myself:
Am I glad I have recovery? Yes. Mostly.

Quote, Unquote

"There is nothing I detest more than people who use air quotes when they talk," I used to say. And then I caught myself using air quotes *the very next day*!

There's a saying: "When you point one finger, there are three fingers pointing back at you." While the math on that saying doesn't totally add up, I get the point. And that's exactly how it goes, now that I'm working a spiritual program. The moment I start to focus on someone else's dim-witted behavior, I inevitably find myself doing the exact same thing they were, or something *more* dim-witted.

Some people call it "karma." I call it my Higher Power sending me little reminders that we're all just doing our best to get through life and that detachment works better than faultfinding or condemnation.

Since I began applying the principles of Al-Anon to my life, I've been getting more reminders from my Higher Power. Reminders for me to focus on my own behavior and less on other people's stupid behavior. Not stupid, as in people who are stupid. Just people, like me, who do stupid things sometimes.

"People like me," she said, using air quotes. Although she secretly despises people who use the third person when referring to themselves.

In spite of myself:
God, help me keep my fingers, judgments,
and air quotes to myself today.

Captain Justice

I used to feel—who am I kidding, I still do—that it is my job to right the wrongs of society. To put on my cape of justice and stand up for the oppressed, the forgotten. The little guy.

My particular area of superpower expertise is the express line at grocery stores.

Seriously, if people have made it past the age of ten, they can likely estimate how many items they have in their cart. So why must they insist they've met the criteria for the express line when they haven't? Do they think they're invisible? Or that the rest of us can't count?

Why must *I* be the one to remind folks that their full cart contains too many items for them to use said line? Why must *I* be the one to announce, "I guess you didn't see the sign that says twelve items"? Why must *I* be the one who recommends people consider taking a basic math course, if needed, so they can identify the correct line? Why? Because if *I* don't, no one else will. And grocery stores around the world will be overtaken by inconsiderate express lane abusers.

So despite my desire to stay out of it, *I've* been chosen to wear the cape of justice, and while others stand by in silence, *I'm* compelled to make things right, even at the cost of my own happiness. Yes, there are times when *I* get tired, but I don't quit, because . . . it needs to be done. Honestly, there really *are* more important things I'd prefer to be fighting about than this.

In spite of myself:
Do not make me put my cape on today.

Act As If

The unspoken motto in my home growing up was "Act as if nothing has happened, no matter what has happened." What? Mom, dad, drunk and fighting? Where? Clothes on the front lawn? Who? Sister climbing out the window at 3:00 a.m.? Huh?

My thinking was, no matter how crazy something looks, if I pretend it's not happening, it just might go away. That approach worked for a little while, but it's a pretty kooky way to go through life—ignoring, minimizing, denying. It catches up with you.

When I got into recovery, I had to tell the truth about the things that had happened and accept responsibility for my reactions to those situations, as well as my own unhealthy behaviors. And that's when I started to think, *Hey, maybe "acting as if" nothing ever happened is an easier way to go through life.*

In fact, some of the time I *still* prefer to pretend things are fine when they aren't.

Except now I have a recovery program that shows me how to face challenges, disappointments, and losses. Today I have friends to reach out to, and I don't have to pretend I don't feel the way I do, or that things aren't happening when they are. Unless things really aren't happening. Then, of course, there's no reason to pretend anything.

In spite of myself:

Things happen. With the help of God and my fellows
in recovery, I can handle them.

Regrets

One of the promises of Twelve Step programs is that we will no longer "regret the past nor wish to shut the door on it."

When I first heard that, it sounded lofty and a bit unreasonable. But as time passed, I began to see it as a reminder—a promise of what will happen if *I do* the work in recovery.

There are times when I wish I could change my past—things I wish I'd done differently, paths I should have taken. When I do that, my Higher Power reminds me that there are people I might help *because of* my past. When I look at my past as a way to be of service to someone who's in deep pain due to addiction and codependency, I start to relax. I stop freaking out about the things I've done, or not done.

"Relax" might not be the correct word. I'm not *totally* relaxed. It's not as if I roll through life in a state of bliss, on perpetual mental vacation or floating on that fourth-dimensional pink cloud. "Relaxed" for me is, in all probability, highly amped for most other human beings.

Today, I don't struggle as much over what I did in the past, because there's nothing I can do to change it, and God might be able to use it. And although I haven't totally "shut the door on the past," I make sure not to throw the door wide open and invite the whole neighborhood in for lasagna. Unless I want to. Which I may, especially if it's a Thursday night. I love lasagna on Thursday nights!

In spite of myself:
I'll leave the door wide open for recovery.

Caves

I heard a guy explain the difference between a James Bond–inspired man pad and a man cave: A man pad is cool and organized, slickly furnished. It's what a man uses to lure a woman. A man cave is where he escapes to once he gets her.

I kind of relate to this, even though I'm not a man and I don't have a James Bond–inspired flat. Also, I'm straight. What I'm saying is, I am plenty experienced at hatching plans and manipulating people to get what I want, and then not wanting what I've gotten the minute I have it.

Once I've achieved the goal, there will surely be a time when I no longer desire it. From relationships to kitchen appliances to eyelash extensions, once I get what I want, I lose interest. It's tied up in my impatient nature and my need for *more* and *better*.

My solution is to write out a gratitude list the moment I start to feel like something is lacking in my life. When I begin to appreciate the things I do have, my joy increases.

Right now I'm going to thank God for everything I've been given. Even if I'm not sure I want those things anymore. Because even if I don't want them now, I will undoubtedly want them as soon as they're taken away.

In spite of myself:

My life is fine. No escape plan needed today.

Super Right-Sized

"I acknowledge that some of my reactions to life were strong when I came into Al-Anon," I admitted.

"Strong?" my friend laughed. "If reactions were Happy Meals, you'd be the super-sized version of everything."

"Are you calling me fat?" I asked.

"No," she said. "I'm saying you weren't 'right-sized.'"

"This has nothing to do with the size of my butt?" I asked.

She said my reaction to alcoholism had caused me to be a little extreme, and she was right. I carried the baggage of my past into every new relationship, and I kept a mental list of every slight or disappointment I'd suffered. When I was hurt or angry, I'd pounce on people with lists of what they had done wrong or how badly they'd hurt me. As a result, my reactions were way over the top.

"Right-sizing" myself was something that happened as I worked the program of recovery. I learned the appropriate response for what was happening in the moment without bringing the past into every interaction.

Or, as my friend would say, I "don't use a shotgun to bring down a fly" anymore. Nope. I keep my responses "right-sized" now. Although there are times when I'm tempted to go super-sized. Especially when curly fries are included.

In spite of myself:

"Right-size" me today, God.

Movin' On

Before Al-Anon, I simply didn't know when to cut my losses and move on. Even when I had a bad feeling about a situation, I would stick it out because I'd spent a lot of time or invested a lot of emotions. Walking away never occurred to me. Instead, I would spend more time and energy trying to fix the situation.

As I've grown in Al-Anon and have gotten clearer about what I want, I've learned that I have to decide where to spend my time, which includes knowing when to walk away. Sometimes relationships don't work out. People grow apart, opportunities change, situations stop working for me, and sometimes I have to move on. And just because something worked years, months, or days ago doesn't mean that it won't change or stop working at some point.

I don't say this lightly. I have a hard time with this aspect of life. I want things—when they're good—to stay as they are. And even when they aren't so good, I'd rather keep them that way than risk the unknown.

I'm glad I have a program and people to give me a soft prodding at times to remind me that it's okay to move on when the time comes.

In spite of myself:
God, show me when it's time to move on.

JUNE

What Defects?

Step #6: "Were entirely ready to have God remove all these defects of character."

Defects. Of character. Such harsh-sounding terminology. *Why can't we just refer to them as flaws?* Flaws are so much softer.

It's like the adorable guy in my office I have a crush on. What makes him so totally irresistible is his crooked nose. Aside from that one flaw, he's next to perfect. It's that single imperfection that makes him so endearing and approachable.

If we replaced my crush's nose, he'd be perfect. Like a model. Unapproachable. When you're normal looking, there's nothing worse for your self-image than hanging out with a model. That's why models never hang out with normal people. Perfection requires perfection.

I'm all for having my major defects removed, but all of them? It's the small ones that keep me humble, which is the way I would rather stay. If all of my defects were removed, I'd be the equivalent of a spiritual supermodel. Impeccable. Boring. No fun to hang out with. And above anything, I always strive to be approachable and lovable. And need I say it—humble?

In spite of myself:

God, thank you for keeping me so "approachable."

Judgy

Yesterday I was freaking out about why I'm not further along in my recovery.

It's become excruciatingly obvious to me that my life should be better than it is today. Frankly, my life's a mess. Pointless. Hopeless. I mean, why get out of bed anymore? Why even bother finishing this sentence, really?

After a few hours of crying and a handful of episodes of *Snapped,* I called a friend in Al-Anon, who reminded me that we're not in a race to recover. He told me that whenever he starts harshly judging and comparing himself, it leads to pain and desperation.

"Comparing and judging myself have never, once, ever led to feelings of pleasure or motivation," he admitted.

"But judging myself harshly used to spur me on," I replied. "It was what kept me on my diet, allowed me to work harder, and improve myself."

My friend then told me the reason judging myself doesn't work anymore is that I'm on a spiritual path that is about connecting to and experiencing God's love. He told me I'm exactly where I'm supposed to be, and God's not in a hurry. I want to believe my friend, really I do, and I know he's right. But you know what? Sometimes I wish God were in more of a hurry, and I wish I were further along.

I know, I know. But not all of these meditations can be light and breezy.

In spite of myself:
Thank God there's no "race" in recovery.

Plant Life

A recent study has proven that plants can do math. Apparently, plants have internal mechanisms that tell them how to preserve the minerals, water, and food they need to survive. These mechanisms calculate exactly what the plant needs to live and rations the nutrients if it isn't being properly fed.

This study is a load off for folks like me. While I love being surrounded by plants, they don't stand much of a chance around me. I've gone months without remembering to water my plants. It's very mean, and I'm very sorry about it.

I carried a lot of shame about my inability to care for my plants until someone in Al-Anon explained that if I'm not taking care of myself, I'm going to have a hard time keeping track of a plant. When I'm being all Al-Anony and obsessed, I forget about myself. And, of course, I forget about the plants.

If I'm not taking care of myself, it's gonna be a free-for-all when it comes to the flora and fauna.

I'm not proud of my actions, but I can't shoulder all the blame for what happened. Obviously the plants I picked weren't that great at rationing their reserves; perhaps they should have alerted me. And, with technology as it is now, maybe I'll teach the next batch of plants I get to text me when they're feeling parched or in need of a snack.

In spite of myself:

I'll do my best to take care of what's important today.
(Hint: That starts with me.)

Masterminds

At first, I loved the business "mastermind" group I'd joined.

However, it soon became apparent to me that several of the members might have done better with a good psychiatrist. I recall one of the members saying, without a hint of irony, "I can't return anyone's e-mails or phone calls because I'm practicing self-care."

"Wait a minute! We take your calls and respond to your e-mails!" I wanted to shout. But I didn't. I held my tongue instead of reminding this bonehead that he'd joined a group to support others, and responding to e-mails was part of what we'd *all* agreed to do.

This guy was constantly trying to conceal his self-centeredness with healthy-sounding psychobabble, and I had to refrain from calling him out on it.

Just because people have access to handy verbiage and terms that sound considerate doesn't mean they *are* being considerate. And likewise, I don't have to call them out on their behavior. Self-care can consist of a lot of things, like suppressing my self-righteous urge to throttle people who use psychobabble to mask their self-centered actions.

In spite of myself:
Is it self-care? Or selfish-care?

Types

I like simple stories and articles: "The Top 10 Careers" . . . "The 5 Best Cities to Live In" . . . "The 3 Types of Men."

Why? Because I'm lazy and don't want to do a lot of thinking. I'm quite satisfied with having the answers spoon-fed to me by intelligent people who do studies and researchy-type things.

It gives me a sense of comfort, in this overly kinetic, hyper-digitized world, to know what the five best cities are should I decide to move. And what a relief it is to know that there are only ten real careers left! As for there being three kinds of men, I'm simply overjoyed because that means I've met them all. In that case, no news is good news.

I've decided that recovery, much like the articles I read, could use simplifying because working a spiritual program can be hard. Honestly, if I'd known how hard it would be, I probably wouldn't have done it. So I'm currently working on an article I plan to call "3 Quick and Easy Ways to Recover." It's the best way I know to get people like me to a meeting.

In spite of myself:

I don't mind recovery being less than difficult.

Fort Me

I used to enjoy isolating and hiding out in my house. Don't get me wrong; it's not as if I was some weirdo with a fort in my yard or anything like that. I mean, if you think it's bizarre for a person to drape sheets over the sofa and chairs and hide under them in their living room with a flashlight, a crossword puzzle, and a bag of red licorice, then right back at you!

Now that I'm in recovery, and I'm learning to reach out more, my desire to hide out has lessened. It's not entirely gone, but I no longer feel compelled to hide under the covers in order to keep my sanity. It's probably my Higher Power's design that I'm still living in an apartment the size of a postage stamp and I don't have a yard, because there are times when I'm tempted to build the world's largest tree house with its own elevator. And a brick pizza oven so I'd never have to talk to anyone again. Except the squirrels. And the pirates, but only if they were nice pirates.

In my gigantic yard with the large tree house with an elevator and a pizza oven, there would be plenty of s'mores. In fact, s'mores—and pizza—would be all we'd eat. Me, the squirrels, and the nice pirates. Of course, that doesn't sound so good, now that I'm learning to reach out more. Except for the pirates part. I still love pirates!

In spite of myself:
Reach out; don't hide out.

Spirit Animal

Years ago, before we knew about cultural appropriation, I made an appointment with a shaman. If knowing my spirit animal would help in my search for a better life, I was all for it.

When I arrived at the shaman's studio, she had me take off my shoes and lie down on the floor, on top of a bamboo mat. She played ancient drumming music and waved her hands over my body. After fifteen minutes, she lay down on the mat next to me and began chanting loudly.

"Your spirit animal is a . . . *pterodactyl*."

My life is being guided by a 145-million-year-old flying lizard?

"I was hoping for a tiger, or a kangaroo," I said, disappointed. "I'm not sure about a pterodactyl . . ."

"Pterodactyls are beautiful creatures," she breathed heavily. "Fiercely independent and loyal, they're able to reinvent themselves when the need arises."

I wanted to say, "So why didn't they save themselves as a species, if they were so reinventive?" But I didn't want my inner pterodactyl to turn on me.

"The pterodactyl's agility and majestic presence reflect balance. It's a gift to those who receive it."

I went home and told my family about the superiority of my spirit animal, in case they wanted to benefit from my many gifts.

When the laughter subsided, one family member suggested medication, and another recommended therapy. They'd best pray their spirit animals aren't T. rexes. Nothing's worse than a bird the size of an airplane hovering over a freshly washed T. rex.

In spite of myself:

I don't need a spirit animal to offer my gifts to others. So there.

The Pause

I didn't have a Pause button before I came into Al-Anon. I had to *get things done right now!* Pausing before I made a major decision, such as moving to a new state, seemed totally absurd.

What was the purpose of life if I wasn't doing—or thinking about doing—something? How could pausing be useful? It took a while in Al-Anon for me to accept pauses, whether they are in my day, my life, or my career. Pauses in relationships were the worst because the terror of not knowing what other people were doing or how they were feeling—about me—was scary. What if they paused and never pushed the Play button again with me?

Eventually, I learned that pauses are important in every aspect of life. They give ideas and feelings time to settle. Pauses allow me to connect with my Higher Power and get clarity about situations and relationships. When I can settle in and pause, I find the answers come to me. Problems work themselves out when I allow a little space.

Nowadays, I consider myself an aficionado of the "pause." For example, yesterday I was on the phone with a friend who was going on and on about something—I don't even remember what it was. I thought it'd be a good opportunity to practice pausing, so I did. All of a sudden, she hung up. When I called her back, she said she thought I'd fallen asleep.

Maybe next time I will tell people when I'm practicing using my Pause button.

In spite of myself:
God, help me use my Pause button today.

Missing Persons

I didn't know I was the person I was until I wasn't that person anymore.

When I came into the program, I thought I was an easygoing chick; in my mind I was like Drew Barrymore in, well . . . in any movie she's been in: tolerant, compassionate, understanding, chilled out.

It wasn't until I'd been in recovery for a while that I realized I was a spastic, impatient control freak. I was about as mellow as a hawk with a bleeding hangnail.

How could I have lived this long and not known myself? I pondered. *After the work I've done and the money I've spent on therapy and facials, I still have no idea who I am. What gives?*

It's taken a lot of work, but with the help of people in Al-Anon, I've learned to look at myself realistically, make changes in areas I've needed to make changes in, and manage my emotions and reactions. The results have been deeper, more meaningful relationships, with others and with my Higher Power. I've calmed down and matured. And I *am* more easygoing.

It doesn't hurt that I carry a printout of the WikiHow entry for "How to Be Easygoing" and a picture of Drew Barrymore with me at all times.

It's probably best that I didn't know I was the person I was until I wasn't that person anymore, because if I'd met that person before I wasn't that person anymore, I probably would have stressed myself out.

In spite of myself:

In Al-Anon, I'm getting to know myself, and I kind of like me!

Nick of Time

There are times when I fear I'm running out of time. When I see a really hairy old man with a teenage supermodel, or hear about the housewife who's having an affair with her tennis coach, I fear my mortality. I fear I'll end up like that woman who lay dead for two years before police found her in her London apartment. No exaggeration, I saw it on the BBC. Her TV was still on!

I fear I won't fit everything in before I die. I fear God has forgotten all about me and I'm the only person who won't recover. That the world is coming apart at the seams and I'll die alone, without a retirement plan, which is weird, because I do have a retirement plan. I just worry it's not enough.

There are times when I give up before I've begun.

But that's not happening today. Because I have an Al-Anon program, and at this moment, I have everything I need.

Or as one of my friends says, "Look, kid, if ya got food and ya gots a place to sleep, ya ain't got nuttin' ta worry about." This friend doesn't really speak like Tony Soprano; it's just more dramatic when I write him that way.

Today, I have a program, and that's all I need to know.

God is in charge, and he hasn't forgotten me. I'm not running out of time. I'm also not taking tennis lessons, so there's no need to worry about me hitting on my tennis coach.

In spite of myself:
I'm not crazy; I just write myself that way.

Premeditation

I was expectant (not of the pregnant kind) when I came into Al-Anon. Specifically, I was expectant when it came to other people's behavior. I believed there were ways my friends—and enemies—should behave, personality traits my family members ought to change, and ways my boss needed to treat his staff differently.

I even had a "code of ethics" for salesclerks and customer service representatives, and I was sure there should be a list of dos and don'ts for drivers to follow. I just wanted to make the world a better place.

One day I heard someone in Al-Anon say, "An expectation is a premeditated resentment," and boy, did I have an issue with that. *What's wrong with expectations?* I thought. *Somebody on this planet, other than me, ought to have some standards!*

It took a little time for me to understand that my expectations are fodder for resentments to feed on. The easiest way for me to understand it was: *Sometimes I don't even know why I do the stuff I do, so how can I possibly know why other folks do what they do?*

Expecting other people to do things or not do things my way just doesn't work. I can only have expectations of myself, and that makes me feel pretty good, because when I expect good things from myself, I always deliver.

In spite of myself:

No premeditations or expectations of others for me today.

Anti–Ritz

The meeting room is filthy. It's cold and uninviting, too! It's like the Anti–Ritz Carlton of meeting halls! I thought as I arrived at my first Al-Anon meeting.

The church basement is dingy and the coffee is mediocre.

Folding chairs? Seriously? This is nothing like the plush leather chairs and decorative pillows in my therapist's office.

This stuff is obviously working for people, and it is free, but they might want to consider making the place more comfortable. It's not like I'm expecting concierge service or a pitcher of mint-infused spring water, but would espresso and a few croissants be asking too much? How about a fresh coat of paint on these walls? I'd recommend Alabaster White and some crown molding. Anything to distract from the hideous orange shag carpet and those burgundy velvet chairs!

That was five years ago. The room has not changed, or probably even been vacuumed since then. Definitely no changes in the carpet or wall color. And yet, this is my favorite meeting because of the amazing people who show up here, week after week.

I used to think that good was the enemy of great, and that the best was the only thing that mattered. Not anymore. I can appreciate what goes on inside the rooms of recovery without being bothered by what they look like.

If, however, someone asks my advice about how the rooms might look better, I will eagerly offer my opinion. But not until I'm asked. See? I've already learned so much from Al-Anon.

In spite of myself:
If it ain't broke, I don't need to fix it.

Over

I didn't want to meditate today. Honestly, if my recovery were rated on a scale of 1 to 10, today would have been a −25. The truth is, I was seriously miffed at God. So I called my sponsor, and she suggested I start the day over by asking for the willingness to just do what was in front of me.

I did. I began the day again. At 5:00 p.m.

Recovery doesn't mean there won't be days when I'm unhappy about some of the situations I'm facing. When I awake feeling out of sorts, the best thing I can do is accept that not every day will be a 10 out of 10. In fact, 10 out of 10s are rare—even in recovery. I like to aim for a solid 7, and if I get to a 6, I'm thrilled.

So, what to do when I wake up feeling a −25? I do the only thing I know: I ask for the willingness to trust that I will receive whatever I need from my Higher Power, even if I'm seriously miffed at him. Then I go on with my day and try to be of service to someone else. The feelings still come and go, but inevitably when I take action, I go from a −25 to at least a 3 on the recovery scale. And while I'm no math wizard, that seems like a fairly decent improvement.

In spite of myself:

I may have to start my day over again today. S'alright.

Reflections

"You can't fix the self with self," the Al-Anon speaker said, sharing about Steps #6 and #7.

I decided to look up the definition of "self," which is "an individual person as the object of his or her own reflective consciousness." While "self" is not a word I can clearly explain, I know it when I see it. As in, I know when I am "in self" or "of self" or being "self-centered."

I've learned over time that, try as I might, my "self" cannot fix me. Because my "self": (1) is too obsessed with me to be objective, (2) isn't very good at fixing much of anything (I've tried), and (3) is what gets me in trouble to begin with.

The whole "self" thing is complex. Philosophers, psychologists, and the major figures of world religions have studied it extensively, and if those guys can't figure out why humanity is so screwed up and bizarre, what makes me think I'm going to?

Here's what I *do* know: I have to take my "self" out of the center of my universe on a daily basis and put God in the center, because "self" is often the core of the problem.

When I don't put God in the center, I'm gonna be looking out for Number One: me, my "self," and I. When I'm in charge of looking out for myself, something's inevitably gonna need fixing. Or reattaching. At the very least, gluing back together.

In spite of myself:
For today, I'll just give my "self" over to my Higher Power.

Unmanageable-ish

When I came into Al-Anon, I experimented with what I called "things that are unmanageable-ish." These were areas of my life that were uncomfortable, but I could accept them. There was no need for my Higher Power's help or input. "Let sleeping dogs lie," and all that.

Most of my life was manageable. I was handling the groceries, the bills, and my job. But the big things—love, relationships, my anxiety, the future, my family, and alcoholism—I could definitely use some help in those areas. In fact, I welcomed my Higher Power's help there! But the rest, I'd hold on to. Obviously, I would check in with my Higher Power every so often to see how things were going. Was my help needed? Did my Higher Power need feedback, perhaps a little coaching?

I ultimately discovered that I couldn't split my life up into "manageable," "unmanageable," and "unmanageable-ish." I couldn't turn some of my life over to God, ignore other parts, and take control of the rest.

I had to turn *every* aspect of my life over to my Higher Power. And today, I still do. Well, except for the groceries. I can manage the groceries. Most of the time anyway.

In spite of myself:

There's no such thing as "unmanageable-ish."

Important

It is my opinion that Al-Anons who throw around the slogan "How important is it?" do so only because whatever particular issue they are applying it to is not important *to them*. In that moment. Because if it was something *they* were obsessed about, you'd be listening to an entirely different refrain!

The thing is, I can't know for sure if my problem will still be important ten years from now. More than likely, it won't, but today it is. And since, according to you people, all I have is today, and this issue is pressing, let's stop with all the "it's-not-that-important" baloney.

Plenty of things in life are important. In fact, *most* things in life are important! At least, more things *are* important than *are not* important. Look, all I'm saying is, things matter.

What I mean is, yes, we're Al-Anons, yes, we're dramatic, yes, we overdo things, but maybe we could give a little love and some respect to things that might not *seem* important, but are. Let's not whitewash everything with the words, "How important is it?" There are times when it might be okay to freak out a little, or obsess just a tiny bit.

The next time someone uses the slogan "How important is it?" on me, I might need to respond with "A heck of a lot more important than *you* think it is."

In spite of myself:

How important is it?
As far as I'm concerned, pretty darn important!

Jessie's Girl

Occasionally, I feel like the female version of Rick Springfield when it comes to love. Especially when it comes to the old song "Jessie's Girl": "I've been funny, I've been cool with the lines, ain't that the way love's supposed to be?"

Like Rick, I've always been in love with the idea of being in love. I wasn't, however, always in love with the actual person with whom I was in a relationship; I was in love with the possibility of love, the fantasies I'd conjured up. Valentine's Day, hugs, holding hands, the matching eighties jumpsuits. The less romantic aspects of a relationship: being vulnerable, afraid, jealous— those emotions rarely factored into any of my love fantasies.

As an Al-Anon, I have plenty of illusions about how love is supposed to be, and honestly, they're about as realistic as a pop song. My idea of true love is total passion and ease, minus the hard work or the sorrow. My version of love is a lot like a music video: guys with shiny hair, perfect teeth, with guitars playing in the background and two good-looking people dancing on top of fast, expensive cars.

In reality, love is a consistent action, a choice I make on a moment-by-moment basis. It's not a feeling, and real love has little to do with big hair, fast cars, guitars, and cute talk. But I guess that "point is probably moot."

In spite of myself:
Moot: subject to debate, dispute, or uncertainty.

The Unknown Al-Anon

Back in the day, there was The Unknown Comic. I don't know what his act was about; I just remember this strange guy in a brown corduroy jacket and plaid slacks running around with a brown paper bag over his head.

He kind of faded away. Not surprisingly—it's hard to sustain a long-term career when you're known as The Unknown Comic.

I was kind of like that comic when I first came in to Al-Anon. I kept my authentic self hidden, terrified that someone would get to know the real me and reject me. I didn't wear a paper bag over my head or anything, but I definitely didn't want to be exposed.

And I definitely wasn't laughing much.

The thing is, I can't build or maintain a relationship when I'm hiding out in plain sight.

Today, when I see newcomers skulking quietly in a meeting, I try to remember how I once felt, and I try to gently let them know that it's okay to let themselves be seen. I try to show newcomers that Al-Anons are a group of kind and loving people who accept others exactly as they are.

However, I never recommend that a newcomer show up in brown corduroy or plaid slacks and a bag over their head. Of course, that might go without saying.

In spite of myself:
Unless they're The Unknown Comic,
most people want to be identified.

Coach

Before Al-Anon, I was arguably one of the best coaches that ever lived. Vince Lombardi and John Wooden had nothing on me— and not because I know anything about football or basketball, because I don't. Actually, when I've attended football or basketball games, I rarely remember who's played, much less the final score. I'm much more into the peanuts and the people watching.

It was the Game of Life in which I excelled as a coach. I had an uncanny ability to see where other people had blown it, and a knack for making the right calls. My strategic and tactical solutions, as well as my ability to advise "teammates," made me a legend in my own mind.

With lightning speed and dexterity, I could coach people on what their next move should be with 100 percent accuracy, and advise them on how to improve. It's like I had a running video in my head of all the plays my friends and family had made, and I'd review it over and over, eagerly offering my feedback.

While I can't claim to have a prodigious career as a coach, I was adept at identifying mistakes and bad calls. The thing is, people didn't always want my feedback.

Recovery has shown me that my coaching skills aren't always needed, or desired. But, just because I've never once been hired for my sensational coaching skills, doesn't mean I don't have them. Because I do still have them. And I will use them, if need be.

In spite of myself:
I'm not a paid coach. God, please help me refrain
from yelling at the ref!

Groupie

I'm a groupie. I don't mean I hang out with rock stars—I just love groups. There's the Al-Anon group, the writers group, the fitness group, the time management group, and the money management group.

Recently, my sponsor said, "Enough with the groups, already. You're overcommitted, and it's making you crazy."

I started thinking about why I needed to be in so many groups. Perhaps a part of me is afraid I won't get things done on my own. If I'm beholden to a group, I won't procrastinate or get a jelly belly. I'll be a better writer (as opposed to just sitting down and writing), and I'll be able to master my finances.

If I'm not pushing myself, I won't accomplish anything ever again. I'll lose everything, end up on the streets, and be forced to forage for my meals from the back alley garbage of that French bistro down the street . . . and I'll die from escargot poisoning. I hate escargot.

I finally stopped thinking about why I'm in so many groups and decided to ask my Higher Power for some direction. The message I received was: "Group accountability can be good, and it can also be taken too far." I took it as a sign that I should spend more time listening to God, as opposed to listening to a "group."

Case in point: Yesterday, Google sent me a notice saying I was a member of too many online groups. They blocked me from joining any more.

In spite of myself:
I can respect the group, but ultimately I have to trust myself.

Summer Solstice

Today is the first official day of summer, the summer solstice.

There's a lot of information out there about the summer solstice—how it occurs when the Earth's semiaxis is most inclined. And a bunch of other stuff about the North and South Poles, and how the sun reaches its highest position in the sky. Basically, it's a lot of information I'm not prepared to go into because too many details can cause Al-Anons to fixate. And today, my little chickens, is an obsession-free day. There'll be no fixating, because today is the first day of summer!

It's summertime, summertime . . . sum-, sum-, summertime!

For the next twenty-four hours, I'm declaring a moratorium on obsession. No preoccupation with *anyone* or *anything*. No thoughts about death (your own or others'), no anxiety over UVB rays, the economy, or any subject that causes you to be anything other than happy. *Capiche?*

In honor of the first day of summer, call or send a card to someone and wish them a "bitchin' summer solstice." Then go outside and twirl around in the sun.

But don't stay out too long. UVB rays are very strong on the first day of summer. Okay, you can worry about UVB rays.

In spite of myself:
Today, no worries, only joy. *Capiche?*

Canoes

"Not only were they up a creek without a paddle," the greeting card read, "they also had a hole in their canoe."

I can relate. Sometimes it feels like I'm stuck in a canoe in a torrential monsoon in an Indonesian rain forest, and I've lost my oars and my compass—as if I've ever even owned a compass—and I can't find my way out.

In fact, I was feeling that way this morning. The rapids were rising; the water was pounding my canoe. I was bailing as fast as I could, but I couldn't keep the tidal wave of emotions at bay. I could only see two options: (1) keep bailing and hope I could overpower the waves, or (2) jump out of the boat and swim to shore.

So, I decided to say the following prayer: "God, please remind me that I'm not out there in the rain forest paddling on my own. Please help me remember that I'm not drowning and there is no monsoon. In fact, I'm not even in a canoe; neither am I within 20 miles of a body of water. I suppose I can stop bailing now."

You know what? I felt much better. Mainly because I realized things weren't as bad as I imagined, and because I turned the boat over to my Higher Power. Also, because I stopped bailing.

In spite of myself:
I'll stop bailing now and let God take the oars.

E's Theory

According to some law developed by Einstein, if I focus all of my energy on a single problem, the intensity of my thoughts is powerful enough to change things.

And yet, Al-Anon says recovery doesn't happen overnight, and I can't expect a problem I've had for years to be resolved right away just because I think about it. Al-Anon also says that true joy comes from letting go and not by focusing on problems—because focusing on problems leads to more pain. According to Al-Anon theory, my job is to *not* try to change things, or people.

So who's right? Einstein or Al-Anon? I like the people in recovery—but who's gonna take on Einstein? I personally prefer Einstein's theory because I want to believe I can change things, but I suppose the final vote goes to the folks in Al-Anon.

Realistically, focusing my energy on my problems has never directly resolved them. Instead, it made me irritable, and a bore to be around. So today I've decided not to focus on fixing my problems, but on all of the things I love about my life. I can always go back to focusing on the things that depress me if I want to. Tomorrow.

In spite of myself:
Today I'll use my laser-like intensity
to focus on things that bring me happiness.

Checklist for Maturity #1

Yes, I've read Al-Anon's Checklist for Maturity and the part that says, "A mature person . . . does not automatically resent criticism, realizing that it may contain a suggestion for self-improvement."

I didn't automatically resent your criticism, and I did spend some time thinking about the feedback you gave me. I appreciate you saying it was "for my benefit." The funny part is, your criticism got me to look at myself, and I also noticed a few things about you, too!

I heard what you said about my communication style and how it could be improved. However, I've noticed the way you speak to your assistant could be a little nicer. I know this is a separate issue, but you aren't exactly the best dresser I've ever met, either. I also noticed you playing solitaire on the computer during our last staff meeting.

I hope you don't take my comment about your clothes the wrong way. You're not atrocious looking. Not at all. It's just that, for example, the suit you had on yesterday added some weight to your frame—a frame that doesn't need any adding to. And I mean that in the most positive way possible! You're not big. You're what they call "healthy." "Sturdy." Remember that line of kids' clothing called "Huskies"? Clothing designers would never get away with that today.

Sorry. I digress. I have a tendency to do that when I've been the subject of constructive criticism. Can we talk more about this later?

In spite of myself:
Maturity, schmaturity.

Checklist for Maturity #2

Al-Anon's Checklist for Maturity says that a mature adult "faces reasonable delays without impatience, realizing that some adjustment for the convenience of others is necessary."

There are times when I enjoy reviewing this checklist. I find it best to read when I'm in a great mood and feeling particularly recovered.

Today, I was feeling emotionally healthy, so I reread the checklist.

A question immediately popped up. *What is a reasonable delay?* You see, I've been waiting for this one particular thing in my life to come to pass for, oh, fifteen years or so. That doesn't seem like a reasonable delay. In fact, it seems a bit unreasonable, in my opinion.

Funny, I've never noticed the "adjustment for the convenience of others is necessary" part. *Just how much convenience? How and when do you draw the line? And what is the definition of necessary?*

Odd, I've read the checklist before, but never saw the fine print in quite this way.

It's a pretty tall order, maturity. It's not that I don't want it; it's just that it takes . . . maturity . . . and time . . . maybe a long time. Hopefully not an unreasonable amount of time. I'm not big on long delays.

In spite of myself:
God, help me have reasonable expectations
about my growth and maturity.

Checklist for Maturity #3

According to the Al-Anon pamphlet *Checklist for Maturity*, "Maturity lies in accepting reality, not in demanding perfection."

So, is it wrong of me to desire perfection, as long as I'm not demanding it? What about gentle requests for slightly higher standards?

I'm not looking for total perfection; that would be pretty crazy and immature. I would, however, settle for 71.5 percent on the perfection chart; 71.5 percent seems fair. If a perfect life were 100 percent of a marionberry pie, to hope for 71.5 percent perfection would allow for a bit of imperfection. Say, a handful of personal failures, three major screw-ups by other people, and one natural disaster per lifetime.

Or, if you sliced the marionberry pie up differently, 71.5 percent could include two natural disasters, a handful of major missteps, and, at a maximum, two personal failures. Or, barring a natural disaster, a handful of major missteps (e.g., prison), and a minimum of five personal failures. Trust me, I did the math, and those percentages work out.

I struggle with the idea of achieving perfection. Which is why I'm so glad I have Al-Anon. It reminds me to lighten up and lower my unquenchable desire for excellence, and it's the one place where I find people who understand my need to create pie charts about the likelihood of perfection.

In spite of myself:
My need for perfection *might* be slightly over the top.

Bad Day

I had been talking nonstop about how bad my life was. Problems galore, money was tight, work was hideous. My love life was fruitless.

My sponsor finally broke in and said, "Just because you're having a bad day doesn't mean you're having a bad life."

"But what if I have a string of consecutive bad days over a long period of time and it adds up to a bad life?" I whispered back. I figured that would shut her up, or at least garner some sympathy.

"Okay," she responded, "I want you to keep track of how many bad days you have in a row. When you get old, give me the list, and I'll let you know if it adds up to a bad life."

Surprisingly, I didn't have a retort, so I agreed to her silly request. I started keeping track of my bad days.

Unfortunately, there have been a few really fantastic days in the midst of my otherwise dismal life since I started keeping track, so I can't confirm that I'm actually having a bad life. Yet.

At least, not today. But there's always tomorrow. And I am keeping track.

In spite of myself:
A bad day doesn't equal a bad life.

Prediction

While it's not something I do regularly, today I'm willing to put my entire reputation on the line with the following prediction: Within our lifetimes, an Al-Anon *will* change the world.

Friends, I have received word from ancient yet reliable sources that this is, indeed, possible. According to my sources, which have made over two hundred accurate historical predictions, this incident will occur between 2021 and 2030, when Al-Anons around the world will join hands and embrace the magical, rainbow-sherbet, strawberry-swirled core of their collective soul as they chant in unison, "All things are good, and all people are perfect. Starting right now!"

On this miraculous, eventful day, Al-Anons around the globe will rejoice, as the people, places, and things that have been bothering us will finally fall in line. When this worldwide shift occurs, it will signify the beginning of a universal plan of order, which will cause the planets to align and lead to total perfection of the species. Of course perfection will reign—an Al-Anon will be in charge!

My sources also say this momentous occasion will coincide with a major shoplifting scandal within the royal family and the death of a B-list celebrity.

In spite of myself:
God, help me remember that it's okay
if things don't change today.

Blurred Lines

Sometimes I lie awake in the morning with the sound of a freight train running through the middle of my head. And then I wonder, *Am I confusing my life with lyrics to a Springsteen song, or am I hearing this because I live near a train track and a train really does pass through my backyard at 5:00 a.m.?*

If I don't stay in contact with my Higher Power and close to Al-Anon, it can be easy for a person like me to confuse my stories with someone else's. My loved ones' worries become *mine,* I start to take on their struggles, and eventually, if I'm not careful, I start trying to solve their problems.

I can tell myself I do this because I'm "down with the people," but in reality, I've been affected by alcoholism. My reaction has always been to take on other people's dramas and—at times— their characteristics and personalities!

This is why I seldom watch reality TV shows. It can be confusing to separate the lives of the TV characters from my own. Do I have a personal chef? Am I in the midst of launching my own fine jewelry line? And where, doggone it, did my personal assistant run off to? He hasn't shown up for work in weeks!

Al-Anon reminds me that I can love and support people without taking on their problems, identities, or even their nonsensical song lyrics.

In spite of myself:
If you don't show up for life, I'll be tempted to do it for you.

What's in a Name?

In the nineties, I was obsessed with Ikea, the colossal do-it-yourself Swedish home store, because they named all of their products, and I loved that.

Drinking glasses weren't just glasses, they were "Brukbars," or "Bistas." Beds had names like "Duken." The spoons and coffee tables, like the meatballs and shortcake cookies sold at their restaurants, had names. I thought it showed *a lot of* caring and creativity.

Once, though, I bought some furniture there, and it sort of put a damper on my enthusiasm. How would I reconcile my love for their sugar biscuits and oversized shopping carts when I couldn't sleep on the futon or close the drawers on that damn entertainment center I'd assembled at home?

I was gravely disappointed. I wanted to hate Ikea, and never go there again because I tend to be an all-or-nothing type of thinker. Instead, I gave it some thought and got feedback from a friend, who suggested that I find a middle ground with my formerly favorite Swedish home center.

And I did. Every once in a while I'll stop by for some meatballs, and I eagerly await the arrival of their catalog, but I shy away from anything that's not preassembled.

I've learned that nothing has to be either-or anymore. I can take the good and leave the not so good. So nice how it all worked out. Ya know?

In spite of myself:
Today I'll take the good and let go of the not so good
without any fanfare.

JULY

Making a List

Step #7: "Humbly asked [God] to remove our shortcomings."

There is no greater joy to an Al-Anon than being able to complete things and check them off a list. We are achievement driven. We get a thrill out of settling and accomplishing things: groceries, house repairs, acne flare-ups, laundry. And shortcomings.

Unfortunately, when it came to my own shortcomings, I couldn't check them off the list and move on with life.

"I've been praying for nearly three months for God to remove my impatience. Nothing's happening," I whined to my sponsor. "Why is it taking so long?"

My sponsor laughed aloud. "Welcome to humanity, honey."

"And my anger is still a problem," I continued to rant. "I mean, thank God I have my ego under control—but what about all those other defects? I could die before they're removed!"

"God will remove your shortcomings in his own time. Which is almost never our time," she said gently.

She was right, of course. She always is. I'll never be able to remove *my own* shortcomings. That's when I have to say to my Higher Power, "I can see that I'm growing and changing, even though my defects aren't gone. I still rely on some of them, and they make my life unmanageable. For today, I'll trust you, and accept myself just as I am."

Then I think about a friend of mine whose defects are *way* worse than mine, and I feel a whole lot better.

In spite of myself:
I'll let my Higher Power do the removing
and step out of the way today.

Slips

If an Al-Anon has a slip and falls in the forest and there's no one around to notice it, is the forest still at fault?

When an alcoholic or an addict "slips," it's often apparent. But Al-Anon and codependent "slips" are seldom obvious to the outside world. Does that mean they don't matter?

For those of us with a mental obsession, our slips are not recognizable to others. That is, unless you're an innocent bystander who happens to get in our way. When I feel a slip coming and I don't talk to anyone about it, I'm fooling myself if I don't believe my slip won't lead to a fall.

Which leads to the often asked question: What if I'm not even in the forest and I slip and fall? What if I slip and fall in a parking lot? Or at a skating rink? At the grocery store?

Since I am neither a philosopher nor a defense attorney, I'll leave it at this: When an Al-Anon slips and falls in the forest and no one else is around, it might not make any noise. But trust me when I say the vibrations will *most definitely* be felt.

And, as any good Al-Anon would, we will do our absolute best to make the forest wrong.

In spite of myself:
You betcha, Al-Anon slips leave wakes.

Indie Groove

Today is Pre-Independence Day. While it's not a big day for greeting card makers or retailers, it *is* a holiday for many.

This annual precursor to Independence Day is special in many Al-Anon circles because it gives us the opportunity to reflect on what our lives were like before we got lives of our own.

Try to remember what you were like before you got your own Al-Anon indie groove on. When you compare your life before recovery to the life you have today, would you not agree that, even on the worst of days, your existence is a heck of a lot better than it used to be?

So why not celebrate your own personal independence and whip up a big, white coconut birthday cake with vanilla buttercream icing to celebrate your Al-Anon independence and freedom? If you're a vegan, maybe you could find one of those bakers who makes vegan chocolate cakes. If not, you could toss up a great big bowl of broccoli salad—although that sounds like a complete bore, if you ask me.

Vegan, vegetarian, gluten-free, or meat-eater—take a few moments today to acknowledge how far you've come on your road to recovery, even if it isn't all that far.

Please don't put this off. Commemorate yourself today—because you deserve it! Besides, you want to be ready to party with your good friend, the United States of 'Merica, tomorrow, don't you?

In spite of myself:
Celebrate your Al-Anon independence today!

Happy Birthday!

Happy Birthday, America! Are you excited? Do you have your outfit planned? Something red, white, and blue, no doubt! Are you gonna enjoy fireworks, maybe hit a BBQ or two?

Did you wake up this morning thinking, "Yay, it's my birthday, and I can eat *anything* I want! Hot dogs, hamburgers, chili, cupcakes, even French—oops, I mean—*Freedom* fries!"?

I hope you're in the mood to *partay*! Because it's *your* birthday, America, and you're just getting started!

I won't send you a card making fun of your age or how you need a face-lift. No, I'll celebrate your awesomeness because yours is my absolute favorite birthday ever. Aside from my own.

I'm sure there are Al-Anons reading this right now who are dreading this day, or who might be nursing a resentment. For you, my little chickens, I'd like to recommend that you find a way to be of service to someone . . . anyone. If you can't do that, then how's about doing something sweet for your friend and mine, the good ol' U.S. of A.? Try sending America a greeting card. Or, call her up and sing "Happy Birthday."

If you want to score points, open with, "Hey, America, you don't look a day over thirty!" The best part about America is that, unlike the Al-Anons and codependents I know, she never expects a gift, and if you don't get around to calling her, she won't hold a grudge.

If none of this helps to lift your spirits or resentments, you can always feel sorry for yourself and have a bad day. But I don't think you will.

In spite of myself:
I get to choose how I feel today and every day.

Non-intense

I used to be addicted to intensity. Intense alcoholics, intense relationships, intense jobs, intense music, intense intensity . . . Calm was unfamiliar.

When I came into Al-Anon, all I wanted was a saner life. Sort of. I *was* a little worried—what would life be like without all the shouting and the broken dishes? If there were nothing for me to rail against, or be incensed about, what would I do with my time?

The longer I'm in recovery, the more I cherish tranquility. I actually take pleasure in moderation and enjoy being in harmony with others. I spend more time being quiet, I have hobbies, and I forge relationships with people who share my desire for serenity and joy. I no longer need things to be big and bold or extreme to feel like I'm truly living.

In fact, there are times when I have the desire to cuddle my serenity, like one of those Gund stuffed teddy bears. I never, ever once wanted to cuddle my intensity.

Tell me, how much do *you* love your serenity today?

In spite of myself:
Today, I love and cuddle my serenity.

Missing Life

There are times when I miss the life I don't have. What exactly that life looks like, I'm not sure—I just know it's *not* what I'm currently experiencing.

I admitted this to a good friend the other day, and she looked at me like I was mad.

"You have a fantastic life. I mean, you're healthy and smart and you have a job. What if you were missing an arm? What if you'd been born without a mouth?" she demanded.

I considered my life without an arm or a mouth, and I felt even worse. While I know my friend wanted me to appreciate what I have instead of dwelling on what I lack, it was clear my friend didn't understand that I wanted to whine and wallow. Or, as I like to call it, "to be heard and understood."

I called my sponsor. I told her I wasn't pleased with the way things were going.

"I have the solution to your horrible life," she said.

"You do?" I perked up.

"Yes. I want you to get out of your house and help someone else. The solution to self-pity is service to others."

I hate it when she's right.

When I spend time doing for others, I forget about the life I think I should be having. I don't have time to worry about missing out on *anything*, and I become grateful for *everything*. Especially my arms and my mouth.

In spite of myself:
I have all I need today. I'm not missing anything.

Feelings, Not Faxes

One time I was at an Al-Anon meeting and I swear I heard a woman say, "Feelings aren't faxes." The interesting thing was, I could totally relate. When I first came into recovery, it felt like I was carrying around a fifty-pound fax machine stuffed with resentments, old wounds, and hurt feelings. My moods and emotions ran my life, and I was convinced I had no choice about the way I felt.

Then it hit me. The woman was saying, "Feelings aren't *facts*," which made much more sense to me!

The way I feel is not necessarily related to the facts of the situation at hand. My feelings *may be profound*, yet they may not reflect the truth.

In Al-Anon, I've learned that I can have feelings, but they don't have to dictate the way I live. I can be angry with people and still love them. I can feel hurt, and it doesn't have to ruin the rest of my day. I can be sad and know I'll feel happy again.

I no longer automatically assume my feelings about situations are correct, and I no longer rely solely on my feelings—because they can change. And feelings aren't facts. Nor are they faxes. They aren't laptops, either.

In spite of myself:

Alexander Bain received a patent for a fax machine in 1843.

Bestest

There are times when my efforts to do my "very best" cause me to be thoroughly obnoxious. Hypercompetitive, overachieving, driven by the need to be more, better, best. Best of the best. Better than the best of the best.

My best often pushes people away, because when I go into overdrive, I can be daunting.

It's not easy for me to allow myself to "be" without having a goal or accomplishment in sight. I have to remind myself that I'm not a machine. I am a human being who needs love. I wouldn't mind a deep tissue massage and a week at an Aruban resort, too, but they aren't required.

When my focus is on *how* I'm doing or being the best, I miss out on the beauty of life.

When I feel myself getting rattled and panicked about being the best, I get quiet and ask for God's guidance because I know I'm more attractive to others when I'm not pushing myself to be the best.

The thing is, not everything I do calls for my very best. Sometimes, good or average is precisely what is required. This is important for most of us Al-Anons to remember—because being average is such a rare occurrence!

In spite of myself:

All right, all right, already. Better isn't always best.

Dirt

You can grow flowers from where dirt used to be.
—KATE NASH

I've noticed that dirt doesn't get much love in our society. "Digging up the dirt," "dishing dirt," "getting the dirt"—none of these are upbeat portrayals of dirt.

When I came into Al-Anon, I saw my own dirt—the losses, grievances, and mistakes—as liabilities, and I wanted to get as far away from them as possible.

Yet I learned that the dirt, those unseemly parts, if you will, the things I perceived as bad or shameful, could be the foundation on which better things can grow.

I'm learning to spend less time worrying about the muck from my past and more time planning my future.

To continue with the garden analogy, what I plant in my soil determines what I will grow. If I plant and nurture the seeds I want, then I'll grow more of those things, like kindness and love, serenity and peace, joy and contentment.

I'll abstain from listing all the other things I'd like to see more of in my garden, but I wouldn't mind designer shoes and fine jewelry. And heirloom tomatoes.

In spite of myself:

Today's the perfect day to plant
or buy something for the garden!

Maximization

Last night, I spent hours struggling with one question: Should I call my Al-Anon sponsee and make sure she's set up her retirement accounts properly? I'd just gotten a book on investing, and I was concerned she hadn't been maximizing her accounts.

This is how my mind works. Things that are absolutely none of my business become my business. Other people's finances or savings plans, the person they marry, the place where they work, their dry cleaner.

I picked up the phone to call my sponsee but stopped myself, first, because it was 4:30 a.m. and second, because I remembered that I'm not a banker or a financial planner. Also, this woman has never once asked me for advice about her finances or where she should take her dry cleaning.

When I start "caring" about people and not working my program of Al-Anon, in a short time, I'm working on a plan for how they could improve their lives, complete with advice on how to implement said improvements.

I've decided I will not call my sponsee and inquire about her retirement accounts until after I've finished reading the investing book myself. And I *may* even wait until after I've figured out a plan for *my own* retirement account.

In spite of myself:

If I'm not being asked about it, or paid to do it,
I'll keep my opinion to myself.

Conveniences

One of the things I love about convenience stores is that they're so . . . convenient. I like things to be fast and easy, and if I'm feeling cranky, I want to remain anonymous. When I'm in a bad mood, I don't want to have to talk to my neighbor about the weather or who'll be playing in the World Series.

And yet, while I love convenience, if I'm honest, I actually dislike the impersonal nature of it. Truth be told, I want very much to be recognized and well-known enough to go to the store and get hot wings and a Diet Coke on credit because the owner knows I'm good for it. And if I don't stop in at my local coffee shop for a few days, I want someone to miss me.

It's kind of like recovery. I can't just stop in at Al-Anon, grab whatever I'm craving, and leave, and then be irritated because people don't really know me. I have to show up and be seen. Consistency is imperative.

I have to sacrifice convenience if I want a quality life. There's no quick way to build relationships, and there's no fast track to intimacy.

When I slow down and take time to invest in others, I am happier and more fulfilled. Showing up and allowing myself to be a part of a recovery community makes life better, but it's risky. It's not nearly as risky as eating a corn dog from a convenience store though. Trust me.

In spite of myself:
Convenience doesn't lead to a happier life.
Neither do corn dogs and hot wings.

Keys

Recently, I got a fortune cookie that read: "The key to your problem is the ignition key."

Before I was in recovery, staying still when a problem came up was like nailing peanut butter to the wall: Next to impossible. And very messy.

When problems came up, my first question used to be, "Where is the exit?" I believed my problems were much more powerful than I was. At the hint of a conflict, my car keys were the first thing I grabbed.

Now that I'm in recovery, I can stay somewhat calm when conflicts or problems arise. I'm able to sift through what I'm able to do, or not do. I can ask for help from people I trust, identify my part in the situation, and turn the rest over to God.

I now know that I'm bigger than my problems. And sometimes it's better to gently walk away and turn my problems over to God, or at least give things time to settle before I try to figure out what I should do. Sometimes, I've found that going for a bite of Chinese food or watching *The Karate Kid* or an episode of *Kung Fu* works, as well.

In spite of myself:
Find the problem and you will also
find the key, Grasshopper.

Suffering

When I first heard the phrase "Pain is inevitable, but suffering is optional" in an Al-Anon meeting, I wanted to clock the guy who said it.

I didn't, because he was on the other side of the room. Besides, punching someone over the age of eighty, even if he is self-righteous and smug, is generally frowned upon in Al-Anon.

He looked right at me when he said it.

As if I was choosing to suffer. As if I was getting some kind of sick joy from my despair. As if I was more comfortable wallowing in my problems and kicking around my woe. As if I was using my angst to get attention.

After the meeting, I went over to the old man. I smiled first, and then I told him that although I appreciated his insight, I thought the part about people choosing to suffer was slightly harsh. That pain and suffering happen all the time and people don't always choose it. That he couldn't possibly understand what I was going through and how I deserved my pain.

Then I clocked him. As he howled in pain, I said, "Pain is inevitable, but suffering is optional."

All right, I didn't punch him; I didn't even go up to him after the meeting—because I was too scared. But saying I did made today's meditation ending a lot more interesting, did it not?

In spite of myself:
No pain, no punching, no suffering.

Ways and Meanings

Before Al-Anon, I was a decent armchair psychologist. In fact, I owned a copy of the *DSM* (*Diagnostic and Statistical Manual of Mental Disorders*, a manual professionals use to diagnose psychological disorders), and I used therapeutic phrases, like: "I get in my own way," "I am a self-saboteur and I create chaos," and "I abandon myself."

I had a lot of head knowledge, but I never connected it to my own actions. I was parroting what I'd heard other people say without understanding the real meaning, or the consequences, of those phrases or my actions.

In time, I was able to step back and observe my own behavior. I could feel when I was ramping up to "get in my own way" or "create chaos" or do something I knew I'd feel crappy about later. Once I'd put things in motion (usually my mouth), it was too late. I hurt people, including myself.

I was powerless over my own behavior.

Yes, I had the terms down, but knowledge about my self-destructive behavior was useless without God in my life. I needed a spiritual path and the help of a recovery community.

Today, I ask God to help me express what I'm feeling by writing or talking about it, so I can heal. Self-will and head knowledge don't show me how to do life better. Instead of saying things like, "I need to get out of my own way," I'll try, "God, get me out of my own way." Trusting a Higher Power instead of a manual requires faith, but it's worth it.

In spite of myself:
God, keep me out of my own way today.

Warning!

After I did Step #6—"Were entirely ready to have God remove all these defects of character"—I expected the results to be fairly instantaneous.

When some of my defects began to pop back up after a few days, I felt like a failure. I don't like failure. I know, I know, it makes you stronger, demands that you overcome fear, challenges you to change. Yawn.

"Why are my defects still hanging around?" I asked my sponsor.

"Defects don't just disappear overnight," she replied. "Some take a while, and some never go away."

"So how will I ever have a good life?" I asked.

"You aren't in charge. God is, and you don't know what he has planned. You may have a certain defect in order to be a blessing to someone else."

Could being a know-it-all be a blessing to someone else?

I don't know how, but my defects *might* help people, and my honesty about it may be exactly what they need. Or, as I like to say: *My entire purpose in life may be to serve as a warning of what not to do.*

While that part isn't so comforting, it *is* comforting to know I don't have to remove my own defects. Which is good, because I'd rather spend my time helping other people remove theirs.

In spite of myself:

God, you can remove my defects whenever you want to.
Just so you know.

Fair

I saw a guy wearing a T-shirt that read: "New York Ain't Fair." I've been to New York many times, and the guy's right. New York ain't fair.

I've decided to make my own T-shirt that says, "Recovery Ain't Fair." Because truthfully, I need to be reminded that even though I'm in recovery and I'm getting better, bad things still happen. Even though I "work a spiritual program," people may leave my life or move away; they'll get sick, lose jobs, run out of money, die, etc.

I used to think recovery was linear, and the more work I put into it, the better life would get. While that may be true on a spiritual level, it certainly isn't circumstantially.

My commitment to recovery does not guarantee me a problem-free life. The only guarantee I have is that if I use the tools and work the Twelve Steps of Al-Anon, I will (1) discover a relationship with a Higher Power of my own understanding, (2) find serenity to deal with whatever life hands me, and (3) have the support of a community of people who share my commitment.

Recovery has given me more peace and serenity, and that seems pretty fair, even though New York isn't. But I don't live in New York, so I guess I don't have to worry about that. Which is good; I've got enough to worry about.

In spite of myself:
There ain't no "fair" over there.

Beat It, Harlequin!

Announcing: The Codependent Romance Novel Series!

These heartwarming, contemporary, feel-bad tales of co-dependent women rescuing mysterious, dangerous alcoholics are filled with tawdry whispers, broken promises, and romances unlike any you've ever read!

These fabulously dysfunctional romantic novels feature controlling women and their feckless, charming lovers in overly dramatic, romantic, suspenseful plots. These intriguing, Al-Anon-inspired fantasies deliver a swift emotional punch and exaggerated story lines that only a codependent can relate to!

You'll fall in love with these overly emotional, sunset-hue-haired, azure-eyed heroes and heroines who learn nothing as they throw themselves into one perilous situation after another. And you'll be on the edge of your seat as you watch these maniacs race straight into the arms of danger. Over and over again.

Will there be a "happily ever after"? Most likely. But, with every happy ending, we guarantee drama and chaos, and knee-jerk reactions that lead to unmanageability and insanity. Plus romance—as always, there must be romance.

In spite of myself:

Thank God I just read about the dramas these days.

Codependent Haiku

Originally developed by Japanese poets, haiku was created to capture strong feelings or images inspired by nature, or used to describe powerful emotions and reactions to personal experiences.

Haiku are short, three-lined poems. The first and third lines contain five syllables, and the second line contains seven.

Most Al-Anons are well acquainted with strong emotional reactions, so please, take a moment now to honor the haiku author inside of you. Here's a start:

> I am giving up.
> You are the kind of whack-job
> Who could go postal.
>
> I don't want the guilt.
> You'd machine-gun a skate park
> And say I did it.
>
> I'm not giving up.
> I will love you forever.
> *It is all your fault.*

Haiku can be very therapeutic for Al-Anons. You can be funny or serious, just express yourself and let your inner haiku master be your guide. Go on, give it a shot.

In spite of myself:
Haiku you!

Reactionista

She is what is known as a full-fledged Reactionista™. You know, she tends to overreact to everything. Especially things she knows nothing about and other people's bad behaviors.

Never one to "kill 'em with kindness" when it comes to dealing with impolite people, she prefers a swift, verbal slicing to nip rudeness in the bud. Her nature is to return insults with a snide remark and respond to stupidity with pointed indifference.

In Al-Anon, she's come to realize that reacting to impolite people seldom changes them, but it *always* changes her. When she's constantly reacting, she's never really free. She's always at the mercy of that situation, that person she loves, or that moron in the other car. It never ends. When she's reacting, she's in bondage, and she can't be open to connect to others or her Higher Power in a thoughtful, conscious way.

She's now trademarked the term Reactionista™ and uses it when referring to herself because it reminds her to, well, stop being such an oversensitive brat. It's odd that she would refer to herself in the third person, because she detests people who refer to themselves in the third person.

In spite of myself:

You may use the term Reactionista™, provided you honor
the trademark. Always honor the trademark.

Un-permission

I signed up for a company's online newsletter because I liked their products. I gave them permission to market to me. That permission to market to me quickly turned into stalking.

Almost every day, I'd receive a new update from the company, as well as offers from random affiliates, or stories about things I couldn't care less about. Exhausted by the onslaught of e-mails and special offers, I unsubscribed to the newsletter. Before I could unsubscribe, I had to write an essay about my reasons for wanting out. As if they deserved an explanation from me!

Their marketing strategies were a lot like mine before Al-Anon. Once people asked my opinion, the floodgates would open. I would give it to them, completely uncensored, and as often as possible. I'd frequently remind them of my opinion and check in: *Have you taken my advice? Are you handling things properly? If not, could I help you further?* Once they'd opened the barn door, it was hard to close. Eventually, people would un-permission *me*.

Of course, I'd demand an explanation. And although I never asked for a written essay, I definitely didn't allow people to un-permission me easily.

Especially if I had their home addresses.

In spite of myself:

Has my opinion put me on anyone's un-permission list?

Now, Now

There are many things I say to myself that I'd *never* say to a friend: "You're such a pain." "You're an airhead." "Your life is a total mess." And if I heard someone else say that about a friend or someone I love, I'd stab her in the knee with a potato peeler, provided I had one handy.

Although I'm doing well in many areas of my life, it's embarrassing how cruelly I talk about myself, to myself. It's like I'm talking trash about myself behind my back, only I'm not behind my back, I'm standing there, right in front of myself. Sometimes I'm looking at myself in the mirror when I say those mean things!

It's strange how automatic these thoughts are. They pop up constantly, and they run through my head, scattershot, throughout the day. Or until I'm conscious enough to tell myself, "Hello, self, you can change your thoughts!"

When I'm ready to change my thoughts, I will sit down and imagine Julie Andrews as Maria von Trapp marching through my front door with her guitar case in hand, in that dress made from green-and-white damask drapes. She pats me on the shoulder and smiles as she says something sweet, like, "Now, now. There, there, my dear. You are fine, *exactly* as you are!"

Sometimes I say Maria's words aloud when I'm berating myself, or during a stressful time, because they remind me to be nice and gentle with myself. How could I say anything mean about me with Maria von Trapp listening?

In spite of myself:

Now, now. There, there, my dear. You're doing just fine.

Coming Back

No matter what I shared during my first few months in Al-Anon, people would respond with the same phrase over and over. "Keep coming back," they'd repeat as they hugged me or patted me on the back. While I appreciated the kindness, I couldn't quite understand what coming back to the meeting would do. How would sitting in some church basement among strangers—albeit thoughtful strangers—improve my situation?

If I have to keep coming back, it doesn't bode well for your program, people, I thought. *Honestly, can't you just give me the answers to my problems right now? Just because some people are slow on the uptake doesn't mean all of us are. Those other folks might need to keep coming back, but me? Hardly!*

I figured if I had to keep coming back to hear the same message over and over, I had bigger problems in my life than a little alcoholism!

In the beginning, I came back to the meetings because the snacks were tolerable, the people were supportive, and I loved the coffee. It wasn't because I was dense and didn't "get it."

Now, years later, I come back because the people are supportive, I love the coffee, and, ironically, I've *never* heard the same message twice. No matter what the focus of the meeting is, I always get something new from an Al-Anon meeting.

The jury is still out on the quality of the snacks.

In spite of myself:
Same people, same snacks, but the message in Al-Anon
is *always* different.

Recovery + Fun

Today I wasn't feeling particularly inspired to write a meditation, so I researched a pair of words, "recovery + fun" online. I found a story about a celebrity's plastic surgery mishap, an article about a governor visiting a state that had just endured a natural disaster, and a recovery-based chat room with some really bad knock-knock jokes.

I might try again later because the things I found were so dismal.

I was stuck, but forcing myself to be creative makes me uncomfortable. *What if I run out of ideas? What if I have nothing interesting to say? What if I have nothing to say about anything?*

It happens all the time. It's called "creative block." People lose their mojo. People also lose their minds.

But today I don't have to worry about losing my mind or my creativity. For today, things are acceptable and I still have a few decent ideas, although I can't, for the life of me, articulate any of them right now. Which is okay because it's *your* turn to come up with a humorous, creative thought about your *own* recovery.

Yes, it's *your* turn to participate in the fun. Your job is to come up with a fun/humorous/lighthearted thought about recovery. Go on, give it a try. I'll get you started: There once was an Al-Anon from Nantucket . . .

In spite of myself:
R-E-C-O-V-E-R-Y spells F-U-N!

Patient

My sixth-grade teacher was Mrs. Benson, and the thing I remember most about her—aside from her giving me detention for talking every single week—was the Precious Moments doll on her desk. The doll held a heart with words on it: "Be patient. God isn't finished with me yet."

I hated that phrase because by the time I'd gotten to elementary school, I'd already run out of patience with other people, with everything. Even in grade school, I hated precious things, like stuffed pastel-colored unicorns from the county fair, those browless characters with humongous, watery eyes, and the mystifying seventies cartoons that said things like, "Love means never having to say you're sorry." Even as a kid, I knew that love meant you *should* say you were sorry when you were wrong.

Today, when I hear, "Be patient. God isn't finished with me yet" in a meeting, I always think of Mrs. Benson, who was also the first teacher I ever heard use the phrase "make love."

Perhaps my disdain for anything precious and my lack of patience makes me a bad Al-Anon. But please, be patient with me. I'm learning to be patient with myself, and with things over which I have no control, like corny phrases, stuffed unicorns, and antiques.

In spite of myself:

God, please feel free to speed things up.

360

It used to be that when I changed my viewpoint about something, I would say, "I did a complete 360."

What I *should* have been saying was, "I did a complete 180." Apparently, 360 degrees is a full circle. So, actually, if I'd done a 360, it would mean that I had not changed my position, and I would've ended up right back where I'd started. A half-circle is 180 degrees, which is the correct way to say I've reversed my position. Half a circle, opposite viewpoint.

In Al-Anon, I have changed my viewpoint on many things, which is good, because most of my opinions before recovery were based on things my kooky family had taught me, superstitions, misinformation, stuff I'd read in books or on Wikipedia, or words I'd overheard while standing in line at Starbucks.

Part of the work I've done in Al-Anon includes forming my own opinion on things, not just parroting things I hear other people say because they're smart—or they act that way.

Today I may have one viewpoint on something, but after doing research, my viewpoint changes. Which is to say "I do a 180," which is another way of saying my position has moved 45 degrees, which is one-half of a right angle (90 degrees), which happens to be a quarter of a circle.

If I change my opinion again, it'll require the use of a protractor, which I do not own. So it's doubtful I will.

In spite of myself:
Recovery has taught me that I can do a 360, a 180,
or even a 110, if I want to.

Travel Light

I would consider myself to be an expert at traveling light. In fact, I once traveled through Europe for three months carrying only a backpack, a Swiss Army knife, and a jar of Nutella.

I can travel light, but I'm not that great at living light. I need a daily reminder that I Am Not Responsible for Everything and Everyone. And I Am Not in Charge of Everything and Everyone. And I Don't Have to Carry the Weight of Everything for Everyone.

Just for today, I will use the Twelve Steps and my Al-Anon program to live more lightly, which to me means taking whatever life hands me and doing my best to accept it while staying in communication with my Higher Power.

Spreading the light, for me, is the equivalent of having patience with myself and being of service to others, wherever I am.

I have a little trouble when I try to *be* the light. I think I've got quite a ways to go before I'm ready for that one.

In spite of myself:

Today, I'll be happy with any kind of light I can get!

Pants Day

While it doesn't appear on most calendars, today is Take Your Pants for a Walk Day.

This is one of my favorite holidays, although it isn't honored equally by all. This reminds me of the importance of Tradition #10, which says that Al-Anon has "no opinion on outside issues; hence our name ought never be drawn into public controversy."

The best part about Pants Day is, even if you don't celebrate it, no one in Al-Anon will make a big deal about it. I've never been asked at a meeting whether I'll be honoring Pants Day. Nobody's ever inquired what I'll be cooking or if I'll be hosting relatives. It's comforting to know my friends in recovery respect my decisions on this matter and won't force me to get into a big discussion about what Pants Day means to me. They respect my right to honor it in my own way, without judgment. Or controversy.

One of the main reasons I love Pants Day is there's relatively little preparation involved. The only requirement is that I show up with my pants on. And go for a walk.

I wear pants a lot. In fact, I am wearing pants right now, and since I'll be doing some walking and my pants will be coming with me, by definition, I'm honoring the holiday. And that feels great!

In spite of myself:

Take a walk, preferably with your pants on. But, no pressure!

Personal

I had arrived late to the Al-Anon meeting and noticed an empty seat next to a woman whom I thought of as a new friend. The room was packed, and I wanted to be inconspicuous, but when I attempted to sit down next to her, she shook her head and threw up her hand.

"This seat is saved," she declared tersely.

"You can't save seats, especially this late in a meeting," I sniped back and sat down beside her. She sighed loudly, climbed over me, and took an empty seat in the row behind us.

During a break in the meeting, I turned and gave her the stink eye. She responded loudly, "Don't take it personal."

"You mean *personally*?" I barked back at her.

It was early in my recovery; I was hypersensitive, and angry as hell, so her response bothered me for many reasons. First, she had embarrassed me. Second, people aren't supposed to save seats in meetings for people who aren't there. But it was her grammar that bothered me most. Incorrect adverb usage really irks me.

If that situation were to happen today, I'd probably find another seat and laugh about it. But I can't be sure I'd be able to stop myself from correcting poor grammar. There is simply never an excuse for poor grammar.

In spite of myself:

I'd like to buy you an adverb.
Will you promise to use it *properly*?

Buts

I carry a lot of "buts" around in my head. *"I like that meeting, BUT I don't like the room. I like that guy, BUT he's a little full of himself. I like that restaurant, BUT the food is overpriced. . . ."*

When I first started listing all the "buts" in my head, I thought, *Wow, I had no idea how negative I was!* Negative thinking had become so automatic, I didn't even notice it anymore. Until I started listening to myself, and then I had to say, *Self, listen to me! You've become one of those "but people"!*

I knew I had to change. But how? I started using a trick I learned years ago in an improvisational comedy class. We were taught to replace the word "but" with the word "and" as a way to keep the conversation and the creativity flowing.

For example: Instead of "I like that meeting, but the building's gross," it becomes, "I like that meeting and the building is retro. That 1950s paneling reminds me of Grandma's house. She was nice, *sometimes,* my grandma."

Instead of a "but," you have a whole new perspective, which opens the floodgates of creativity. "And" opens things up, where "buts" close them down!

The "buts" will continue to pop up here and there, but now you have something to replace them with!

In spite of myself:
I won't let the "buts" go to my head today.

Tools

When my sponsor spoke about using the "tools of the program," you might say I was less than thrilled with the idea. What tools? I don't even own a Phillips screwdriver, much less a jackhammer. And I'm no good with anything that requires assemblage. Assembling, whatever. The last place in the world I want to spend any time is in a home improvement store. Unless it's filled with categorically great-looking men.

Even after I learned that the Al-Anon program tools had nothing to do with chainsaws or pulling copper wires from buildings, I was still disturbed. I don't like physical or mental exertion, and I was enough into recovery to know that this would require a lot from me. It may be a simple program, but Al-Anon *does* include some heavy lifting.

Mind you, I *did* do the work as directed by my sponsor—sometimes sloppily and usually without a smile on my face. And while, at first, I didn't like the tools (meetings, service, prayer, sponsorship), they were vital to my recovery.

I wouldn't have the life I have now if I hadn't picked up the tools and learned how to use them.

It was not easy, but it was definitely worth it.

Learning to operate a jackhammer, however, probably would have been simpler.

In spite of myself:
Today I will pick up and use the tools of Al-Anon.

Value

It was my third meeting with the potential client who ran a lucrative med spa. As she sipped tofu soup, she glanced over the proposal I'd spent days preparing.

"No offense," she said, looking at herself in the mirror, "but I don't really see why my business needs a marketing plan. Besides, I don't read."

I tried, again, to explain the necessity of a marketing plan, while she checked her cell phone and e-mail.

Finally, it dawned on me. This woman didn't want what I had to offer.

My work life began to pass before my eyes—images of me pitching various clients and thinking: *If I could just explain things better, they would understand. If I could prove my value.* That was me—constantly trying to convince people who didn't want my help that they needed it.

Hmmmmmm . . . where else have I been repeating this pattern? I thought as I stood up and said, gently, "You know, I might not be the right person for this job."

I removed myself from the meeting with the famous med spa guru as graciously as I could and never looked back. Okay, I looked back. In fact, I agonized for days over how I could have done things better.

Eventually, I came to realize that I was, as Al-Anons say, "going to the hardware store for milk." Or, in my words, "selling vowels and consonants to a woman who doesn't read."

In spite of myself:
No shopping for milk at the hardware store today.

AUGUST

Right?!

Being right can be an issue for an Al-Anon like me. It isn't as if I always *have to be right*. I just need to *not be wrong*.

I panic about not knowing the right answer to important things and not-so-important things—things like: Is it wild or farm-raised salmon that causes mercury poisoning? Should I yell and try to look big if I have a run-in with a grizzly bear in the forest, or is it better to roll over and play dead? And: Who, in truth, *was* responsible for discovering that the Earth is round?

These might seem to be irrelevant questions in the grand scheme of life, but for an Al-Anon like me, they represent larger questions that I also might not have the answers to. Questions that lead to other, larger questions, which lead to more questions about those larger questions.

Losing control of our thought processes and not knowing the right answer are many Al-Anons' greatest fears. That, and eating mercury-filled salmon. I would also add: death by running into a grizzly bear in the forest. Or death by choking on a pen cap— which, by the way, is twice as likely to happen as being killed by lightning.

In spite of myself:

God, help me remember:
I don't always have to know the answers.

Close Encounters

The Al-Anon speaker was talking about Step #8: "Made a list of all persons we had harmed, and became willing to make amends to them all." She said, "We can be someone's encounter with the effects of alcoholism, or someone's encounter with the effects of God."

I thought about how irritable I'd been all day and wondered: *What if the last person I was rude to died right after meeting me? Or, what if I'd been a jerk to a friend and then she got E. coli and died? Or, after seeing me, my friend succumbed to transient global amnesia and all he could remember was how boorish I was?*

Plagued by such horrible thoughts, I called the Al-Anon speaker and told her about the lives I'd inadvertently ruined that day. She said I should make amends, if necessary, but the thing to remember was that we affect others. And when we are kind it affects *us, not just the other person.* Treating all people kindly makes *us* feel good. When we bring God into our encounters, instead of responding out of codependency or reaction to alcoholism, life is better for *us all.*

I gave it more thought, and here's my take on it: What I do directly reflects who I am inside. If I say I'm pursuing a spiritual life, I need to act like it. If I bring God into all my encounters, there's less chance of me ruining someone's life. Especially my own.

In spite of myself:
Today I'll bring God into all of my encounters.

Motivation

My former business coach had an office filled with motivational posters. One of them was of a bald eagle perched on a branch. At the bottom of the poster was the phrase "Your Life Begins This Moment."

As time passed, I grew to hate this coach. Not only was he overpriced and egotistical, but also I resented those motivational posters!

Images of college rowers in a boat with a phrase like "Fear Is a Four-Letter Word" or a general on a battlefield with "A Leader Is a Man Who Can Adapt Principles to Circumstances."

What I first saw as encouraging reminders to do and be my best became subtle judgments and covert condemnations. What the posters should have said were, "Boy, You Are Sure Screwing Things Up," "Time's a Wasting, Loser," "99 Percent of the Population Has It Figured Out, Lamebrain—What's Your Problem?"

When I found myself flipping the bird to one of those motivational posters, I knew it was time to say good-bye to my coach. The pressure to improve myself had become too much for me.

In Al-Anon, there's no schedule, no right way to do life or recovery. My fellows offer me love and grace no matter how long it takes me to figure things out. My Higher Power has a pace that's perfect for me. There's no rush to improve.

And, thank goodness, in Al-Anon I don't have to sit and be mocked by stupid, soul-crushing motivational posters.

In spite of myself:
I'm glad God's not rushing to motivate me.

Low Heat

*Truth hurts. Maybe not as much as jumping
on a bicycle with the seat missing, but it hurts.*
—*The Naked Gun 2½*

That's an incredibly painful image, jumping onto a bicycle without a seat—but it's an accurate description of how I've felt at times in Al-Anon. Super-duper uncomfortable.

When I did my first moral inventory, I was faced with my bad attitudes and dysfunctional behaviors, and I was forced to look at the secrets I'd kept—things I thought were making me safe, but were actually harming me. I ended up feeling like I was riding a bicycle without a seat. The truth can be painful.

Not to put too fine a point on it, but there have been times in recovery when it's felt like I've shoved my hand into a garbage disposal while it was on. Or, like I'd put my finger on a hot burner on the stove. Or, like I'd tried to use a steam iron on the collar of a dress while I was still wearing it. (That one I actually did.)

The bruises, bumps, and near loss of digits during my time in Al-Anon have not been for naught. I've learned from every difficult situation I've encountered. Recovery has taught me to accept the good and even the not-so-good things.

Yes, there are some who might ask, "If you could do it all over again, would you do things differently?"

To those people I would say, "Hell, yeah. Second-degree burns take a long time to heal."

In spite of myself:
The truth is easier when the heat and the seat are low.

Wisdom

Most of the wisdom I've received from my family has come from those who've passed on. Historically, my dead relatives have been much wiser that those who are still living.

"Your dead Aunt Leona always said . . ." "Uncle Saucy used to tell us . . ." "Thomas Jefferson once said . . ." Actually, no one in my family has ever quoted Thomas Jefferson. But the point is, in my family, the dead were pretty clever. Those of us who were living, well . . . we weren't so clever.

As I got older, and more family members began to pass on, it occurred to me that they'd said some intelligent—one might say profound—things while they were alive, and it seemed such a shame that we'd waited to quote them until after they'd passed.

There are plenty of people in Al-Anon who say wise things as well. In practically every meeting I go to, I hear something worth writing down. Unfortunately, I rarely have a pen handy, and it's rude to text myself during a meeting, and even though I think I'll remember it later, I never do.

No matter, because I'm certain that at the very next meeting, I'll hear something helpful or profound, because in Al-Anon, wisdom isn't relegated to the dead.

In fact, I've come to the conclusion that there are people in Al-Anon who are truly profound. And the best part is, they are often sitting right next to me.

In spite of myself:
God, help me find the wisdom in this moment.

Wiggle Your Toes

Today is national Wiggle Your Toes Day. Some people see this as an unnecessary, frivolous holiday. And there are some who don't even observe it!

Since most Al-Anons make little time for play, you're officially encouraged to commemorate Wiggle Your Toes Day by doing the following: Take off your socks and shoes and wiggle your toes in a pool or a public fountain. Perhaps even a tub. Heck, you could run some warm water in the sink at work and stick your toes in it, then add some lavender oil and rose hips. If anyone winces, simply explain that you're honoring a highly personal holiday and you'd appreciate a bit of reverence.

Look at it like this: Those little piggies at the ends of your feet don't have a recovery program. *They* can't get out to a meeting on their own. They don't get calls from caring friends when they're feeling kind of lonely. There are times when they feel chubby, ignored, and uptight. Kind of like you did before you got into recovery.

Your toes deserve some love and attention. So go on, wiggle them, massage them, soak them. Party on! Just, please, don't ignore them. At least not today.

In spite of myself:

Ten percent of the population
has two toes partially joined together.

Conspiracy

I'm not really sure *exactly* what my Al-Anon sponsor said, but what I heard was, "Stop being a victim and acting like the world is conspiring against you."

At first I thought, *Who has she been talking to? Has she been listening in on my phone calls or reading my e-mails?*

The truth is, I'm not *acting* like a victim—I *am* being singled out. While I can't go so far as to call it a plot, there have been several "incidents" that have caused me to pause. There was that altercation with a parking attendant, and the way the teller at my bank behaved the last time I went in. The people in my Al-Anon meetings haven't been very pleasant or welcoming. As for God, we haven't connected in weeks.

I can't say for sure, but yes, indeed, I believe there might be some "meeting of the minds," some conspiring to take me down. I have my suspicions.

I'm not some doomsday prepper who has a bunker stockpiled with dehydrated peas and ammunition, but there *are* times when I wonder if the people who love me and the people who can't stand me are actively planning my demise.

And just because I don't have proof doesn't mean it's not happening. I'm an Al-Anon, and we are experts at this stuff. The signs are all around.

In spite of myself:

I have seen the signs, and they are all around me.

Break

God and I took a break last week. As in, I felt the need for some space. I'd spent the night panicking about my career, my relationships, and my finances, and I straight out told God I was over him. I told him I'd let him know when I was ready to talk.

"It's not personal," I said. "It's me, not you."

I used to harbor guilt about feeling distant from my Higher Power, as if that was a sign that our relationship was in big trouble. Now I understand that's it's just the nature of our connection. Sometimes we're really close; at other times we aren't. And at times I get irritable and fearful, and I need to stomp around the house and slam doors.

The great thing is, I can struggle with God without fearing he'll punish me or say something like, "You want space? You got it! How's about you call me when hell freezes over?"

Nope, my Higher Power lets me throw a fit and gives me my space, and then welcomes me with open arms when I'm ready to talk. The best part is, this is my first relationship in which I've never been scolded for squeezing the toothpaste tube the wrong way or leaving the toilet seat down.

In spite of myself:
Sometimes I need a little break. It's okay.

Gaiety

I noticed something recently while looking at the appendixes of several Al-Anon meditation books. None of them had entries under the word "fun." One of the daily readers had an entry for "humor," but I could barely get through the meditation because it was so *dull*. It suggested the way to experience more humor in life was to "nourish gaiety," and "spark things with a dash of rosy pink." Huh?

While humor can't be analyzed, it can be cultivated. It's about perspective, and it starts with your attitude. Yes, even an Al-Anon can learn to lighten up.

Begin paying attention to other people. Be curious and ask questions. Set a goal of seeing humor, because the irony is, the more you look for humor, the more you'll find it. Although I don't think that's an accurate use of "irony."

No matter. Just start looking at your problems with a new perspective and relate things that don't ordinarily go together. Look at your life—say, from the viewpoint of your dog. Find one element of your situation that could be considered humorous, and share it with others.

Life is absurd, but a slight twist in your viewpoint can turn tragedy into comedy.

Humor isn't easy to explain. And as I've proven, it's impossible to do it in a funny way. But I'm sure of one thing: Humor never, ever includes "gaiety" or "dashes of rosy pink."

In spite of myself:

*I'll find three things about my situation
that I can laugh—or at least smile—about.*

Bridges

I've burned quite a few bridges during my time on this planet. Not that I'm counting, but if pressed, I'd estimate the number to be 12,408. Give or take a few. There have been times when I've taken a match to one of those bridges gleefully, watching it all go up in flames as I stood by. And there have been times when I've burned the bridges out of ignorance, unable to stop myself. I've made major decisions knowing full well that I was destroying the only remaining route home and blowing any chance for a future.

I simply didn't know better than to douse everything I loved in kerosene and ignite it.

Al-Anon shows me how to do things differently.

Today, I avoid creating disasters or crises in my life, and in the lives of others, by walking away from situations with as much dignity and grace as possible.

Most of the time.

There are times when the temptation to pull the gas can out from the back of my trunk is strong. . . . That's when I ask for God's help, and I take contrary action by picking up the phone and calling someone who understands—someone who will talk me out of the urge to start burning things because they've been there and know it's hard to get back home when you've burned all your bridges.

These days, when I see a bridge, I rarely feel the need to set it on fire.

In spite of myself:
I won't even think about burning that bridge
when I come to it.

Wheels

I'm constantly asking my Higher Power for directions. Sometimes I receive clear indications about what I should do.

The ironic part about this is that once I feel I've been led in a certain direction, I immediately start to question it. . . . *Did I hear what I thought I heard? Should I ask again, in a different way, just to be sure?* And when the path seems obvious and I feel I'm being led, I immediately want to take things over. Even after I've asked for directions!

I want to trust my Higher Power, and while I'm down with trusting God to be my GPS, I prefer to keep my smartphone with Google Maps handy, and a Thomas Guide in the car, just in case. I've had enough life experiences to be able to look back and see that I can trust my Higher Power. And yet, when the rubber hits the road, I still try to take over.

The only solution is to trust, once again. It's never easy, but I know that when I allow God to lead, the results are infinitely better. The ride is smoother, the road's not as rugged, and I don't get pulled over as often.

Even though it's killing me, I will suppress every urge I have to insert lyrics to a Carrie Underwood song right here.

Just for today, I'll let God be my GPS, and I promise to keep my hands off my smartphone.

In spite of myself:
I'll let God provide the directions today.

Slo-Gos

I used to hate all those corny Al-Anon slogans. I seriously doubted that repeating such simple, hackneyed sayings would help people who were in a desperate situation—especially if they were smart and sophisticated, like some folks I know.

I thought about the phrases I'd been repeating to myself before Al-Anon. Some of them came from adults in my life; others were made up, based on my experiences. Most of the sayings I repeated were variations on the theme of "Boy, are you screwed." Some of the printable ones included:

- You're such a loser!
- When will you ever learn?
- Why can't you get it together?

When I compare *my* slogans to the Al-Anon slogans, it's obvious the Al-Anon ones are better, and a lot kinder; they help me focus on what's important:

- Keep it simple
- Easy does it
- First things first
- Let go and let God

Now, when I hear the old slogans echoing in my head, I immediately replace them with ones I've learned in Al-Anon. Yes, they are simple, but they actually work, even for people who are smart and sophisticated. Like some folks I know.

In spite of myself:
I'll never be too smart for recovery.

Summer Dreams

It's summertime, a season for memories: children running through the public fountain, teenagers lying by the pool with their friends, firing up the backyard BBQ on weekends and basking in the sun without fearing skin cancer or worrying about global warming.

I'm in love with the idea of the perfect summer, and I still buy the fantasy that summer is the most magical time of the year, when flirtations become flings and *anything is possible*. The reality is this: Memories of summers past and fantasies about things I *should* be experiencing *are all made up*.

Is it that I'm bitter because on a bright summer Saturday I'm in an Al-Anon meeting—which I do love—but I'm working on myself instead of my tan? Perhaps. More than likely, it's because I'm obsessing about something and wishing I wasn't. Or freaking out about parties I've not been invited to.

Perhaps I *am* bitter. But thanks to Al-Anon, I *am* also *better*. Yes, I worry that my life's dreadful and will never improve. That my friends have it made and are all out having the best summer ever. But like the perfect summer, that's just an idea from an active imagination.

While I'm on my bitter rant, is it too much to ask that people learn to stop capitalizing seasons inappropriately?

In spite of myself:
There's no such thing as a perfect anything.

The Universe

There's a sentence that begins, "I'm putting it out into the universe . . ." I don't know how the rest of it goes, though, because I always tune out once I hear those first words.

I've never, ever been able to put anything out "into the universe," mainly because, unless NASA's involved, things sent into outer space rarely return.

I *understand* that people want to trust that their problems, relationships, or issues are better off in the hands of something bigger than themselves. However, when you throw something willy-nilly out into the massive black vortex of space, it has a tendency to stay there. Ask an Al-Anon. There is nothing more disturbing than things being removed without prior approval—preferably written.

I'm all for trusting a Higher Power, but it's my opinion that, as a society, we ought to practice caution and show some respect for the cosmos. Nonchalantly tossing any "situation" into a universe that is also responsible for keeping track of a billion stars and the Milky Way simply seems unwise. Trusting that the cosmos is going to resolve my little problem is assuming a lot. As for me, believing that there's a loving God who cares about me personally and is going to take care of things is much more comforting.

The universe may be friendly, but it is not a dumping ground, or a conflict resolution center.

I'm not trying to be preachy; I just thought I'd "put it out there." God can and does answer prayers. I have no idea what the universe does. That's way above my pay grade.

In spite of myself:
Hey, God, thanks for caring about my little problems.

Platinum Rule

I worked for a retailer that promoted what they called the Platinum Rule: "Treat others as they would like to be treated."

While I think this is admirable in theory, the reality is, I don't always know how others *want* to be treated. Say, for instance, I've just met someone at a party, or they're temping at my office and they'll only be there for a week. How can I possibly get into that level of detail in five days' time?

I can appreciate the Platinum Rule, and while I admire the good intentions of that retail company (which, by the way, had the highest turnover rate of any business I've ever worked for), as an Al-Anon and a codependent, I have to steer clear of trying to figure out what someone else wants. Doing that can lead me to a whole new level of manic-fueled craziness . . . law enforcement . . . yellow caution tape . . .

Instead, I try to treat others with dignity, kindness, and respect. It's the way I like to be treated, and I'm fairly certain it's what other people want.

Of course, there will always be those who want to be treated *unkindly* and even disrespectfully, but that's a whole other reality show, *if you know what I'm sayin'*. I'm not touching that subject with a ten-foot pole. A platinum ten-foot pole, that is.

In spite of myself:

If I stick with courteous and kind, things will probably be fine.

First Dates

Within a month of ending a relationship and starting Al-Anon, I began to worry about my next relationship. Already planning how I'd inform my future husband I was in a Twelve Step recovery program. The scene, as I imagined it, would begin on our first date, which, of course, would include dinner at a spectacular restaurant, high on the cliffs near the ocean.

MAN: I think I'll have a beer. What would you like, darling?

ME: Would you say that drinking is a problem for you? You see, I'm an Al-Anon, and I have this attraction to alcoholics. I have all my life. So, if you have a problem with any substances, please tell me now. But only if you think it's a problem. I don't want to put a damper on our relationship, as it's just starting and all, and so far it's going very well, wouldn't you agree? Anyhoo, we can avoid a big mess if you'll just tell me the truth. Right now.

And then, he'd smile and cradle my face in his strong hands.

MAN: I have no substance abuse problems or strange habits. I'm happy and emotionally available. I work out every day, and I help the homeless on Sundays. I eat only organic foods, and I make guacamole from scratch. Honestly, I'm as close to perfect as a man can be. I'm so glad you're in Al-Anon. It confirms that you, too, are emotionally healthy. You're exactly the kind of woman I could spend the rest of my life with. I like you already. In fact, I think I'm in love with you.

In spite of myself:

God, help me remember that sometimes, less is more.

Dear Abby

I had a colleague who was constantly asking my opinion about her relationship problems. At first I felt honored, in the way that codependents do, because I thought it was *my* unique brand of advice she wanted. And I assumed the hours I spent comforting her in the women's bathroom marked the beginning of a lifelong friendship.

One day, I happened to find this same friend in the women's bathroom being consoled by another coworker. My feelings were really hurt. It wasn't *my* particular advice that was so valuable to her—she simply wanted an audience. This chick would tell her sob story to *anybody who'd listen!*

That's it! I thought. *I won't waste my hard-earned wisdom on her. The next time that dummy asks for my opinion, I'll tell her to call Dear Abby, even though I don't think she's alive anymore.*

Although I really *do* know what's best for my colleague, and I'm utterly convinced she would have flourished under my supervision, I've learned to smile and hold my tongue whenever she stops by my cubicle to complain.

And when holding my tongue doesn't work, I pretend my phone is ringing—and it's someone who actually *listens* to my advice.

In spite of myself:

Could it be that my special brand of advice really isn't?

Poker Face

The radio host suggested that people try "acting happy," even if they aren't feeling that way, for a week. "Don't deny your feelings of sadness, or whatever else you're feeling. Just don't act on them," he advised. "You can have your feelings, but you can't take them out on the people around you."

Now, I've never been a big card player, mainly because I don't have a poker face. When I'm sad, I wear my sad face. When I'm upset, I wear my upset face, and my bitchy face when . . . well, I guess that's pretty obvious.

I decided to take on the radio host's challenge, and I began by watching my face. I noticed I was quite comfortable sporting the snarky face. And the irritated face. And, well, the angry face popped up a lot more often than I'd previously been aware of. The truth is, I wanted to try out some new faces, like the sweet face and the friendly face. Eventually I wanted to try out the whole "acting happy" challenge, so I smiled, even when I felt crabby. I acted as if things were okay with me, even when they weren't. After much practice, my feelings began to match my face.

It didn't feel like I was telling a lie—it felt like *I* was telling my face what to do, instead of my face telling *me* what to do.

To this day, there are times when I put on a happy face, even though I'm not really feeling it. Strangely enough, after all this practice, my face is starting to look a lot younger!

In spite of myself:
Today I will feel better, even if I have to work at it.

Acquit

For most of my life—say, from the age of six on up—I've had a difficult time handling criticism.

Like many Al-Anons, I thought I was above criticism. I was a decent person; I'd never been to jail or assaulted anyone, at least not at work. But unless feedback included the words "you're amazing," I didn't feel the need to hear it. High praise was simply all I was interested in.

If I discovered my position was replaceable, or the work I was doing wasn't considered magnificent, I assumed the problem was with the massively incompetent people around me. No matter the job or position I held, my attitude was essentially, "This place would fall apart without me!" Conversely, I felt so poorly about myself that the slightest bit of criticism made me feel like I was on trial. And since my value was based solely on my accomplishments, if everything I did wasn't considered fabulous, I'd lose it. If I couldn't be perfect, there was no point.

How can one person have so many diverging opinions about her worth? Honestly, I don't know the answer to that question. I'm human, and human beings are complex.

Al-Anon has taught me that criticism isn't an indication of my value. Criticism can be useful, and if I take the time to listen to it without reacting, it can improve my life. Criticism can be a reflection of my behavior, but it doesn't determine my value.

I don't think I'll ever love hearing criticism, but today I'm able to listen to it without falling apart. Unless it's a Monday. I can't be entirely responsible for my reaction to criticism on a Monday.

In spite of myself:
If the criticism doesn't fit, I must acquit.

Groundhog Day

Frankly, some days it feels like I'm living out the movie *Groundhog Day*—the same exact day over and over . . . and over.

There are times when I want to throw my hands up and say, "Somebody get my agent on the phone, dammit! I'm not being paid nearly enough for this job!"

Except I'm not an actor, and I don't get to walk off the set and eat and drink all the champagne and gluten-free, organic duck pâté I want when the director yells, "Cut!"

That's when I begin to wonder: *What if my life isn't just a seemingly monotonous replay of problems? What if the days that seem like repeats are just refresher courses? What if I'm not going in circles, but instead, moving up into a bigger circle, and the things I'm experiencing are a reminder of what I already know? And what if, at the end of the journey, I'll be rewarded with a tasty ice cream sundae with whipped cream and a (parallel) lifetime Netflix membership? What if the remuneration is my very own leprechaun and a mountain of jelly donuts? What if?*

Although it may be second nature for me to fall into the dark hole of despair over and over again, because of Al-Anon I know how to stop myself. For today, I'll try to be grateful for the spiritual lessons I receive, even though they seem to be slightly repetitious, and I'm not very well paid.

Instead of complaining about my life, I'll be thankful to my Higher Power for the gifts that might be on their way to me. And if that doesn't help, I'll call my agent and fire him.

In spite of myself:

I think I get the point, God. At least, I did yesterday.

'Splanations

I have a business-related website, and naturally there are trolls who leave messages on my blog. I read this post recently: "*You really make it seem so easy, but I, in finding this matter to be really one thing which I feel I'd never understand. It feels too complex and very vast for me. I'm having a look forward in your subsequent post.*"

I don't think that troll really read my article. I also don't think that troll has spell-check. Or grammar-check.

As an Al-Anon, it's common for me to feel misunderstood, and not just by trolls. Sometimes I feel unheard and undervalued. My solution used to be to try to explain things more, and louder, so that people would understand.

This generally led to *more* misunderstanding. It would go on and on like this for days, until I learned that it's not my job to get anyone to understand anything. *I* can't make *anyone else* understand *anything.*

The only thing I *can* do is increase my conscious contact with my Higher Power. The more time I spend with God, the less I find myself feeling misunderstood or needing to explain things.

The thing I *can't* do is know if the trolls will ever get what I'm saying.

In spite of myself:
I don't have to 'splain nothin' to nobody!

My Business

It was a few years before I found Al-Anon. I was at my highly intense, hypercompetitive job at an entertainment company, crouched on the floor, holding my ear to a drinking glass I was pressing against the wall. I wanted to hear everything my conniving, power-mongering colleagues were saying about me in the office next door. It wasn't pretty!

After I'd gotten an earful (I wasn't just paranoid—they *were indeed* conspiring against me), I pulled myself together and concocted a plan. My main goal from that point forward: enhancing and managing my reputation, and proving those jerks wrong about me. I vowed to be the smartest one on every project, and if I weren't, I'd settle for being the nicest. I knew if I worked hard enough, I'd get those idiots to change their minds about me. This, of course, was insane, because I had an intense job, the requirements of which didn't include being the most likeable.

It took a great deal of work in recovery for me to admit and accept that not everyone I like will like me, and it's none of my business. I have to allow people to think what they want about me. And more importantly, *I* don't have to change if *they don't* like me.

I've learned to go where the love is, and I no longer worry about folks who can't offer me love. I've also learned not to take drinking glasses to work. I simply don't need the temptation.

In spite of myself:
God, I give you other people's opinions of me.

Broadcasts

A father confessed in his blog that his eldest son was his favorite kid because he was more fun to play with. People went crazy, posting comments about how insensitive the guy was—how he'd undoubtedly damaged his children for life.

I thought, *Well, he may be daft, but at least he's honest! All of us have favorites; we're just not supposed to admit it.*

It's okay to admit I have a favorite food, a favorite song, a favorite movie. But it's entirely different to say I have a favorite person. The thing is, I think, like most people, I'm fickle, and my favorites change. This was just a dorky dad who said something dumb. But he'd put it in writing and couldn't take it back.

How many times have I said things that I've wanted to take back? While it's important for me to know what I'm feeling and thinking and work through it—especially with my Higher Power—I don't need to broadcast my innermost thoughts or feelings to everyone around me. They might not always be received in the way I've intended.

Sometimes it's better to keep my feelings to myself until I've sorted them out, and prayed about how to deliver them. And it's always best that I think about things before I say or do something I can't take back.

My feelings and opinions change. A lot. I don't always have to report or record them. In fact, I've learned that it's wiser and safer for me to keep some of my bright ideas to myself!

In spite of myself:

I don't have to report all of my feelings all of the time.

Happy Guilt

Pssssst! Did you know that it's actually okay to enjoy a good day? Stay with me, because, if you're anything like I was before Al-Anon, good days weren't really good days, they were the "calm before the storm"—the tremor before the massive earthquake that destroyed everything. Happiness was *not* something I was accustomed to.

I used to feel there was something virtuous about suffering. It's like my brain had tricked me into thinking that enjoying my life meant I was being disloyal to the friends or family members who were having problems.

One day, I sat myself down and took a look at those beliefs. *Now that's a pretty silly way to live,* I thought. *I don't have to be unhappy just because others are. I'm not being disloyal by having a great life.* And my mind replied, *Okay, maybe that's so. But what if you aren't having a good time and you're in denial? What then?*

I didn't have a reply at the time, but today here's what I'd say to myself, should that question come up: *It's okay to have a fantastic day. An amazing day does not have to be met with feelings of guilt or fear. It isn't necessary to look in the mirror and examine your flaws in order to keep yourself grounded. You don't have to create problems where there aren't any.*

A stellar day is a gift from God. I no longer have to analyze it; I can even savor it. In fact, I can feel a stellar day coming on right now. It's either that or a big storm with heavy rain.

I'll grab my umbrella, just in case.

In spite of myself:

Today I'm going to assume that
the feeling I'm having is a good one.

Promos

Tradition #11: "Our public relations policy is based on attraction rather than promotion."

When I read this Tradition, I often think of Vivien Leigh and Audrey Hepburn. Audrey Hepburn was an elegant beauty; she made Holly Golightly attractive in *Breakfast at Tiffany's* by animating her grace, her style, and her sense of amusement. And Vivien Leigh transformed Scarlett O'Hara from a vain, self-centered woman-child to a strong, determined woman in *Gone with the Wind*. Although Scarlett made some poor choices throughout that movie, she did command loyalty from brave, handsome men. Both of these characters lived like the rest of us, except one of them survived a civil war and tricked her sister's fiancé into marrying her. The other character had no job, yet wore designer clothes and threw outrageous parties. They also had men like Clark Gable and George Peppard after them.

Okay, admittedly, those women lived like no one I have ever known. Unless you include my mother.

What Scarlett and Holly *do* have in common with this meditation and Al-Anon's Eleventh Tradition is that, by being who they were, they attracted others. When we absorb the principles of Al-Anon into our lives, and we're living spiritually centered lives, we change. We're more at ease and comfortable with ourselves. Our lives are an attraction. Hopefully, for good. Hopefully, we don't trick our cousins into marrying us or behave outrageously at parties and ignore all of our responsibilities. Hopefully.

In spite of myself:
God can use me the most when I'm being myself.

Rags to Riches

My favorite Disney characters—Elsa the Snow Queen, Cinderella, and Snow White—were orphans, and my favorite success stories are about "underdogs"—Steve Jobs and Michael Jordan, people with seemingly no help who managed to succeed.

I love the rags-to-riches stories of loners who did it all without anyone's help, because I suffer from the illusion that I, too, should be able to do it without anyone's help, thank you very much. The lie I tell myself is this: *I have to beat the odds and overcome obstacles through my will.* That whole "me-against-the-world" thing makes for interesting fairy tales, but it doesn't work that way in the real world.

The reality is that those hugely successful people—the Jobses and the Jordans of the world—had a ton of support. Not only did they have the assistance of a team, they each had mentors, coaches, and angel investors. None of the hugely successful people "did it" alone.

Al-Anon reminds me that hard work alone isn't the answer. I need the help and guidance of a Higher Power, a recovery community, and a set of guidelines to live by. I can take risks because I have the support and love of other people.

I can't do life alone, and I no longer dream of doing it that way. I will, however, never give up the fantasy of having a tiara and wearing glass slippers while creating and developing the next Facebook.

In spite of myself:
Thank God I don't have to do life alone.
Really, thank you, God.

Seeking

I'm what they call a "seeker." I want to know the purpose of All That Is, every day of the week and even on weekends. I don't do well when I don't understand the *meaning* of *everything*.

Being a seeker requires more mental effort than, say, skipping stones or playing a game of Rock, Paper, Scissors. In fact, seeking can be strenuous.

As a seeker, I can often be found in an existential dialogue, if you will, with my Higher Power. *What is the meaning of my existence? What is my purpose? Am I on the right track? If I'm not on the right track, how do I get back on it? Am I missing the point here? And if I'm missing the point, is there a way to get more clarification—perhaps, in the form of a DVD, a book, or a pamphlet?*

There are times when my seeking nature exhausts other people. Sometimes it exhausts me. That's when I have to sit myself down and say, "*Stop it, with all the seeking. There is nothing more to know at this point. Especially because you already know a lot! At least more than your friends, who are pretty dense. I mean, for God's sake, they're out skipping stones and playing Rock, Paper, Scissors!*"

I feel much calmer when I remind myself that I already know more than most of my friends.

In spite of myself:

There's probably nothing more I need to know today.

249

Resistance

Whatever you resist persists.
When you allow it, it will disappear.
—CARL JUNG

This sentiment, which might actually be based on some scientific theory, has never really worked for me. It's not logical. If I don't put my effort into making "it" go away, or if I don't rail against "it" or gather votes from my friends about how bad "it" is, then how on earth will "it" possibly go away? Isn't applied force directly proportional to the movement of something? I have no idea what that means, but I think you get my point.

Allowing something to fall away, and not pushing it along, doesn't make sense. Letting some things go, and allowing other things . . . to just be? That's peculiar.

Even though I'm in recovery, I cannot, with 100 percent confidence, buy into the idea of allowing things to be—in particular, when I don't want them to be. I will, however, give it some consideration. I'll try nonresistance, and I'll begin by not resisting the dirty dishes in my kitchen sink. Instead, I will welcome those dishes and allow that sink to stay full until it isn't anymore. Now that, as they say in recovery, is progress!

In spite of myself:

I'll try to allow whatever is to be what it is today.

Love Actually

One of my all-time favorite movies is *Love Actually,* and my favorite part is when Mark, one of the central characters, finally expresses his unrequited love for a woman named Juliet by showing up at her door on Christmas Eve. He shows her a stack of poster boards one by one, including one that says, "To me, you are perfect."

In the movie, Juliet doesn't share his feelings. In fact, she marries someone else in a massive ceremony at a church where the groom surprises her with a brilliant serenade by a gospel choir and an orchestra playing the Beatles song "All You Need Is Love." Lucky girl.

My point is, wouldn't it be nice if someone just showed up at your door with a poster that read, "You are perfect exactly as you are"?

So, here it is. You are perfect.

I know, I've never met you, but I still like you and I want you to try this on for size. Spend today believing that, despite your flaws, that extra weight, and those past mistakes, you are absolutely perfect.

Now, I'm not your Higher Power, but you can trust me on this one. *You are perfect exactly as you are.* And, in this moment, things are precisely as they should be.

In spite of myself:

Reread this page should you *ever* start to doubt it.

Hysterical

It used to be that Al-Anons had cornered the market on overreacting. But lately I've noticed that most people are no longer capable of handling life without histrionic outbursts or excessive exaggerations.

For instance, I was at a restaurant listening to two women next to me. One woman said, "This is the most amazing shrimp I have ever eaten in my life!"

Her friend replied, "This sticky rice is literally better than anything they make in Vietnam."

"You've been to Vietnam?" the friend asked.

"No. But I've heard they invented sticky rice. And I've heard it's beautiful there. Plus, I'd love to check out the Great Wall."

"OMG, me too! Seeing that wall would be the best thing in the whole world."

It was comforting to know that, as an overly dramatic Al-Anon, I'm not the only one who thinks life should be one huge hyperbole (BTW: That Great Wall is in China).

I no longer have to be the one who makes a major ordeal when my gym runs out of clean towels, or the one who freaks out at people who decide to stop and converse in the middle of a busy sidewalk or slow their car in traffic to take a phone call. Now, I can count on other people to do those things.

I'm grateful to Al-Anon because, while I appreciate a daily dose of laughter and tears, it is nice to be the saner one in most situations these days. Literally.

In spite of myself:

This is *literally* going to be the best day I've ever had.

Adventure

When I was a kid, I rode my red Pixie bike to school, to the store, on highways and sidewalks, wherever I wanted. I set up jump-ramps from pieces of plywood and got into fistfights with boys who purposefully tried to stop me from mastering a wheelie. I had Adventures.

As an adult, I stopped having Adventures, like most of us did. Friends, today, we're going to change all that!

Today is Adventure Day. The activity is up to you, whatever you think would be fun or different, such as roller-skating, eating lutefisk, riding on a Ferris wheel, or having candy for lunch. The only requirement is that you try something new. Get out of your comfort zone and explore.

Alas, you're probably an Al-Anon, and ergo, you want to know the purpose of Adventure Day, yes?

There is no point to Adventure Day. There is no goal, nothing to expect, nothing to conquer. Maybe you'll send a card to someone you admire or see *The Muppet Movie.* Maybe you'll go out dancing with friends or try karaoke. It's entirely up to you.

Have an Adventure. No matter how big or small the activity, just have an Adventure.

It doesn't have to include riding a bike, popping a wheelie, or getting into a fistfight. Unless you want it to.

In spite of myself:
Happy Adventure Day!

SEPTEMBER

Amends

Step #9: "Made direct amends to such people wherever possible, except when to do so would injure them or others."

One of my amends in Al-Anon was to a former boss. My behavior while working for him had been crazy; I'd been obsessed with my alcoholic boyfriend, and I was a wreck.

I started the meeting by telling him I was working a Twelve Step program.

"You're a drunk?" he asked, shocked.

"No, I am an Al-Anon," I said, slowly and evenly.

"What, you do drugs?"

"No."

"What the heck is that, Ala-what? You overdo it on the ice cream?" He went into a litany of substances, but I kept shaking my head. Exasperated, he said, "I don't get it!"

"No food, no drugs," I said. "My problem is people. I'm codependent."

Suddenly, I was embarrassed. I couldn't explain Al-Anon or codependency, and I couldn't blame a substance for my whacked-out behavior. The source of my problems was my reaction to life, which manifested itself in my relationships.

I acknowledged that my actions had negatively impacted my work and other people, and I asked him if I could make restitution for it.

When the meeting was over, it occurred to me that he might always think I was just a jerk and that he still had no idea what an Al-Anon was. It's okay—sometimes I'm not so sure myself.

In spite of myself:
I don't need a substance. My head is enough.

Likable

One of my favorite pastimes before I found Al-Anon was trying to get people who didn't even like me to . . . love me.

I once spent hours doing damage control over an article I'd written online. It was a comedic piece about dating, and I'd received some harsh responses. I was so shocked that I stayed up until 3:00 a.m. responding to these people, totally ignoring the ones who had expressed support.

I want people to love me and agree with me. If they don't agree with me, they don't love me. If I can get them to understand what I mean, they'll write me back and say, "I'm sorry I was so mean. I understand now, and guess what? *I love you!* Let's go out for coffee. Better yet, I'll treat you!"

That did not happen. Those people didn't want to like me, and they didn't want to have coffee with me. Come to think of it, I honestly didn't want to have coffee with them, either. But I didn't think about that part. When I'm in the throes of "Like me, like me!" I never stop to think if *I* like the person I'm wanting to like *me.*

Recovery has shown me that not everyone will like, understand, or love me. For an Al-Anon of my type, accepting this truth was about as easy as doing twenty military pull-ups. But I'll bet doing twenty military pull-ups would be easier than having coffee with someone who hates me.

In spite of myself:

Not everyone likes me, but I'm still lovable!

Sidewalks

Most people in recovery know the poem about the hole in the sidewalk: A man walks down the street and doesn't happen to notice the humongous hole in the sidewalk. He falls in the hole, and it takes him a long time to crawl out of it. The next time the guy walks down that same street, he pretends he doesn't see the hole, and he falls into it again. To cut a long story short, this chap walks down that same street a few more times until he wises up and takes another route.

When I first heard this poem, I thought, *Time to contact the department of transportation about that hole, buddy.* The next time I heard it, I thought, *What is up with this yahoo? I saw that hole coming from a mile away!*

Now that I've gotten some recovery under my belt, when I hear that poem, I think, *Why can't I write a goofy poem about a clueless guy falling into a pothole that becomes a cottage industry and makes me a million dollars?* Then, I say to myself, *You're being snarky. Might there be a few potholes in your own life?* And I respond, *Of course there are potholes! I live in L.A. The other day I saw a pothole so big there were car parts in it, but I'm not dumb enough to fall into it!*

While I'm trying to stay off sidewalks and paths that lead to cynicism and resentment, I do believe that people who knowingly step into gaping potholes deserve to get run over. And that's just the truth.

In spite of myself:

Are there any potholes in my life that I'm ignoring?

Trust Falls

In the nineties, many companies would send their employees off to corporate retreats—the kind where a group of employees spends days trying to bond with their unlikable coworkers and engage in pointless exercises like "trust falls," where one person falls into the arms of another who, hopefully, catches them. Or where people sit in circles and say thoughtful things they don't mean to colleagues they despise.

I've been to a few corporate retreats, and I've never felt like I could suddenly trust my backstabbing coworkers just because we did a scavenger hunt together. I've never been able to "bond" with anyone who works in the human resources department of any company, and I always wondered what falling into the arms of the creepy web developer in an ice-cold hotel ballroom had to do with increasing trust.

I love that Al-Anon doesn't ask me to do meaningless exercises in order to force a false sense of intimacy. Other Al-Anons don't expect me to trust them, the program, or a Higher Power until I'm ready. Trust takes time.

I'm also glad Al-Anon doesn't ask anyone to do "trust falls" in meetings, especially not at my home group, because there are some cranky old broads who sit in the back row. I'd bet a dollar to a donut they wouldn't even *try* to catch me if I fell.

In spite of myself:
Al-Anon meetings are trust-fall-free zones.

Squeeze

I once picked up a greeting card that had a Barbie doll on the front of it. The card read, "I wish I had real arms, instead of these pink plastic ones, 'cause then I could squeeze you like I want to without my arms popping off."

When I saw the card, I couldn't think of anyone I wanted to squeeze in the same way that Barbie did. This was before I discovered Al-Anon; I was miserable and unhappy with most of the people in my life. In all honesty, I doubt many of the people in my life wanted to squeeze me like Barbie did, either.

Al-Anon shows me how to focus on the good parts of the people I love and not discount those people because of their not-so-good parts. I can let the folks I love be who they are without (as much) judgment, and I can show my love and appreciation for them.

Today, I can think of at least five people I would like to squeeze, in that good, Barbie kind of way. It makes me wish I'd bought that greeting card when I had the chance, because I've looked all over town and I can't find it anywhere.

But it's okay, because I have real arms and not those pink plastic ones. Today, I'm proud to say I can squeeze the people I love, and even prouder because my parts won't fall off if I do. Most of my parts, that is.

In spite of myself:

Do you want to squeeze me like I want to squeeze you?

Devices

Al-Anon talks about what happens when we are "left to our own devices" to figure life out.

Before Al-Anon, my own devices included a combination of behaviors, such as being rescued, mind reading, sulking, controlling, and, if those didn't work, breaking things. The funny part is, there were plenty of well-meaning people giving me indicators about how ineffective my own devices were. Some gave me verbal hints or threw me looks. Some had their attorneys send me cease-and-desist letters. But those things didn't deter me.

I won't go into specifics—the case is public record now—but it took something pretty darn big to lead me to the conclusion that I am way better off when I let my Higher Power take the lead, especially when it comes to relationships. Each and every day, I turn my will over and ask God to show me the person he would have me be.

I no longer rely on my own devices anymore, which is good, because they don't work most of the time. Besides, it's probably time I replace them with more elaborate, expensive devices, which, no doubt, I'll have to spend hours standing in line outside the Apple store in order to buy.

In spite of myself:

I'll let my Higher Power manage all my devices today.

Reasonable World Sanity

Yesterday I was lying in a field of grass, staring up at glorious clouds, and I began to visualize a world where there was no war. A place where all people lived in complete peace.

Then I began to worry. If things were perfect and there was nothing to be concerned about, what would I do? Nothing but hang around all day in existential bliss? Sounds like a total drag. Although I strive for perfection, I'm not really sure what I'd do if I looked perfection in the face. If perfection had a face.

Instead of world peace, I've decided to visualize world sanity. I'll paint a mental picture of a world where people behave reasonably sanely, and I can contribute to making things better by connecting to my Higher Power and working a program of recovery. And while I don't know what world peace looks like, I'm fairly certain reasonable world sanity means people get along and are smartly dressed, with good grooming habits and sparkling white teeth. And no one ever wears pleather.

World peace may not happen in my lifetime, and reasonable sanity might not either. But honestly, is it too much to ask folks to groom themselves and resist the pleather?

In spite of myself:
Peace. Sanity. Serenity. Please, no pleather.

Pardon?

Today is National Pardon Day. As you might have guessed, millions of Al-Anons will be holding their collective breath . . . waiting for apologies they are due but will never receive.

In spite of the fact that it's National Pardon Day, I've decided not to wait for the apologies that should be coming to me. And believe me when I say that for an Al-Anon, this is a magnanimous feat, because I'm due a boatload of apologies. Biiiiiiiigggg apologies.

But you know what? Instead of lamenting how the people I've loved and sacrificed everything for have let me down—essentially shattering my hopes for a better life—I have made a decision to be the bigger person and let bygones be bygones.

That's just the kind of individual I am.

Sure, I could hold on to those grievances and wear them like a cloak of misery. I could recall the tears and the worry I've experienced because of other people's selfish, narcissistic choices, but I refuse to hold a grudge or rub their noses in it. Yes, I have justifiable reasons to treat *some* people as poorly as they've treated me, but I'd *never* do that.

The power of National Pardon Day allows me to let it go.

The people who owe *me* the apology will no doubt continue to be . . . themselves, but *I* will be gracious *as always*, on National Pardon Day. I'm an Al-Anon; I've done my part in pardoning. For today. I cannot prognosticate about tomorrow.

In spite of myself:
Pardon me, while I pardon you!

Negative Nelly

If you're a Negative Nelly like me, you can relate to dark times—days spent lying in bed watching *Bridget Jones's Diary* and listening to every sad George Michael love song. There is only one thing that consistently gets me out of negativity: service. When I am being of service to someone else, I break the cycle of pessimistic thoughts and behaviors.

The problem is, when I'm being a Negative Nelly, I don't feel like being of service to others. I want to *be* served! When I'm being morose, I couldn't care less about helping other people. I'd rather focus my attention on the savagery of humanity while reading books about vampires or articles on pesticide poisoning and bowel cancer.

When I feel myself descending into negativity, it helps to put a time limit on it. I always give myself exactly five minutes. After I've given myself the time I need to feel bad, I *have* to take contrary action that leads to my long-term serenity. No matter how small or how bad I feel when I start, I always feel better when that action includes service.

At heart, I'm a Negative Nelly, and the things my mind can conjure at any given moment, especially when I'm down, are quite dark. Places where Bridget Jones and George Michael would never go. Okay, places where Bridget Jones would never go.

In spite of myself:

Today, I will not wallow; I will be of service to someone else.

The Whisperer

I have a friend whose dog, Shakespeare, has his own dog whisperer. Once a month my friend takes Shakespeare in for a session to make sure he's on track emotionally and mentally.

Once, she took Shakespeare in for an appointment because he had been chewing on the furniture. After an hour-long session, the dog whisperer told my friend the dog was chewing on the couch because he was craving a burrito.

"A beef or chicken burrito?" I asked my friend, laughing.

"Shakespeare's a vegan," she snapped at me.

At first, I wrote the whole thing off. My friend is from Venice, California, where fellow residents include a woman who swallows flames, a boy who sniffs needles, and an old man who puts his dog in a bikini to earn money.

But maybe the dog whisperer's right. Who am I to say a dog can't have the munchies? If I were a dog and I wanted a burrito, the best way to communicate it—aside from scratching the word "burrito" in the dirt—might be to chew on the sofa.

I felt bad when I hadn't heard from my friend after a week, so I called her.

"I'm sorry I was insensitive," I said.

"Thanks," she said, "for honoring Shakespeare's feelings."

Al-Anon has taught me to accept people, places, and things exactly as they are: dogs, dog whisperers, and people who swallow flames. I will not, however, accept a guy who puts his dog in a bikini. I have standards.

In spite of myself:

Today I'll accept people, places, and things exactly as they are.

Job Hunt

Recovery can be like job hunting. It often requires the same skills and strategies needed for an intensive career search: plenty of hard work, a ton of useless research, and a lot of waiting around for something to happen. Without any pay.

In recovery, like in a job search, the harder you grasp at results, the further away they seem. And when you finally give up trying, you get multiple offers.

In Al-Anon, we discover that the answers don't come by grinding it out. Recovery comes when we acknowledge and accept our powerlessness. It's known as "surrender."

The thing is, when you're on a job interview, you can't exactly say to a recruiter, "I don't need to go into details about why I'm unemployed or how great of an employee I'll be, do I, because we all know people lie." And you can't just show up at the interview with the hiring manager, and say, "You might not know it, but you're not really in charge of hiring here. God is my employer."

In that sense, recovery and job hunting are wholly and utterly unrelated and have absolutely nothing in common. But on the other hand, in recovery you never have to spend time with a hiring manager. That is, unless you want to.

In spite of myself:

No hiring managers were harmed
during the writing of this meditation.

Zones

We all have areas in our lives where we feel relatively safe and in control. These comfort zones might include our workplaces, our living rooms, or even certain Al-Anon meetings.

When it comes to trying out new things, many Al-Anons get kind of wigged out. Why do we get this way? I don't know. That's just an Al-Anon for you.

Situations that might cause an Al-Anon anxiety could be, say, going on a blind date or going to watch a live professional hockey game when you have no idea how hockey is even played. But you go to the game anyway because you want to get out of your comfort zone and practice being spontaneous. Before you know it, you're in the thick of things, having a blast, eating peanuts and hot dogs, and screaming profanities at the referee, just like everyone else in the arena. And by the time the night is over, you find yourself with a tattoo of the name of some hockey player you'd never heard of until that very night!

That's one example I've heard of an Al-Anon getting out of the comfort zone. I'm sure there are many other ways, but that's one I know of. Intimately.

Now it's your turn. Try doing one tiny little thing that gets you out of your comfort zone today. C'mon, you can do it!

In spite of myself:

They key to a comfort zone is knowing when to leave it.

Service

I couldn't afford to pay for the traffic ticket, so the judge sentenced me to community service at a thrift store. I was excited. All those castoffs waiting to be cared for!

My first day, I organized the women's clothing section by textures and color. Within a week, I had the mannequins in the men's section looking like Abercrombie & Fitch window displays, though most of my time was spent apprehending kids who were hell-bent on destroying pure silk with their filthy hands. It broke my heart to see cashmere treated like roadkill.

"You won't believe how mean people are to mohair!" I cried to my sponsor, my resentment festering. She suggested I become willing to be of service and stop judging the customers. I reluctantly agreed, even though she was wrong. Before my thrift store sentence was over, the customers were approaching me for fashion tips and I was hosting mini-makeovers in the aisles of the Salvation Army.

On my last day, the supervisor pulled me to the side.

"I'll miss you," he said. "You're a hard worker, and I like how you organized the store by color and textures."

To show his appreciation, he sold me a gorgeous pair of caramel-colored suede pants for $1.00. I cried, because they were marked at $63.00.

While I may not always start out with the desire to be of service, I can always change my mind. When I do, things usually turn around. I mean, real suede for a dollar? Now that's service!

In spite of myself:
Hey, God, help me turn things around today, if need be.

"Psychi"

I was going through a really dark time before Al-Anon, and I'd broken up with—*another*—alcoholic. I was desperate.

While out for a drive one night, I saw a house with a sign that read, "Psychi Readings." The missing *C* should have been a red flag, but I was in no mood to be discerning.

Sela, the psychic, looked intently at my face and spoke slowly, in a haunting Eastern European accent. "You are old soul . . . theees is not first time you have been to Earth. The last time, you are . . . an angel."

According to Sela, the reason I'd returned to Earth was to bring love, by way of the "wounded warrior."

One day, I told my sponsor this story. After the laughter subsided, she said, "I hope you didn't spend much. And I hope you didn't fall for the old there's-a-curse-on-you-that-I-can-remove scam." She hugged me and added, "I think finding a Higher Power might be more reliable than a psychic. And a lot less expensive."

I never told my sponsor, but Sela did inform me that I had been cursed. But, thankfully, she was able to reverse the curse at a discount.

In spite of myself:

I can rely on my Higher Power,
and I never have to pay for the answers.

Al-Anon Olympics: Opening Ceremonies

Though not generally known, Al-Anons around the globe have been gathering every four years at the Al-Anon Olympics to celebrate the achievements of the world's finest in Al-Anon.

The exact date of the original Al-Anon Olympics is unknown, so for simplicity's sake, let's call this one the XVII Al-Anon Olympiad.

Over the next few days, we will pay homage to the crafty, quick-thinking behaviors that make Al-Anons who they are— the lovable codependent types who can always be counted on to do their very best, especially if it's for others. Together, we will hold our breath in anticipation, as we watch these elite Al-Anons who have trained day in and day out in their quest for world domination and complete control!

Whether they're preparing for the grueling *200-Liter Booze Dump*, the *Victim Pentathlon*, or the brutal *Long-Distance Resentment Relays*, Al-Anons who compete at this level don't merely push through adversity. Nope. They relish it!

So strike up the band (here's hoping they show) and let's honor the twisted thinking and the extreme, fanatical, distorted behaviors that make Al-Anons so beloved the world over! Because no matter who wins the gold or the silver, we'll celebrate together—whether anyone else wants to or not, the Al-Anons will demand it.

Let the XVII Al-Anon Olympiad begin!

In spite of myself:
In honor of this day, let's spend ten minutes
obsessing about something.

Al-Anon Olympics:
Long-Distance Resentment

The life of long-distance resenters can be difficult. The training is torturous: They wake before dawn to rehash scenarios or conversations they've already had—sometimes years ago. They toil for hours upon hours on metaphorical treadmills like champions, despite the emotional injuries they've sustained.

Few are as dedicated as the long-distance resenter. In fact, while most try to let things go, the long-distance resenter will travel thousands of miles, organizing cross-continental trips in order to set someone else straight. These amazingly single-minded Al-Anons spend years fanning the flames of anger and resentment, dreaming of the gladiators they will one day conquer.

We mere mortals admire these resenters, who continually resist the urge to quit—despite the pain. Instead, they soldier on, in hopes that they'll finally be able to exhibit their superiority. They could've been content to just sit on the sidelines, *but no*—members of this class of Al-Anon refuse to be comfortable, to relax, or to let one injustice escape them!

Today, we honor the long-distance resenters for their passion for passion, for their unwavering commitment to clutching onto the past, and using anger to fuel them for, well, a lifetime.

That, my friends, takes a great deal of talent and skill. Put your hands together for the long-distance resenter!

In spite of myself:

Long-distance resenters give new meaning
to the term "unwavering commitment."

Al-Anon Olympics:
Track-and-Stalk

Much has changed since the early days of the Al-Anon Track-and-Stalk event, but even so, participants are always honored and revered the world over for their epic rivalries and the controversies that surround them.

With the introduction of Google Maps, Facebook, Twitter, and Instagram, Al-Anons are no longer limited to second-hand information or the drive-by for details about their stalkee. Technology has greatly impacted this sport, leading to increased speed, skill, and dexterity—in some cases by thousands of seconds! In fact, in order to compete, Al-Anons must qualify for the 100-meter stalk by gaining access to their stalkees within 10.79 seconds via GPS, a wireless camera, credit cards, or a smartphone.

But enough of this scientific talk. The truth is, the Track-and-Stalk event is simply a reminder that Al-Anons continually raise the bar on their performances, proving time and again that their efforts to get the dirt on the person they love-slash-hate are Herculean. Way beyond mere mortals.

And to the competitors, I say, "Track-and-Stalkers, your victory is my victory, and your triumph is my triumph. You bring pride and joy to those of us who lack your courage. I celebrate your speed, technical skill, and your infinite paranoia."

In spite of myself:

I'm so inspired, I'm going to look up
a few old friends online today!

Al-Anon Olympics: Victim Pentathlon

The crowning jewel of the Al-Anon Olympics, the Victim Pentathlon, is among the most beloved events in the history of the games. The five-event competition combines the skills that make Al-Anons so, well, Al-Anony—talents that the world's most accomplished Al-Anons have spent years honing.

As impressive as it is to compete in other Al-Anon games, the versatility and dedication required to compete at this level is what makes the Olympic Al-Anon pentathlete the greatest and most admired the world over. In order to participate, competitors must be able to achieve complete perfection—of course—with a mixture of speed, accuracy, and dexterity.

The Victim Pentathlon brings together the most compelling display of martyrdom, victimization, and manipulation, while maintaining a masterful level of grandiosity. Only Al-Anons with the belief that they are simultaneously the best and the worst would dare challenge themselves at this level.

While no one has ever been able to understand the Victim Pentathlon scoring system, we are confident that someone will win. And we know we can trust the judges—they're Al-Anons!

Traditionally, the title of the World's Greatest Al-Anon has been given to the person who wins the Victim Pentathlon. Mainly because they're the most dramatic competitors

Whatever happens, this year's event will no doubt be historic. Or, histrionic. It will most *definitely* be histrionic.

In spite of myself:

Today, I'll honor my inner athlete
by not being overly dramatic.

Al-Anon Olympics:
Unbalanced Beam

To be present when a nimble Al-Anon dominates the competition on the unbalanced beam at the Al-Anon Olympics is one of the best natural highs imaginable!

These Al-Anons are artists and strategists in the purest sense of the words, calm and composed throughout their impeccably timed manipulations—er, routines. These Al-Anons approach their targets with utmost precision; they are masters of the verbal twist, the emotional turn, and the subtle walkover. They should be—they've had years of training, dealing with all their friends, family members, and previous employers! The mixture of dexterity and speed that enables these Al-Anons to make massive leaps of logic in midair while maintaining control and garnering sympathy is almost supernatural. They never cease to amaze the crowd with their proficiency at moving on and off the beam with grace and aplomb.

Their determination is often accompanied with a frown and an intense stare. "I *must* win," their eyes seem to say. Even after they've completed the most difficult moves, they're seldom satisfied.

The beauty of the Unbalanced Beam event is that, although Al-Anons fall off the beam due to their own mistake, they're able to make it appear as if someone else caused it. There's nothing like an unbalanced Al-Anon to remind us that no matter how spiritually centered and humble we may strive to be, those who master the beam will always be able to put one over on us.

In spite of myself:
I'll try to stay on the balanced beam today.

Al-Anon Olympics: Closing Ceremonies

As the XVII Al-Anon Olympiad comes to a conclusion, spectators will undoubtedly agree that this year's closing ceremony was unlike any other. There's no other way to say it than that it truly redefined the term "emotional experience."

While details are limited to the public, sources say that a choreographed show performed by fellows in the Al-Anon community was followed by the traditional parade of Al-Anons from around the world.

There are rumors that this Olympiad had its share of controversy. Unfortunately, several Al-Anon competitors were thrown out of the games, due to allegations of overexaggeration, excessive manipulation, and poor sportsmanship.

The big shot of some really important Al-Anon committee was reported to have said, "Sadly, we come to the end of the XVII Olympic Games. As always, the Games were performed amid an inordinate display of chaos and drama. Al-Anons are among the most over-the-top, hypersensitive people on the planet. What else can we expect? And while we're very proud, we're also definitely glad they're over." And with that, the big shot declared the XVII Olympiad formally over.

In spite of myself:

Elaborate and dramatic.
What else is there for an Al-Anon?

World Gratitude Day

Today is World Gratitude Day! On this day in 1977, the United Nations Meditation Group celebrated World Gratitude Day to encourage people around the world to express their appreciation for the good things that have been done to make life better for others.

You might be thinking to yourself: *Wait, don't we already have a day of thanks-giving, called Thanksgiving?* Well, yes, you are correct, we do have Thanksgiving in the United States—and it'll be here before long—but the UNMG thinks everybody could do with another day to spend in gratitude. And you know what? I agree with them!

Today, you won't have to stuff a turkey, or spend a day with people who trigger your childhood "issues," or deal with your brother's vegan wife who insists on making a lentil and soy non-meatloaf.

Instead, the UNMG suggests you find a group you are grateful for and show your appreciation.

This year I'm honoring Al-Anon because of all the wonderful things the program has done for me. While there are many creative ways I could express my thanks to people—making homemade cards or cooking a turkey meatloaf—I've decided to present each person in my home group with their very own pair of recycled socks!

Hopefully, you will find a unique and individual way to show how much you appreciate the people and groups that matter to you. I can vouch for the recycled socks.

In spite of myself:
Happy World Gratitude Day!

Meetings, Not Misdemeanors

There's a nonprofit organization whose motto is "Hugs, not drugs." While I'm all for that, my personal motto in recovery has become "Meetings, not misdemeanors." Because for an Al-Anon, there are times when the slope between sanity and homicide can be shockingly slippery.

No, I've never been charged with a misdemeanor (or a felony, for that matter), but I can tell you there is a fine line between self-management and murderous rage. One wrong move, one slip of a foot onto the gas pedal instead of the brake, one fourteen-inch serrated kitchen knife thrown in the wrong direction, and we're talking handcuffs, an orange jumpsuit, and three square meals a day.

Meetings are pretty darned important for Al-Anons because they remind us to keep our hands and our comments to ourselves.

So the next time you feel a surge of self-righteous anger or an overwhelming desire to set that "certain someone straight," please remember: "Meetings, not misdemeanors."

Pass it around. It just might save a life. Or a foot. Or at least a set of quality kitchen knives.

In spite of myself:

Meetings, not misdemeanors.

Better, Worse?

Despite the personal work I've done in Al-Anon, if I were forced to label myself, I'd say I am more superficial than deep, more impatient than patient, and more entitled than, say, whatever the opposite of entitled is.

For instance, when I hear the wedding vows "for better or for worse," I spend no time focusing on the "worse" part. I'd rather plan for the "better" part. I say "Heck, no" to the sickness and "Yeah!" to the health! Rich? Definitely. Poor? No.

I figured I'd experience some emotions in Al-Anon, but I imagined they'd be good ones. I knew there'd be hard times, but I didn't think they'd last. For the first few years in the program, I struggled—emotionally, financially, and mentally—and I was peeved! Things were supposed to get better, not worse.

I had to learn that recovery doesn't guarantee an easy life—just a way to handle things that come my way, support and concern from others, a set of tools, and a God of my own understanding.

That being said, my nature hasn't completely changed. I'd rather go to a party than suffer from indigestion. Rather eat cake than shed tears. Rather get a massage than pay the IRS the money I owe from that amended tax return I never filed.

I'd prefer to hear about deep spiritual principles and problems that turn into blessings, versus experiencing them.

You might call me a shallow, easy-way-out Al-Anon. And if you did, you'd be right. Most of the time.

In spite of myself:
I will always take cake over tears.

Corners

I'll admit it: Sometimes I cut corners. It's a character defect that I have an ongoing flirtation with.

For instance, when it comes to writing these daily meditations, there are days when I want to type "ditto" after the previous day's meditation, or repeat another one I've already written. Most people probably wouldn't even notice.

But my recovery program demands that I practice rigorous honesty, and rigorous honesty does not include writing "ditto" or "see June 2 entry" just because I don't feel like writing. Nope. Not an option.

Rigorous honesty means going the extra mile and sharing my gifts and talents, even when I don't think my talents are valuable, or when I feel like someone else could do things better than me. While that may be true, I still have to do my part, especially because no one else has shown up to write these meditations for me.

The truth is, I feel good when I'm being authentic. Even when being authentic means I have to admit to embarrassing things, like wanting to cut corners, which I sort of did today. But I suppose my authenticity makes up for my laziness, no?

In spite of myself:

Today, I will practice rigorous honesty.
Or, if you prefer, see "In spite of myself" from June 2.

Wise One

An ancient, wise man once said we have a choice when we awaken. We can see the world as lacking, or we can look at the world through eyes of love.

When I open my eyes in the morning, I don't see love. I have thoughts like, *I can't believe Joe said that to me; I should tell him off!* Or, *Sarah never called me back. Is she mad at me? I'll bet she won't show up for my party.*

Yes, I'll admit that, when I awaken, I do not automatically look at the world through eyes of love. I'm lucky if I can manage to view life through eyes of love until rush hour. The only way I can carry compassion throughout my day is to constantly remind myself that I can't do love alone.

I need a Higher Power to help me view people, places, and things with gentility. Most mornings, I awaken and say, "God, please be my eyes today." And then I turn my will over. It always makes for a better day.

That's not to say I drive with my eyes closed. It's a figurative thing, asking God to be my eyes, just so you know.

In spite of myself:

God, I'll let you be my eyes, but I'll keep mine open, too.

Action

Sometimes I confuse *thinking* about taking action with actually *taking* action.

There have been times when I *thought* I had accomplished something simply because I fretted about it for so long. I had expended so much energy thinking, that my brain got confused about whether I had actually done it.

Did I remember to send the check to that humanitarian mission in Haiti? Did I ever send Sam a text saying, "It's not you, it's me"? Have I mentioned to Marie that she should think about covering those gray roots? Did I actually tell my therapist I think I'm a "love avoidant," or did I just post it online?

Thinking about acting on something and *taking* the action are *not* the same thing. I often have to remind myself that the degree to which I worry about taking an action does not equal the actual effort I put into accomplishing said goal or task.

Worry ≠ Action (worry does not equal action)—or did I already make my point?

In spite of myself:

I don't need to worry about the action if I pray first.

Codependency, Schmodependency

For a while, it seemed like everyone was calling everyone else "codependent," and the word got a really bad rap. For good reason. That word just, well, seems so mealymouthed, weak, clingy—the stuff of country music lyrics. Nothing I want to identify with.

I was resistant to CoDA, Al-Anon, or anything, really, that smacked of me sitting quietly in the corner or playing the dutiful enabler. Anything that reminded me of that old commercial with the woman running after a car, screaming, "Don't take the car, you'll kill yourself!"

Uh, no, thanks.

Thank goodness the Al-Anon group I found was nothing like that. People were happy, spiritually centered, and living big lives. In that community, I discovered interdependency. I don't do life alone anymore, but I also don't expect others to rescue me or make decisions for me.

It sounds so healthy, this interdependency, where I accept and support others and they do the same for me, but I must confess, sometimes I miss the days when people had no judgments about codependency. Back in the day when I could demand loyalty from you, blame you for my problems, and, basically, live my life through you.

I don't always miss those days. Just sometimes.

In spite of myself:

I may be a little codependent,
but God and my recovery buddies still love me.

Hallway Dweller

I've heard people say that when you're in the hallway of life, the best thing to do is start hanging pictures.

But I don't want to hang pictures in the hallway because I don't plan on staying here! And, incidentally, I don't feel comfortable leaving my valuables hanging in some public thoroughfare! Suppose I decide to take a walk and some other hallway dweller wanders in and steals my stuff? Suppose I awaken in the middle of the night screaming, "Help! Somebody get me out of this freakin' hallway!" and I get rescued? I'm not gonna be pulling nails out of a wall at 4:00 in the morning!

I'd been in a particular hallway for a couple of years when I considered hanging up a few photos and doing some other light decorating. But I couldn't, because it felt like defeat—an admission that I was content being stuck in that stupid corridor. And I wasn't.

I finally got so tired of having to guard my things and being on high alert that I just gave up and accepted I was a hallway dweller. I started unpacking.

I started wallpapering, hanging childhood paintings, and going through old boxes. I even found a pair of shorts that I'd forgotten about.

I'm still in the hallway in that particular area of my life, and I don't know how much longer I'll be here, but at least it's pretty now. And cozy. I don't mind being called a "hallway dweller" as much as I used to, and I even invite other hallway dwellers in, as long as they promise not to steal my stuff.

In spite of myself:
I'm a hallway dweller and dang proud of it!

Crybaby Club

My friend's partner used to laugh at him when he started going to Al-Anon meetings. "Are you going to the Crybaby Club tonight?" he'd ask as he was leaving the house.

What a jackass, I thought. *I ought to give him a piece of my mind.*

Months later, I finally met him. "Are you a member of the Crybaby Club, too?" he asked with a sly smile.

"I sure am," I said, laughing. "A proud member."

Although I cried a lot more than my friend did, we both shed a few tears when we came into Al-Anon. But the meeting we attend is so focused on solutions that it's hard to stay miserable and defeated for long. While it might appear to outsiders—or to the less enlightened—that people in recovery are crybabies, there's no denying what happens because of the work we do. It's not easy to explain how it changes lives. Eventually, my friend and I began to love the name Crybaby Club.

"Hey, you coming to the Crybaby Club tonight?" we'd ask each other each week.

The response was always, "You betcha!"

The best part of it was, after the first year, neither of us was crying anymore. We were at peace, on a spiritual path, and enjoying our lives. In fact, my friend's partner saw such a change that he asked us if he could come to the Crybaby Club.

I was tempted to tell him no, but I didn't. Because I'd grown to love him, too. And if he needs the Crybaby Club, we'd be happy to have him.

In spite of myself:
While I'd rather laugh,
it's good to know I can be a crybaby if need be.

Impossibly High Standards

I was infamous in my neighborhood for writing plays and getting kids to perform in them. My favorite theatrical revue, which I penned during the summer after sixth grade, was called *More Than the Sound of Music.*

As a kid, I had exceptionally high standards when it came to theater. As a result, I was constantly discouraged by the lack of artistic consistency displayed by my peers.

The opening night of *More Than the Sound of Music* was a complete disaster. During the final rehearsal, the lead actress vomited on her dress and the boys ran off with all of my hand-made props. Perhaps it was because I paid the cast members with Pixie Sticks and Lemonheads.

I vowed never to work with any of these massively unprofessional types again. And I didn't, until I needed to cast them in my next play, *The Door-to-Door Muppet Christmas Carol Tour.*

There's a saying, "Insanity is doing the same thing over and over and expecting different results." Unfortunately, I didn't hear that saying until I was much older.

Today, I try to live by that saying, remembering that not everyone else lives by the same standards I do. And while I don't believe *Impossibly High Standards* has been adapted as a Broadway play, when it is, I'll be the first in line to direct it.

In spite of myself:

Impossibly High Standards. Such a nice ring to it.

OCTOBER

Change

The words to the song "Waste" by the band Foster the People are, "And every day that you want to waste . . . you can. And every day that you want to change . . . yeah . . ."

What I take from those lyrics is that I get to decide how I'll respond and live out my life. It's always up to me.

I thought I'd come up with a few alternative verbs that might fit into those lyrics, as a reminder to myself that I can make this day whatever I want it to be.

Every day that you want to:

- rearrange
- taste
- paste
- admire
- appreciate

you can . . . you can!

The possibilities of what I can do with my thoughts and my behaviors today are endless! There are actually 6,784 verbs that could fit into that sentence. I know because I tried writing them all out.

I can also love today. And so can you. I hope you do!

In spite of myself:
There are 3,362 ways to have a lovely day.

Admissions

Step #10 says, "Continued to take personal inventory and when we were wrong promptly admitted it."

I figured by the time I'd made it to Step #10 in Al-Anon, I'd be completely recovered. I assumed mistakes would be a rare occurrence. At least that was what I thought, based on having never, ever attended an Al-Anon meeting.

Even after a few years in recovery, I'm surprised at how often I have to admit to doing or saying thoughtless things. Despite what I used to hope for, there will never be a day when I've got it all "figured out." Part of me is relieved, but another part of me is kind of bummed out about that.

Making it through the Twelve Steps doesn't guarantee we'll become saints, or any less kooky than we were when we came into Al-Anon. We will, however, have a spiritual experience and get new tools and solutions for living life on life's terms.

Step #10 reminds me that I am human and need a Higher Power in my life. When I turn my will over to God early in the day, I have fewer things to make amends for. I don't let my attitude get out of control, and I stay centered on being who God would have me be.

When I do that, I feel better and rarely have a big, fat, hairy list of people I've harmed at the end of my day. The big, fat, hairy amends generally only happen after the holidays, when I've been forced to spend a lot of time with my family.

In spite of myself:

Admitting when I'm wrong tends to get easier with time.

Imaginary Lives

There's a woman who's created an Internet photo board based on her imaginary perfect daughter. The photos she posts are of model-perfect kids who are totally composed and gorgeous. It's a spoof on privileged, overindulged kids—a satirical poke at society's obsession with hip, ultra-cool kids and the parents who raise them.

After finally getting over the fact that I wasn't clever enough to come up with the idea first, I considered creating an imaginary "ideal self" that I could post online. You know, images that represent the "me" who is poised and always says the right things. My ideal self, the one who never reacts to mean or irrational people, is a team player and never gets into fights with other kids. The ideal me, who gets everything right the first time and isn't mercurial or demanding and is always content. The one who's also thin and gorgeous.

If I could, I'd post pictures of myself doing things model-y gorgeous people do, like living ideal lives that are problem-free, healthy, and serene.

I'm still trying to find that picture of the ideal me. Till then, I guess I'll have to work with what I've got.

In spite of myself:

There is no ideal, just me.

Mysteries

There's a passage in the Al-Anon book *From Survival to Recovery*, and it says that when we begin to recover, "We will discover we are free to delight in life's paradox, mystery, and awe."

Mysteries and paradoxes were not very high on my list when I came to Al-Anon. I just wanted certain people to stop drinking and all the kooky folks who were making my life difficult to go away. When I came into Al-Anon, I was tired, cynical, and jaded. The highlight in my day was taking a good, long nap.

As for awe? No, thank you. I wasn't after any religious experience. I felt no need to seek out the deeper mysteries of the universe. No existential joy or interest in talking about the miracles of life.

In time, I've come to see recovery as a kaleidoscope of opportunity. Today, I live in a state of wonder and bliss, with each experience being a new passage into some variation of the fourth dimension.

Well, that's not entirely true.

Because of Al-Anon, I'm open and eager to experience life's unknown possibilities. At least, I no longer yell and scream at the mysteries when I encounter them. And as for paradoxes and awe? I'm even slightly open to those now, too!

In spite of myself:

Life is a mystery I don't want to miss out on.

With Me

The Al-Anon slogan "Let it begin with me" is about taking the initiative, being the one who makes things better, apologizes first, and seeks harmony. And I'm all for it. Unless I have to approach people who've really hurt my feelings or are mean. Then I prefer to "Let it begin with them."

My Al-Anon sponsor suggested that letting it begin with them wasn't really an option. If I wanted a new life, I'd have to assume that it would *always* begin with me.

"Why do I *always* have to be the mature one?" I demanded.

"Because it's the right thing to do," she'd say. "And because it's the way we recover."

"Okay. Well, then I guess it will have to begin with me," I said, "if that's the *only* way."

But inside I was thinking, *Let's not take this thing too far. I'm down with fifty-fifty, but 100 percent me, all the time? That's a bit much!*

"'Let it begin with me' is the beginning of healing, the way to peace and maturity," she continued.

"I've never claimed to be aiming for maturity," I said and laughed.

"Oh, yes, you have," she said quietly.

"Well, in that case, never mind," I said.

In spite of myself:
Let it begin with me. I mean it. Really.

Feedback

Once upon a time, when I was dying to give gratuitous advice to a friend but I didn't want to seem too eager, I'd say something like, "I have some feedback, if you'd like to hear it."

Almost never did anyone respond with, "No, I don't want feedback," because they knew they'd sound like a dolt if they did. A closed-minded dolt. Who wants to be *that* person?

Another way I used to give unsolicited advice was by using the Socratic method, which is the way you prove people wrong by getting them to contradict their own statements. It goes something like this:

"Yada, yada, yada," says person in need of correction.

"You really sound like you know what you're talking about," says me. "I had that same problem, but would you not agree that (insert unsolicited advice by questioning here)?"

Socrates believed that knowledge begins with recognition of one's ignorance, so his method focuses on *disproving* the other person's point with questions, which results in puzzlement. It goes on from there.

There's a lot more to this method, but because I didn't go to law school, that's all I can remember. It does work, but I can't cite more examples because I don't use it anymore.

Al-Anon has taught me that unless someone directly asks for my advice, I don't give it. I still want to—much of the time—but I don't. Because I'd rather have friends than give advice.

In spite of myself:
Unless someone's asking for my advice,
they probably don't want it.

Blue Sky

Just because I don't really know what I'm saying, doesn't mean I won't say it.

Before I got into Al-Anon, that was my credo, my dogma, only I didn't know it, because I genuinely thought I knew what I was talking about. Most of the time. And if I didn't know what I was talking about, I'd never admit it. Especially when it came to work.

If I had a general idea about something and I could "blue-sky" it—a term advertising people use to cover up a lack of knowledge about anything—I would. Once I learned a few key phrases about a subject, I'd repeat them, especially if they made me sound smart. I didn't get called out on it often because I worked in advertising, where most other people don't know what they're talking about, either.

The truth is, I only really know what I'm talking about maybe 46 percent of the time. The rest I'm just making up. The beauty of recovery is that I can admit that; I don't have to pretend or "blue-sky" it anymore. My program has taught me to be honest. In fact, there are times when I catch myself saying, "I actually don't know what I'm talking about. Sorry."

I find it's better if I'm honest about what I don't know. The alternative is to hang around people who know a lot less than me, but I genuinely like smart people, so I prefer to stick with being honest about what I don't know. You know?

In spite of myself:
No "blue-skying" it today, unless I'm outside.

Likes

I started the day by making a list of the things that I don't like about myself, and I was surprised by how short it was! When I made those lists in the past, they'd go on and on, for days. They're so much shorter since I started Al-Anon.

Because of the work I've done in recovery, I'm also able to list my positive qualities, like the fact that I'm a good friend. I'm also kind of funny, and I have exquisite taste in home furnishings. I make a mean turkey meatloaf; it's the Worcestershire sauce that gives it a special kick.

Okay, now it's your turn! Just skip the list of the things you don't like, and start with the list of things you *do* like about yourself. It doesn't have to be big, or spiritual, or deep. You can start small.

I'll get you started.

1. You have great taste in reading materials!

You take it from here. Jot down three more things about yourself that are positive. Oh, come on! Don't give me that face. You can do this! Ready? Go!

Keep those things at the top of your mind today, because they're uniquely yours. And you came up with them, so they must be true!

In spite of myself:

There are so many things to like about you,
I don't even know where to begin!

You Are Love

The huge billboard above the gardening center, hand-painted to look like a neon sign, said, "You Are Love." I'd driven by the place hundreds of times but had never noticed this sign.

How on earth had I missed this sign? I turned the car around and drove past the sign again to be sure I'd read it correctly. Shouldn't it read, "You are loved"? Did they run out of room for the letter *d*? Or was the implication that I am the embodiment of love? Or could it be that grammar just wasn't their thing?

When I drove by the gardening center the next day, the sign was gone.

Was there a *meaning* behind the sign? Was the *sign a sign*? Was it a message from my Higher Power to say, "Hi, I love you, and I think you're kind of cool"? I don't know. There are many things I don't know. This is one of them.

What I do know is this: If I think about the spelling of that sign for too long, I'll get irritated, and wonder why my Higher Power didn't use spell-check. Certainly my Higher Power has spell-check! So instead, I'll say, "Thanks, God," and, "You are love, too!" Just in case, I think I'll find a new route home.

In spite of myself:
You are love, and you are loved!

Listen Good

When I came into Al-Anon, I considered myself a decent communicator, although I knew my listening skills could be improved.

Actually, I *knew* I was a poor listener—because for most of my life I'd been asked things like, "Why don't you ever listen?" and, "What part of 'no' don't you understand?"

Over time, I'd gotten good at pretending to be an "active listener" (i.e., nodding my head, mirroring movements, maintaining eye contact), when in actuality, I was just planning my responses. I didn't really want to hear about my friends' dreams, or how much their baby weighed; neither did I give a darn about the fact that they'd once played in a band.

When it came to talking about really difficult subjects, I didn't even pretend to engage; I'd simply walk away if I felt a conflict brewing. I simply didn't know what else to do.

I continued to avoid difficult discussions until I got some advice from one of my Al-Anon friends. "You don't have to respond," she said. "Just listen to the other person and treat them as you would a newcomer in a meeting."

It worked! I'd let other people talk, even when I disagreed. And I didn't run away; I just sat through my discomfort. I pretended they were cute, itty-bitty little newcomers.

I learned to listen without reacting. Oddly enough, I no longer mind listening to others, even when I disagree with them. Most of the time. Over half of the time.

In spite of myself:
God, help me listen well today.

Flames

I just read something that really rocked my world. The words "inflammable" and "flammable" mean the exact same thing.

Apparently, in the 1920s, the National Fire Protection Association began recommending the use of the word "flammable" (instead of the original word, "inflammable") because they were worried people would think "inflammable" meant *not* flammable. Since most people in those days weren't Latin experts, they didn't know that the "in" in the world "inflammable" was derived from the Latin preposition "en" ("enflamed" or "in" flames), not the Latin prefix meaning "un" (as in "not").

My point here is: "Flammable" is a modern term for a material that catches fire very quickly, and "inflammable" is . . . the same thing.

I have spent my entire life being unclear about these very important terms. Now, this may not seem important to you—until *you're* the one sleeping in the "flammable" tent that you believe to be "inflammable," unaware that they are the same thing. So when that campfire inevitably gets out of control and *your* flammable/inflammable tent catches fire, your goose is cooked.

The recovery corollary is this: If I've been wrong about something as important as this, what else might I be wrong about?

In spite of myself:

Words that are their own opposite are called "contronyms."

Passes

I don't know if "This too shall pass" is an official Al-Anon slogan, but I hear plenty of people saying it, and it certainly speaks to me.

Except my attitude has always been, *If it's going to pass, why not give it a nudge?*

Regrettably, the world is not under my tutelage, and, like the rest of the human race, I must ride out the waves of joy and happiness—and yes, turmoil and sadness—that I will inevitably experience without pushing things along.

Although now that I think about it, I've never once uttered the words "This too shall pass" when someone was in the throes of a beautiful new romance. Or at a party, or after they'd lost ten pounds, or when they were skiing down a mountain.

Nevertheless, I find solace in the thought that everything will pass, and no matter what it is, I can trust that God will be with me in every situation. It's comforting to know, especially when I'm having a hard time, that life is a series of seasons passing by. Except I really dislike the phrase "To everything there is a season." I know, I know, it's from the Bible, but still, it's *way* overused.

Whether good, bad, or in between, everything is going to pass, and my job does not include nudging things along. I can trust that God is with me. Whether it's good or not so good, ultimately, it's all good. Can I get a whoo-whoo!

In spite of myself:
I'll let God do the nudging today.

Greener Grass

I recently read a survey which confirmed that 95 percent of the people who live in the city I *almost* moved to are the happiest people in the world.

According to the study, this city, which is experiencing a period of immense economic growth, also got high marks for cleanliness and safety—the subways are pristine and on time, and police are seen as helpful.

The survey suggests that residents of all ages feel positive and are living at their peak potential. They have healthy relationships, fitness, and total freedom to choose from the best that life has to offer. They're the world's most productive people; they earn more and are better citizens. Residents in the city can ski on snow and on water, surf and sail, and attend free museums, festivals, and outdoor theater. Shopping, cafés, and restaurants are plentiful.

As for housing, all of the homes and apartments in this city offer stunning views of both the sea and the mountains, as well as free access to numerous parks, forests, and lakes.

One of the residents was quoted as saying, "This city is the happiest place to live because everyone here is completely fulfilled. The grass really is greener over here. Too bad we aren't accepting new residents."

In spite of myself:
I will not read surveys that support the theory
that my life is not as it should be.

Cake Face

Statistics say that nine out of ten cake-in-the-face weddings end in divorce. I'm not surprised. Even when I was ten, at my first wedding, when the bride (my mother) shoved wedding cake in the groom's face, I knew it was doomed.

I did further research and found out that adults who refused to smile for photos when they were kids were also more likely to divorce than kids who smiled intensely. They were more likely to be psychopaths, as well.

My research showed that professional choreographers have a higher divorce rate than, say, animal trainers or mathematicians.

Although I was trying to be objective, these studies about the state of marriage saddened me, especially when I projected my findings across the entire human race.

I knew I had to shake my bad mood, so I called a friend in recovery. She assured me that although surveys have merit, Al-Anons operate in the spiritual world. She also told me that she'd read a survey that suggested that people in recovery who have a Higher Power are more likely to be happy. It felt so good to know that people with a Higher Power and a spiritual program are more likely to lead happy lives.

I'm still going to keep an eye on those people who refuse to smile for photos.

In spite of myself:

I'm glad my Higher Power doesn't read my made-up statistics.

Whatcha Sayin'?

I'd been on four interviews with one company, and I really wanted the job. After promising me that an offer was on its way, the president of the company stopped returning my calls.

"What do you think he's trying to say," I asked my friend, "by not saying anything?"

"I think it means he doesn't have an answer," he said.

"That can't be it. It must be something else," I said. "What is it he's trying to tell me?"

I spent the next two months wondering what the president was trying to say by not saying anything.

Trying to derive meaning from what someone wasn't saying used to be my stock-in-trade. I wasted time and a lot of energy trying to "uncover" meanings that just weren't there. Sometimes people do something and they mean nothing by it.

One of the things Al-Anon has taught me is that I won't always know what things mean, but I can still accept them. If there's a lesson my Higher Power wants me to get, it'll be revealed in time. I don't have to keep rehashing or inventing meanings for conversations to find the "real" point.

These days, when someone isn't saying anything, I presume it to mean they just aren't saying anything. And that might be *exactly* what they are trying to say.

In spite of myself:
I'll take what is said at face value today.

Impact

My sponsor is a bit of a saint. A Mother Earth type: pretty, kind, loving, together, fashion-forward. Funny. The kind of person who doesn't let things rattle her.

There are times when I have a hard time with the directions she gives me because she's just not naturally anxious or tense, like I am. She lets problems go, like water off a duck's back. I'm convinced she came into Al-Anon way more recovered than I did.

I'll never be like her, and I'm not exaggerating. When I tell people I'll never be as recovered as my sponsor, they laugh and say, "Oh, don't say that, that's not true!" and when they meet her, they pat me on the shoulder and say, "I see what you mean."

She's one of those people who truly makes a positive impact on so many other people, and I'm not writing these things in case she reads this meditation book. It's because I get the benefit of her amazing recovery and the constant guidance she offers, which is to seek solutions in my Higher Power and the Steps of Al-Anon.

While I might not be super together, or close to sainthood like my sponsor, if I can positively impact one or two people today, I'll be happy. Might you be the person I impact? I hope so. And if I'm not, I still hope you have a marvelous day!

In spite of myself:

God, help me have a positive impact on someone today.

Figured Out

"More shall be revealed," or so the slogan goes in most Twelve Step programs. But not for an Al-Anon, for whom the slogan might be, "More shall be figured out."

And frankly, if *anyone, anywhere is* going to figure *anything* out, it will be the Al-Anons.

There are few people who spend more time in contemplation than Al-Anons, and you'd be hard-pressed to find another human who cares as much about *everything* as much as we do. You will certainly never find any as determined or as persistent.

Most will agree that relying on the Al-Anon to figure things out, or at least make sense of the stupid things other people do is a very wise decision, indeed.

With that in mind, today just *might* be the perfect day to let an Al-Anon figure it all out. It could even be the day to forgo the "Higher Power" thing and see how much you can accomplish completely on your own.

Go ahead, see if you can figure out all your problems today. I'll bet you dollars to donuts that you'll come pretty close. And if more isn't revealed, you'll definitely make something good up. Because you're an Al-Anon.

In spite of myself:

I'll let God figure things out today,
because if I don't, we're all in big trouble.

Geographics

My first two years in Al-Anon, I was certain that moving to another state was the solution to all of my problems.

"I don't think a 'geographic' is the solution," my sponsor said when I brought up the idea of moving for the fortieth time that week.

"Why not? This city just isn't working for me. It's crowded, the people are rude, and I need a new job."

"How would things be different in a new city?" she asked. "A place where you have no job, no home, or friends?"

That was *precisely* my point. I figured if I could get away from the *people I knew*, I might *finally* have a shot at a decent life.

"Okay, so, maybe moving isn't the best idea," I relented. "Maybe I just need a new haircut or a massage."

"Maybe," she said gently. "In the meantime, why don't we have dinner and go to a meeting?"

At dinner she explained why doing another geographic—moving from one place to another to escape my problems—might not be the solution. She said geographics don't work because we take ourselves with us when we go. She suggested I think about it and pray before making any moves.

Weird, but after dinner with my sponsor and an inspirational Al-Anon meeting, the urge to move subsided. I did get a haircut the next day, which I hated for at least six months. I am, however, glad I didn't move.

In spite of myself:

Rearranging chairs on the deck of the *Titanic*
rarely changes the outcome.

Out of Fun

Can I be honest? I'm really tired today, and I've hit a wall. I don't have much recovery or humor to offer.

When I woke up this morning and started to write, a little voice in my head said, *These meditations are really dumb. It's October, and you've run out of steam. And funny. In fact, you ran out of funny way back in June.*

I yelled back at that voice, *Well, I don't see you being all that hilarious. You try coming up with interesting things about recovery for 365 days in a row. Not so easy!*

Silence.

Then I said to the voice, *See what I mean? You just love to taunt me and tell me I can't do things. I'm not going to listen to you anymore! I'm going to go sit down and write my meditation today, and you can shove off!*

I haven't heard from the voice since. I wonder if I was a little too harsh with it? Maybe I should do something nice for it, like sending it a greeting card, or my unused Groupon for a luxury bus tour to Las Vegas?

In the meantime, I'm going to ask my Higher Power to help out with an encouraging word for today.

I'm thinking . . . okay . . . I've . . . got . . . it . . . it's . . . "love"! Really. That's honestly what I heard!

In spite of myself:

All you need today is love.

Moody

Studies show that moodiness is responsible for approximately 87 percent of unhappy marriages. While I cannot verify that statistic, or even find the studies, I do know, without a doubt, that it's true.

I know because I used to be moody, and being emotionally unpredictable does not bode well for relationships. When I was an unrecovered Al-Anon, my moods were usually in response to what the people around me did—how they drove, dressed, bathed, breathed, etc. One slight change in plans or one unpleasant exchange could throw off my mood for an entire week.

Al-Anon has helped me see that my moods don't have to depend on my circumstances, my bank account, or on what other people do or don't do. Even though I still have a tendency to be short-tempered, life is better when I don't act on my emotions. And despite what I thought in high school, moody people are not any sexier than the more emotionally consistent folks.

Frankly, life improves when I don't indulge in bad moods or respond to other people's bad moods in kind. And while I don't have one in hand right now, I'm sure there's some study somewhere that will validate that.

In spite of myself:

God, help me indulge in a good mood today.

Promptlies

In my Al-Anon home group, we call working Step #10 "making a promptly," which means we promptly admit we're wrong and make amends for it.

The thing about "promptlies" is that there's a difference between knowing I need to do it and actually *doing* it.

It's not that I don't *want* to do it. It's just that I feel it's important not to be hasty with my amends. I need to think things through before taking full responsibility. If the other person will agree to meet in the middle—in order to establish equal and mutual levels of involvement—I'm more than happy to make my "promptly" promptly.

Ironically, my sponsor doesn't agree with my version of how promptlies should go. According to her, I need to be willing to take full responsibility for my part. Period. It doesn't matter what the other people's parts are, or whether they acknowledge them.

She may have a point, but why would I want to take complete responsibility if my part is only 10 percent?

Yes, life improves drastically when I make my promptlies promptly, even if my part is minuscule. And sure, I feel lighter knowing I've done the right thing. But that's not really the point I'm trying to make here, is it?

In spite of myself:

Today I'll make my promptlies
before I give them too much thought.

Cup o' Misery

There's a song by The Smiths titled "Heaven Knows I'm Miserable Now." I'd quote the lyrics because they are so fantastic, but I can't unless I want to get written permission from Morrissey, The Smiths' lead singer, and if you know anything about him, you'll know the chances of me getting clearance are slim to none.

Basically, the song's about a guy who's looking for a job, but once he finds it, he's miserable. Then the guy wants to find someone to love, and he does, and he's miserable. He sees everyone else as the source of his unhappiness and angst. In essence, he's just a pain in the ass who's never happy.

That song was my anthem for most of my adult life. I was constantly looking for the right situation, but once I got it, I was miserable. People bothered me. I didn't want them to want things from me. I wanted to be left alone to do what I wanted.

Unlike Morrissey, the quintessential purveyor of woe and sorrow, I came off as agreeable, but the minute I was asked to do something I didn't want to, I'd dig in my heels and pull some passive-aggressive move. And I was really unhappy.

It took working the Twelve Steps in Al-Anon for me to see how I reveled in suffering *of my own making.*

I still enjoy a cup of misery at times, but when I ask for help and guidance from my Higher Power, and a fellow in the program who understands, I'm able to stop myself before I drink too much from the cup. A misery hangover is the *absolute worst.*

In spite of myself:
God, help me refrain from picking up the cup of misery today.

Knock-Knock

I've decided, once and for all, that I will never answer the door to another knock-knock joke, at least not to anyone over the age of seven. Knock-knock jokes have *never been* funny, and they rarely result in anything more than a groan, or the desire to pull your own hair out, agreed? And if I make an effort to open the door, I expect to be rewarded with something other than a stupid knock-knock joke!

I'm thankful to Al-Anon for showing me how to be honest about things—like the fact that I've never truly laughed at a knock-knock joke. I also credit Al-Anon with the wisdom to know how to handle things like that uncomfortable moment when someone wants me to go along with a ridiculous knock-knock joke. Here is my way of handling the situation, now that I'm working a program of recovery:

JOKESTER:	Knock-knock.
ME:	No one's home.
JOKESTER:	(Goes quiet. Awkward silence.)
ME:	You might try the Browns down the street.

This generally stops the offenders in their tracks. If they insist, I simply say, "I hope you understand, I once had a bad experience with a knock-knock joke, so I don't answer the door to them anymore."

I'm so glad I can apply Al-Anon wisdom to every aspect of my life!

In spite of myself:

Please don't knock-knock. You can, however, ring the doorbell.

Party On

My friend's husband, Mike, talks to *everyone*. Last week, she waited for twenty minutes in the car while Mike helped an old woman with her groceries. He then wrote out his detailed recipe for the world's best pulled-pork sandwiches.

Recently, my friend's work was hosting an office party, and she told her boss that she wouldn't be able to go. He responded with, "That's okay. Can Mike come instead?"

Everyone loves Mike because he's a genuinely good guy. He also recites Shakespeare and makes up naughty limericks on the fly. But it's his interest in other people that makes him so well-liked.

When I came into Al-Anon, I wasn't interested in other people. I was just trying to survive. Ergo, I came off as self-centered and uninterested in anyone except myself.

After a while, I started to notice more about other people: what they enjoyed, their favorite movies and songs, what they might need from a friend. I started to gain an "interest in my fellows," and life opened up. I became more tolerant and open to friendships with people I would never have been interested in before.

Recovery doesn't promise us we'll become social butterflies like Mike, hanging out in parking lots, sharing recipes for pulled pork, but it does promise us we'll lose interest in selfish things.

As a result, we will probably get invited to more parties. Which means we'd better have a limerick or two in our pocket.

In spite of myself:
Is it just me, or is everyone self-centered?

Yes, No, Wait!

They say that God answers all prayers. Sometimes the answer is yes and sometimes the answer is no. And sometimes the answer is, "Wait . . . I have something better for you."

My immediate reaction? *God may have something better, but I'll settle for "okay" and take mine now.*

My head tells me that a three-week-old-cupcake-with-beige-frosting-that-smells-like-my-refrigerator in the hand is better than two fresh-creamy-red-velvet-cupcakes in the bush. Because the three-week-old cupcake is here now. And I can see it.

"My Higher Power's 'something better' sounds like a great idea," I told my sponsor, "but I don't have much time left."

"Why? Are you sick?" she asked.

"No. I'm not sick, but I'm not getting younger. What if I'm busy doing laundry, or I'm not around when God gets to the better stuff? Or worse, what if I'm too old to enjoy it?"

I explained to her my metaphor about one stale cupcake in the refrigerator being better than two fresh ones in the bush.

"I'm so happy you aren't God," my sponsor replied, giggling. "And I'm even happier you don't cook for me," which I thought was an odd response. She doesn't even have a personal chef, and I have no idea why she wouldn't want me to cook for her. I'm a fairly good cook.

In spite of myself:
I want it *bad*, I want it *now*, and I'll take it so-so.

Try

I've heard that trying to pray is praying.

There are times when I worry that my praying doesn't qualify as praying—that I'm not doing it the right way and God might not be paying attention.

This fear comes as a result of a painful experience I had in my youth. After graduating from college, I was being interviewed for my first professional job at my dream company. I told the interviewer that if I got the job, I would try to be his best employee. He picked up his expensive Cross pen and threw it on the floor.

"*Try* to pick that pen up off the floor," he said.

I quickly picked it up and put it on the desk. He threw it back on the ground. "There is no such thing as 'try,'" he said, in a manner that short men with too much power tend to use.

He demanded that I *try* to pick up the pen again, causing me to burst into tears.

Despite the life-altering, traumatic incident, and the resulting emotional scars it caused, there's a part of me that believes there *is* such a thing as trying.

I believe it's the same way with prayer. It doesn't matter where I am or how I'm sitting, or what I say when I pray, as long as I keep trying. Trying to pray *is* praying.

As I looked back on that interview, I'm glad I didn't get that job. I would have fantasized about "trying" to place that Cross pen you-know-where every time I saw that short, power-hungry jackass. Alas, I did not have the gift of recovery back then.

In spite of myself:

I'm not gonna try. I'm just gonna talk to God today.

Self-Love

I was doing research on dumb relationship advice and found a seminar called "Twenty Days of Self-Love." The book the seminar leader was peddling was called *How Do I Love Me? Let Me Count the Ways.*

Surely I wasn't the only one who found these titles disturbing. Although I was intrigued—just exactly how much self-love *could* one experience in twenty days?

As if people don't worship themselves enough already, here it is, another attempt of this whiny, narcissist culture to improve its self-esteem.

They were charging people a thousand dollars! *Who on earth pays that kind of money for this baloney?* When I went online to sign up, it was sold out. *But I was signing up, too, so what did that make me?*

But then I remembered I wasn't really signing up, I was doing research for humorous subject matters. I called my sponsor and told her about it, thinking she'd find it funny.

"You were going to waste twenty days and a thousand dollars for dumb relationship advice?" she quizzed me.

"Uh, yes. No," I stammered.

"You've got too much time on your hands," she said.

She suggested I go to an Al-Anon meeting and find a way to be of service if I was so bored. She didn't get the joke.

In spite of myself:
In spite of myself, I don't have an in spite of myself.
See what wasting time does?

Plushies

Today is Plush Animal Lover's Day. Although there's been a tremendous amount of controversy over the original date of this holiday's origination, for the sake of brevity and this meditation, we're going with today, October 28.

The objective on Plush Day is simple: Give your beloved stuffed animals appreciation and plenty of attention.

You might consider taking your plushie out to breakfast or tea, or even a movie. Or how about a nice, long drive in the country with the windows rolled down? Your teddy bear or your stuffed giraffe won't care where you go. Plushies aren't demanding; they just want to be with you. For instance, I've never heard of a stuffed unicorn freaking out because she didn't get a Rolex watch. Or a Beanie Baby serving up attitude because she wasn't met at the door with a bouquet of flowers on Plush Animal Lover's Day. How many other things in your life can you honestly say that about?

Despite what our culture of greed and excess implies, you do not have to spend lots of money to prove you care for your plushie.

Just give it a big squeeze and spend as much quality time together as you can today. Trust me, your plushie will love you forever!

In spite of myself:

If you don't have a plushie, today is the day to get one.

Crying & Driving

Before Al-Anon, I would occasionally schedule what I called "Crying & Driving Tours"—road trips solely dedicated to indulging and wallowing in my problems.

The Crying & Driving Tours would begin with a trip to the local convenience store, where I'd stock up on provisions: diet sodas, pretzels, and M&M's. I'd fill up the gas tank and head out onto the open highway, where I'd spend hours pondering what I could've possibly done to have deserved the rotten hand I'd been dealt. I'd continue on for hours, stopping just long enough to grab a slice of greasy cheese pizza or a funnel cake—why bother eating well when life was pointless?—until I ran out of gas. Or tears. Whichever came first.

Since I started working the program of Al-Anon, the Crying & Driving Tours are fewer and farther between.

For instance, the last time I set out on a Cry & Drive, I didn't even finish it because I'd stopped to enjoy the most scenic sunset. Feeling grateful for my reasonably decent life, I took the uneaten McBurger and bag of pretzels and threw them in the garbage before heading back home.

It's hard to eat junk food and feel grateful at the same time.

In spite of myself:

I'm glad my self-pity tours don't last as long as they used to.

Gratuitous Rant

I'd been feeling really down about being single and such a dismal failure at my age until I read that the universe is two billion years old. Now *that* is old! Older than me, anyway. And anything that's older than me makes me feel better.

So, the next time I get anxious about my marital status or where my life isn't headed for someone of my age, I'm going to remember that, in comparison to the universe, I'm just a baby. And even though I haven't accomplished nearly as much as the universe has, I am still lovable.

The fact that the universe has accomplished more than me would normally cause me to spin into a rant about how the universe has a lot more money and support than I do, but I'm a woman in recovery, and today I'll not allow myself to spin out about something that'll do nothing to improve my mental health.

Instead, I shall stick to one rant per subject. The point is, age is relative, is it not? And in comparison to the universe, you and I are but mere toddlers. And despite what we have or have not achieved at our age, if we're in recovery, we can trust that God's in charge. And he isn't grading us on our accomplishments.

So there. To heck with those people who are all caught up in ageist ageism. That's my rant for today. Feel free to choose one of your own. It must, however, be limited to one subject.

In spite of myself:
You may have one totally gratuitous rant right now.
Extra credit if it lasts less than five minutes.

Inventories

If you're like me, at least several times a day you find yourself needing to work Step #10 and apologize to someone for something.

Before recovery, my approach to any apology-type situation (and they were numerous) would go something like this: "Mistake? Oh, yeah, that. Someone else did it. Oh, that mistake? I guess that was me, wasn't it? Suppose we just forget any of that happened? No? Oh, okay, then I'll admit I did it and I'm going to apologize, but frankly, I don't want to. I will, though. Truthfully, I was pushed against a wall, and I made a snap decision. Sure wish I could snap it back!

"Not that I'm seeking sympathy or anything, but the mistake can be directly linked to my dubious upbringing. Things were very difficult for me growing up. It's a miracle I'm even alive. And, mostly, I blame my mother, so really, maybe you should give my mother a call and ask her to apologize to you. Okay, okay, okay! I'll admit I was wrong . . . go ahead, bring in the 'right police' and have me arrested!"

I'm not endorsing the above approach to a Step #10 amends. It is, indeed, not a good apology, but in terms of creativity, I'd give it fairly high marks, would you not agree?

Feel free, however, to come up with a few of your own.

In spite of myself:
What? Sincerity, accountability, and humility
need to be a part of an inventory?!

NOVEMBER

Play Hard

"I've never trusted people who use the phrase 'Work hard, play harder,'" I said to my Al-Anon friend while on a hike one Sunday afternoon.

"Why not?" she asked.

"It contains an implied judgment, and it assumes I'm not doing enough. It makes me anxious just hearing it," I said, quickening my pace.

"That's interesting. I don't feel that way when I hear the phrase," she said. "I just think, 'That person must be hard-working,'" she said sweetly, catching up to me.

"There's a covert superiority to the statement, like the only people with any value are power-mongering corporate drones who are also triathletes," I said, breaking into a jog.

"It's just a phrase. Could you be overthinking this?"

"Overthinking is *not* my problem. It's society's *lack* of overthinking that troubles me. It's like if we're not pushing ourselves to the limit, we're worthless in this society," I huffed as we came to the end of our hike.

"You wanna go get some coffee?" she asked.

"No, I can't," I said. "I have work to do."

On my way home, I thought about what my friend said—about how some phrases contain judgments, and about how our society puts too much pressure on us to do more. She's totally right.

In spite of myself:

God, help me remember that the only critical judge
is the one inside my head.

My Gut or Yours

People used to tell me I should make decisions based on what my gut tells me. The problem was, I was horrible at distinguishing what my gut was communicating.

Before Al-Anon, I'd let my friends' guts answer the bigger questions, like: What university should I go to? Where should I eat lunch? What should I name my new dog—the one I haven't yet adopted?

When I'd ask my friends' guts whether I should break up with "him," I'd frequently get a "yes," no matter who "he" was. It turns out people enjoy advising their friends to end relationships. Especially when they're disappointed with their own relationships.

It doesn't work to trust other people's guts or allow them to make decisions on my behalf. They don't have to live with the consequences.

Al-Anon has taught me to seek my Higher Power's guidance and to ask for support from trusted friends, but ultimately, I'm responsible for my choices. As a result, I've grown to trust myself more, and I feel more empowered and connected to God.

In fact, I love making decisions now. Like that dog I haven't adopted? I'm definitely going to name her Chelsea, and I don't care what anyone else's gut says about it!

In spite of myself:

It's nice to be able to trust my gut.

Me First?

People in Al-Anon often refer to the airline warning that flight attendants give: "In an emergency, put the oxygen mask on yourself first, and then help those around you."

As the saying goes, if I don't take care of my own needs first, I can't help anyone else. The analogy makes perfect sense, especially when I'm at home, doing my daily routine. But when I'm on a plane and I hear that warning, I freak out about the thought of putting *my own* oxygen mask on, much less trying to help someone else.

In my hallucination, I'm on a plane next to some kid who's never flown. Suddenly, the airplane begins to drop rapidly out of the sky—although planes don't just fall out of the sky. I've Googled the phrase "Can a plane fall out of the sky?" and the answer was a categorical "No."

Anyway, I grab the oxygen mask and start to put it on him, until I remember the warning and put it on myself. As I place the mask over my mouth, the plane continues to spiral downward. Finally, I reach out for the kid's mask, but he already has it on.

He lifts his mask and whispers, "Boy, you know how to ruin a flight. Thanks for nothing, lady!"

This is exactly why I don't sit next to kids when I fly. I never want to be responsible for ruining someone's flight. Or life.

In spite of myself:
I'll stop imagining outlandish scenarios.

MYOB

MYOB might sound like something you'd hear at a college frat party, but it's actually an acronym for the Al-Anon slogan "Mind your own business."

The thing is, this saying applies for *almost everyone on the planet*. Al-Anons aren't the only ones who butt in when we aren't invited, or offer advice even after we've been repeatedly asked not to. Al-Anons don't have the corner on meddling.

While the world can fault Al-Anons for making loads of inappropriate and unnecessary suggestions, we are not the only ones to operate under the mistaken assumption that everyone we come into contact with wants to hear our opinions.

Yes, it's fun to put all the blame on the Al-Anons, but we aren't the only people suffering from the sin of "helping too much or too often." Take my aunt, for example. She made her son's bed for him every morning until he left home—at the age of thirty-five. And she wasn't even an Al-Anon!

There are plenty of people who could benefit from some good old-fashioned butting out, not just us Al-Anons. Of course, those people probably aren't reading this book. Perhaps you could suggest it to them?

In spite of myself:
Can I make a suggestion? No? Okay.

Grim Fairy Tale

There's a story about the little girl who had a temper, so her father led her to a long fence and handed her a bag of nails.

"Daughter, every time you lose your temper, you must hammer a nail into the fence."

The first day the girl drove thirty-seven nails into the fence.

As she learned to control her anger, the number of nails she hammered dwindled. She learned it was easier to keep calm than to drive nails into the fence.

Finally, the day came when the little girl didn't lose her temper at all. Her father suggested she pull out one nail for each day she was able to hold her temper.

Then, one day the girl told her father the nails were gone. The father then took his daughter to the fence.

"You've done very well, but see the holes in the fence? When you say things in anger, it leaves scars. If you put a knife in a man and draw it out, it won't matter how many times you say 'I'm sorry.' The wound is still there."

Thank goodness, this all happened in, like, the 1920s or something, and people don't parent that way anymore. Sometimes, however, I do still worry about that little girl.

In spite of myself:
Can I stop counting the nails already?

Closers

I'm at a real estate sales training course. Our trainer, who's wearing a blue suit he's no doubt been recycling since 1984, opens with a story about the fortune he's amassed in real estate.

"Rapport building," he says, dashing around the room, "is developing a *relationship* with a customer. It's getting them to see you as a friend. If they can imagine you at their backyard BBQ, chances are they'll buy a house from you!"

My favorite terms from the course are "porcupining," where the salesperson answers the customer's question with a question, in order to avoid answering the first question, and the "confirming closing statement," which is asking a series of questions that have "yes" answers. If people say yes enough times, it's hard to say no, thus forcing them into buying a massively overpriced home.

Wow, maybe I can do this sales stuff, I think.

"People *want* to part with their money," the trainer declares. "Your job is to help them. No shame in that!" He shows us charts that prove the more expensive and painful the parting, the more the person will value something.

I liken it to recovery. If tears were cash, I would have some major dollars invested in myself. I treasure my recovery because of all the hard work I've put into it.

No matter how good I get, however, I doubt I'll ever be able to hard sell another Al-Anon into doing *anything*, especially if it's something they don't want to do. Al-Anons can be pretty tough customers.

In spite of myself:
Today I'll try some rapport building with my Higher Power.

Winning

This is what I saw when I opened my first e-mail this morning:

Dear Winner,

Your e-mail address has won for you a prize of three million six hundred thousand United States Dollars ($3,600,000.00) in this Year Lottery Awards & Live Promotion, Respond to notification to claim your prize:

Congratulations!! Mrs. Anne W.

Well, there you have it, my friends. I am now worth three million plus, in United States dollars, no less! Therefore, today's meditation shall be short and sweet: You don't have to open your mailbox. Your Higher Power already thinks you're a WINNER!

I will return tomorrow with another spiritually uplifting message. For today, I must concentrate on locating Mrs. W. from the Lottery Awards & Live Promotion Department.

And, please, don't take the fact that I no longer need to work for a living as a sign that my Higher Power is better than yours, or that I am in any way, shape, or form more spiritual or recovered than you are. That is simply not true. Have a great day, WINNER!

In spite of myself:

Lottery or no lottery, today is gonna be a winning day!

Factor This

On the front page of the local paper is a story about the investor for my film.

"Three years after being arrested, the leader of a Ponzi scheme who used investors' money from phony investments in a 'factoring' business, causing $145 million in losses, was sentenced to twenty years in federal prison."

This cannot possibly be the kind-hearted man who invested in me and my film, I think as I fold the paper. *How did I miss the signs?*

True, the story's kind of cool—like a James Bond film. Except I was never escorted on a private jet or sent to Ibiza on a yacht owned by the prince of Dubai. There were no covert meetings with Israeli arms dealers or parties in penthouses on the Vegas strip. I never wore a tight black cat suit while sword fighting a Russian assassin on a roof.

To learn that I've missed out on playing a minor—albeit juicy—role in a tale of almost international intrigue because I was completely clueless is kind of odd.

The thing is, there were signs. Now that I'm more recovered, I can see signs more clearly. Today I know when to walk away from a situation, even if it means looking bad or losing money.

I smile, pleased because I'm much better at reading signs. Just in case, I put the newspaper in my handbag, as a memento. Of course, I'd never be dumb enough to be involved in a mess like that again.

In spite of myself:
I don't always know what signs to look for.
Today, I'll ask God for help.

Justify

When I tell people I'm in Al-Anon, they sometimes confuse it with AA, or they think it's a program where a person can drink or use drugs in moderation.

"Good for you," they'll say. "So, can you still have a glass of wine?"

"If I want to," I say, and usually leave it at that, because it's not easy to explain Al-Anon. If, however, the person wants more information, I'm happy to offer it. This is how my side of the conversation generally goes:

"Well, I tend to be a little controlling, and I have a tendency to obsess about people, places, and things. I also struggle with my temper. Once I tried to run over a policeman because I'd discovered my ex at the bar again . . .

"What? No, I wasn't drunk. I was sober. You see . . . I have ideas about how people should behave, and when they don't behave that way, I get testy. Also, I have voices that tell me I'm a loser . . .

"No, not real voices. Internal thoughts. And I sometimes get thoughts about how I'd like to change things: 'the system,' my job, other people. So I go to Al-Anon meetings . . .

"What do we do? We sit in a circle and share. There's a lot of laughing and hugging. And when we're done, we hold hands and pray. Then we go home.

"Huh? No, of course, we aren't drunk."

In spite of myself:
I don't have to justify my love for Al-Anon.

Embellishing

I was having a hard time figuring out what to do about a certain situation, and my sponsor told me to wait. Actually, she said, "Feel the confusion and the powerlessness, and let it go."

I'm well acquainted with what confusion and powerlessness feel like, I thought. *The question is how do I let go after I've felt them?*

I don't know who she thought she was sponsoring, but I'm not capable of having intense feelings and letting them . . . go. I need to have feelings, announce to the world I'm having them, and report about how it feels to have had those feelings. It's not a simple process.

Against my better judgment, I took my sponsor's advice. I felt the confusion, dread, and sadness about the situation. I tried to let them go. I sat in silence on the living room floor for hours, but I couldn't let go of the feelings.

So I went into the kitchen, kicked my refrigerator, and called it unspeakable names. Then I went to the bedroom and punched my embellished throw pillows until I fell asleep from exhaustion.

When I woke up hours later, I couldn't even remember what I was so upset about in the first place. Maybe my sponsor was right. I had finally let go.

I did, however, feel I should apologize to my throw pillows and my refrigerator.

In spite of myself:
I can have feelings without embellishing them.

Self-y

The quote said, "Self is not something we find. It's something we create."

There were psychics, intuitives, therapists, healers, and astrologists. There was the masseuse who told me my problems were caused by dead spirits that had latched onto me. All of these people seemed willing to help me find myself. But even after tens of thousands of dollars, I'd not been found.

When I came into Al-Anon, I started to get the impression that my definition of "self" had been based on other people's opinions and feedback. I had no idea who my real self was. In Al-Anon, I was gently reminded that my self has nothing to do with what other people think of me or my circumstances.

And I heard that quote about self-creation.

My initial thought was, *How the heck can I create a life when I can barely put a sandwich together?* I've come to discover that life unfolds when I spend less time analyzing and thinking about my self, and more time living. The life I want happens when I get out and do what's in front of me.

Now I start the day with a prayer, asking my Higher Power for direction. I don't spend nearly as much time navel-gazing. And while I spend more time creating than I ever have, I still haven't quite figured out how to create myself. Mostly because I don't even know what it means.

In spite of myself:
Is it self-improvement, or self-obsession?

Brand-New Me

I mentioned this before, but one of the best things I've ever heard at an Al-Anon meeting is from an acquaintance of mine, who said: "I didn't know I was the person I was until I wasn't anymore. I only saw myself after I looked back and saw who I used to be."

To me, it goes like this: I can't look in the rearview mirror and see the reflection of my past. I'm looking in a mirror, seeing the present, only from a different perspective. Okay, that's not what I meant. Let's try this: I don't see who I used to be until I'm not that person anymore. I can't be someone I'm not until I've changed and become someone else.

What I'm trying to say is, in Al-Anon, as we change for the better, we spend less time focused on the past.

For example, there are times when I catch myself saying things that are so kind and thoughtful that I want to add, "Who the heck is talking here? What on earth just came out of my mouth? That was so . . . not me!"

And then I realize that it *is* me. The newer, improved me. Except I'm not even *trying* to be new or improved. I am just being me. A nicer, sweeter version of the me that I used to be.

Today, I can clearly see who I used to be, who I am now, and who I'm becoming. And I sort of like all three versions of myself!

In spite of myself:

I can't wait to see who I'm going to be next year!

Forgiveness

Doling out forgiveness is not something I do with reckless abandon. In fact, there are times when I enjoy holding and nursing a long-term grudge. It feels good to know that I am making someone who has harmed me suffer—a bit.

Before recovery, I was notorious for withholding forgiveness until someone had shown they were thoroughly remorseful and appropriately humbled. I suppose you could've called me the Supreme Judge of the Universe.

I'm doing better since I started using the tools and working the steps of Al-Anon, but forgiveness isn't easy-breezy for me. I have to stay honest with myself and be careful about evaluating other people's intentions and decisions. I still catch myself getting supremely judgy about other people, so I'm constantly asking my Higher Power for help.

Because of Al-Anon, I've learned to be more generous with forgiveness—of others and myself.

I don't know why people do what they do, and besides, I feel better when I don't hold grudges. I forgive now because it makes *me* feel better. And because if I don't forgive, I can get smug and sanctimonious pretty quickly. It wouldn't be a huge leap for me to start believing I could save a nation, or part the Red Sea, or even summon a plague. That is, if the wrong person tried to cross me.

In spite of myself:
My happiness is in direct correlation
to my willingness to forgive.

Hot!

I once worked as a waitress for a bustling Italian restaurant chain. We all hated making hot teas because they were a big waste of time, but one of my coworkers, Joel—a charismatic attorney in training—had a special disdain for people who ordered hot tea.

When customers would request hot tea with their pasta, Joel would give them some bogus story about a broken water pipe. Joel became a bit of a hero among the waitstaff for his ability to pull off this lie.

Once when I was extremely busy and a woman at my table ordered hot tea, I thought I'd try Joel's approach.

"I'm sorry, ma'am, we aren't serving hot tea tonight. The water pipe broke."

"Don't be daft, young lady," the woman said, glaring at me. "Use the damn microwave."

I didn't know what to say, so I got her hot tea. I also got a written warning from the restaurant manager for lying. Joel continued to do it and never got caught.

Even before Al-Anon, I was a horrible liar. I've never been able to try on other people's lies. They never fit, and I always get caught.

Not surprisingly, Joel's now a tremendously successful criminal defense attorney.

In spite of myself:

I don't do well when I take on other people's lies or stories.

Sainthood

We are not saints. The point is, that we are
willing to grow along spiritual lines.
—ALCOHOLICS ANONYMOUS

I've never sought sainthood; neither do I expect it from others. Well, I do expect it from others—in fact, I used to demand it. And so, when I came into Al-Anon, I was disappointed with what I'd been getting from most of the people in my life.

Most definitely.

As for "growth along spiritual lines," I was into it. I had a knack for identifying what could be done better and was always happy to point others in the right direction.

When I started working the Twelve Steps in the Al-Anon program, there wasn't much time to think about other people's sainthood.

Of course, I felt bad about spending so much time on my own growth and potential sainthood, so I bought Al-Anon and CoDA literature for my loved ones. I even highlighted key phrases for them.

In time I came to accept that sainthood is not the purpose of recovery. The purpose is to grow spiritually, focus on my own healing and serenity, and connect with my Higher Power daily. Oh, and enjoy life. While I'm willing to help others along spiritual lines, getting them to sainthood is not my purpose either. I know. That's a bummer.

In spite of myself:

Today I'll stay focused on my growth instead of yours.

Loomies

"You can just f— off!" the woman screamed at me. It was Thanksgiving, and I'd been working at a store, which I'll call Loomingdale's. Our holiday sale included giving customers a $15 gift card for every $100 they spent in our store.

This particular woman hadn't spent enough to get an additional $15 gift card, so I explained to her she'd need to spend more to get another card.

"Why don't you just give the extra card to me, anyway?" she demanded. "I've already spent a lot of money here!"

When I told her I wasn't authorized to give her another card, she began yelling, hurling a string of expletives at me.

What a jerk, I thought. Actually, I thought of my own expletive, but I'm trying to impart a spiritual message, so I'll leave it at that.

I started to spin out about what an entitled, greedy cow she was, until I remembered the times I'd been rude to someone because I feared I wasn't getting my "fair share." It made me reflect on my behavior when I didn't get what I thought was "mine."

I imagined the woman must have been in a lot of fear and pain, or she wouldn't behave that way, and I said a prayer for her. I wished her all the wonderful things that I wanted for myself. And then I imagined what she'd look like falling down the escalator with those damn gift cards in her hand.

In spite of myself:
Progress, not perfection.

Conscious Contact

Step #11: "Sought through prayer and meditation to improve our conscious contact with God . . ."

I was agonizing over Step #11 before I'd even started Step #1, certain I'd never be *the girl* who meditated. Then I heard a friend share about how meditation had transformed his life. I asked him how long it had taken him to get comfortable with it.

"About fifteen years," he said.

Well, there goes that idea, I thought, and gave up the prospect of trying to meditate again.

Meditation used to make my heart leap because I was not a "meditation type." I had plenty of opinions about meditation types, and they weren't positive. My opinion was colored by stereotypes, which included white dudes with dreadlocks and patchouli-drenched bohemian chicks in yoga pants spending a lot of time sitting quietly. And sitting quietly was hugely frightening. I'd had glimpses of what was going on inside of me, and the prospect of delving deeper into that mess wasn't comforting.

To this day, just thinking about meditating still unsettles me, so I've chosen my own way to communicate with my Higher Power. In fact, some of my prayers are still about the stress that my inability to meditate causes me. Instead of worrying about it, I've decided to learn to appreciate any and all conscious contact I can get with God, no matter how unhip or unconventional it may be.

In spite of myself:

Today I'll take conscious contact, any way I can get it.

Greetings

The greeting card read something like, "I'd rather have straw-berry jam shoved into my eye sockets than have you mad at me." I loved it so much that I bought a stack of them.

Since I'd bought the cards, I wanted to be able to use them, so I pulled out my cell phone and scanned all my contacts to see if there was anyone I needed to apologize to, but there was no one.

I really loved those cards, and I began to think I might just be forced to go out and purposely piss off one of my friends so I could send them a card. Then it hit me: I'd been pretty snippy with a pal of mine earlier in the week because she'd canceled our plans to go to a concert at the last minute, for no real reason. I had reacted unkindly, but I'd already called her back and asked for her forgiveness.

Sure, I'd taken responsibility for my part, but was it enough? Should I send the jam-in-the-eye-socket greeting card? Or would it just make things worse?

Keeping my side of the street clean doesn't mean I have to mop up the whole darn neighborhood while I'm at it.

Al-Anon has taught me that I don't have to keep apologizing for the wrongs I've done. Once I've made amends, I have to let them go and give people time to settle. But, honestly, with so many cool greeting cards, it does make it harder to leave things alone.

In spite of myself:
Today I'll keep my side of the street,
and my eye sockets, clean!

2 for 1

Tradition #11 states, "Our public relations policy is based on attraction rather than promotion."

Al-Anon doesn't promote or advertise recovery. This is why you'll never see a sign outside a meeting room that says, "50 Percent Off Recovery, This Week Only!" or "2-for-1 Discount!" or even "Bring a Friend and Get Better Faster!" Admittedly, I'd like to see that last one. I know *exactly* who I would bring with me.

No promotion, no discounts, no early-bird specials, and no waving flags about what I've gotten from recovery.

Just being myself, ironically, is enough. I've become a source of attraction by working the Steps and staying on my spiritual path. I don't have to try to look good or "sell" the program of Al-Anon. People will see the change in me and decide if they want what I have.

I don't know about you, but this takes a huge load off. I don't have to look good or endorse anyone or anything. Don't have to worry about signing up a certain number of people or pawning off cases of "healing" berry juice on all my friends.

Where else in the world is it okay to be my crazy, obsessed self and not have to worry about "doing it right"? That's right. Absolutely nowhere.

In spite of myself:

Hey Al-Anon, thanks for being a place where I can
be exactly who I am.

Coach

Sometimes my Al-Anon sponsor reminds me of Vince Lombardi, the football coach who brought the Green Bay Packers to multiple, successive NFL championships. Except my sponsor's very pretty and not at all hairy.

The reason she reminds me of Lombardi is that they both set high standards for the people around them. For instance, Lombardi considered ten minutes early to be "on time" for players at meetings. My sponsor expects the same. Vince had a "no T-shirts and jeans" rule when speaking or representing the team; my sponsor requires us to wear dresses when speaking, out of respect for the Al-Anon program. Lombardi made sure his team was a cohesive group of "dignified" people; anybody who didn't want to meet that expectation was "free to get the hell out." My sponsor isn't that harsh. She sets the bar fairly high, and the people she sponsors eventually figure it out.

For Lombardi, football was more than a game—it was a lifestyle. That's how my sponsor feels about spiritual growth. She encourages me, and tells me the point of recovery is to live a spiritual practice with grace and dignity. She reminds me that self-esteem is achieved by doing estimable acts.

My sponsor doesn't, however, ask me to do a push-up or sit-ups or anything like that. That might be taking the whole recovery thing a bit too far.

In spite of myself:

Is there any area where I could use some spiritual "coaching"?

Rewriting History

I have a well-deserved reputation for being able to rewrite history. More specifically, my own.

It's a skill I've perfected throughout my lifetime, and if there were an award—an Oscar—for, say, rewriting life stories without a script, a budget, any production value, a crew, actors, or sets, I'd be a serious contender.

"Professional mental health experts" might say my warped viewpoint is a form of denial, but I don't pay them any attention.

Personally, I think most professionals could benefit from some lightening up. The world doesn't need to know every detail of your unpleasant childhood—and, seriously, no matter how bad it was, I guarantee you, mine was worse. And despite what those experts tell you, your partner doesn't really want to hear everything you talk about with your therapist, or every time your feelings get hurt. Trust me. That's called "oversharing," and it's a death knell for relationships. Again, trust me. Try "buttoning it up" for a day or two.

I might also add: *Any* story can be improved with some decent rewriting. If that fails, just go for excessive exaggeration.

Not really. I was being ironic. Trust me.

In spite of myself:

Today I'll try not to do too much oversharing.

Fraud Alert

On some level, deep down, I knew this day would come.

There's no simple way to explain how I felt when I woke up this morning, other than the sense that my biggest fear had finally come to fruition: Today I'm going to be outed as the complete fraud that I am.

I have no proof, but I'm fairly sure that when I arrive at work this morning, my boss will make the announcement—over the loudspeaker, of course—that I am unqualified for anything other than shredding envelopes or licking stamps, and that everything I've done up until this point in my life has been a total waste of time. At that point, I'll be escorted out of the building as my colleagues stand by.

"We've been on to you for years," they'll hiss as they toss staplers and paper clips at my head.

I'm considering calling someone in Al-Anon to go over how I should handle things, but I'm sure they're all busy living authentic lives. Unlike me.

I would call my sponsor, but I won't be able to handle the disappointment in her voice when she discovers she's been sponsoring an impostor, a hack, and a sham of a human being. Instead, I'll go in and face the music, which will no doubt be sad. And very, very slow.

In spite of myself:

Am I creating music that I'll never have to face?

Communication

Everything's okay between us, isn't it? Well, it's just that you've been so talkative and happy lately, I wonder: Are you having an affair?

What? No, I'm not crazy! According to a study in one of my fashion magazines, when a partner, specifically, a man, gives too many details about their day, it's a sign he's hiding something. What do you mean, "What magazine?" Does it matter? Why so interested in the details all of a sudden? Until now, there were, like, four subjects that interested you!

Okay, I will make some sense. When I asked about your day, instead of saying "It was fine," like you always do, today, you told me about a disagreement you had with Jennifer in accounts receivable. And your story—as you call it—was chock-full of insignificant details. Big red flag! I also noticed you paused a lot while telling your really, really detailed story about . . . Jennifer. As if you needed to create more realistic-sounding facts.

Yes, I asked for more communication, but not this kind. Huh? You know exactly what kind I'm talking about. The kind where you make up stories to hide your philandering!

Okay, I'll calm down. Yes, I'll give you some space. In fact, I think I'll go to a meeting. Maybe that'll give you enough time to come up with more details. About you and . . . Jennifer.

In spite of myself:

God, show me how I can improve my communication today.

Rainbows

My Irish grandmother was a tough old bird who chewed tobacco and slept with a loaded shotgun next to her bed. She used phrases like "I'll slap the chops off ya" and "Don't go pissin' on mah rainbow."

Even at the tender age of seven, I could tell Grandma Belle was calling me out for being a downer. She could sense my predisposition toward negativity and neurosis, though I always figured my predisposition toward negativity and neurosis was driven by being the only kid in school whose grandmother slept with a loaded shotgun.

Now that I've spent some time in recovery, I have a different perspective on Grandma Belle. True, she was completely inappropriate, and today, her lifestyle would undoubtedly prompt a visit from the department of social services, but I've come to see her phrases as a reminder for me to "Live and let live."

Now, when I want to tell a friend why she shouldn't quit her day job to pursue her dream of performing with a mime troupe, I think about Grandma Belle in her old rocking chair holding a tin of Skoal. And while it's an intimidating image, it's a reminder for me to stay out of other people's business.

Al-Anon teaches me to allow other people the dignity of having and pursuing their dreams, no matter how insane they may seem. It's their rainbow; who am I to piss on it? More importantly, *how* am I to piss on it?

In spite of myself:

God, help me look for my own rainbow today.

Thanksgiving Pie

There's nothing like a Drama Queen's Homemade Thanksgiving Pecan Pie. This recipe's been passed down in my family for generations, and it's my favorite! Hope ya'll enjoy it!

Drama Queen's Homemade Thanksgiving Pecan Pie
1 freezer-burned piecrust, leftover from last Thanksgiving
8 cups festering anger
2 lbs. of Will your mom show up with her carnival-
    worker beau?
1 oz. I told you there'd be no grocery stores open this late
1 lb. pecans . . . to go in . . . What? I don't know—do I look like
    I know how to make a pecan pie from scratch?
1 dollop of superiority

Place pecans in a bowl and mix with sugar. Offer a fifty-minute lecture on how you keep this dysfunctional family together. Toss in a comment about how all this needless drama makes it hard for you to remember things like what goes into a stupid pecan pie! Storm into the bathroom and refuse to come out until someone turns down the damn TV and asks you how therapy is going. Exit dramatically, and return to the kitchen to finish layering the pecans and sugar mixture in a mostly frozen piecrust. Heave it into the oven and crank the temperature up to 650 degrees. Bake until your mother-in-law and her boyfriend arrive to show off their identical neck tattoos.

Before dinner's halfway over, begin clearing the table, complaining about the long drive ahead of you. Smile and tell everyone you hope they've enjoyed the pecan pie you made from scratch.

In spite of myself:
Nothing like Thanksgiving with family!

QTIP

I have a weakness for Q-tips. In fact, whenever I'm at a pharmacy, the first thing I do is scan the personal care section and ask, *Am I out of Q-tips yet? So many pretty pastel colors . . . I should probably stock up, just in case.* I have so many Q-tips that it takes a crowbar to get one out of the jar, but I've always got the perfect housewarming gift!

In Al-Anon, QTIP, "Quit taking it personally," reminds us that people's reactions aren't personal. It's about them. Or, if I want to get all existential about it, *people's reactions are merely projections of their own reality.*

I have to remind myself that other people's behavior—even if it *is* in reaction to something I've done—is *their* own choice. The truth is, not even my own family knows me entirely, so how on earth could someone I met this year, month, or within the past fifteen minutes . . . know me? They can't. And if they don't know me, why would their reactions have *anything* to do with me?

They don't, and they can't.

So, now, when I start trying to read someone else's mind and anticipating their reactions, I pull out a QTIP—the slogan, not the kind from the pharmacy. That is, unless I'm on my way to a housewarming party.

In spite of myself:
Q-tips should never be placed in the ear canal.
Ears are self-cleaning organs.

Active Listening

I was talking on the phone with a friend from Al-Anon. She was depressed about the state of her . . . entire life.

"I made a list of all the bad relationships, and it occurred to me that I might have a wonderful life by now if I hadn't been so needy," she moaned.

"Don't be silly, you aren't needy," I told her in my most consoling voice. *My God*, I thought, *this chick is so needy!* As she continued to drone on for the next hour about every relationship she'd been in, I started to think: *Could it be that people in Al-Anon are lying to me by not telling me the truth? Are they patronizing me, pretending to be listening while doing other things, looking up the meaning of words like "emetophobia" (the fear of vomit, generally as a result of childhood trauma)?*

Suddenly, I began to feel guilty. Should I come out and tell my friend the truth? Should I say, "Yeah, you're pretty needy, maybe you should consider getting help for that"? Instead, I looked up the definitions of "*passive listening*" and "*active listening.*"

All of a sudden, my friend said, "Thanks for listening, and not telling me to look at my neediness."

I hung up, feeling pretty virtuous for having been of service. And then I began to worry. *What were my friends lying to me about?* More importantly, what were *they* doing while I was on the phone with them?

In spite of myself:

I'm glad God's a better listener than me.

Al-Anon Intervention

SHOW SUMMARY:

Al-Anon Intervention is a riveting series that profiles Al-Anons whose friends and families feel that the only option is to hold an intervention. Each documentary profiles the lives of several Al-Anons struggling with—what else?—a world that won't cooperate with them, and it's making them mad! We'll take an unflinching look at these codependent drama queens and how they create crises, making everyone around them miserable.

Each airing ends at a hotel where friends, family, and a professional interventionist meet for a staged family event. When the Al-Anon arrives and, as predicted, tries to take control and boss everyone around, the surprise intervention takes place. Will the Al-Anons allow someone else to help them? If they do, well, we'll have no show. But more than likely, they won't. In fact, we're banking on it.

EPISODE ONE:

Carol's frequent hacking into her forty-year-old son's e-mail is finally confronted, Amy's blind date asks her to stop introducing him as her "future husband," and Larry's wife discovers him hiding—again—in the trunk of her car when she arrives at her scrapbooking class.

In spite of myself:
Will the Al-Anon allow someone to help?

Hope

Our lives, no matter how battered and degraded,
will yield hope to share with others.
—From Survival to Recovery

Hope is cool, I thought when I heard this in a meeting—*for other people. But what I need right now is a solution to my problems, people. Screw hope!*

By the time I got into Al-Anon, hope was just some corny ideal. I'd convinced myself that things just didn't work out for "people like me," and I was more comfortable riding the Dark Horse of Despair. Even though I didn't ride horses. But if I did, you can be sure it would have been a dark one. A despairing, dark one.

As time went on and I developed a relationship with my Higher Power, I started to believe in the remote possibility that things just might work out. I began to hope for a bigger, better life, and most importantly, I began to believe that I had a loving Higher Power who really was on my side and that, maybe, I might have something to offer and share with others.

Then things really began to change. I took a dance class and voice lessons, and I learned how to ride a horse. I became an expert at solving cryptograms (puzzles consisting of short pieces of encrypted text). This, my friends, is what hope can do for you. Maybe you should give it a try.

In spite of myself:
Today I'll make a list of things I just might hope for!

Intense, Man

In one of my all-time favorite comedies, *The Jerk*, Navin Johnson (Steve Martin) tells his new girlfriend:

> I know we've only known each other four weeks and three days, but to me it seems like nine weeks and five days. The first day seemed like a week, and the second day seemed like five days. And the third day seemed like a week again, and the fourth day seemed like eight days.
>
> On the fifth day you went to see your mother, and that seemed just like a day, and then you came back, and later on the sixth day, in the evening, when we saw each other, that started seeming like two days, so in the evening it seemed like two days spilling over into the next day, and that started seeming like four days, so at the end of the sixth day, on into the seventh day, it seemed like a total of five days. And the sixth day seemed like a week and a half.

This just about sums up every one of my love relationships before Al-Anon, except mine progressed a little more quickly.

I'm so glad I'm in recovery, because I'm learning to take things day by day. Even when one day seems like it's been a week and a half.

In spite of myself:
I'll not confuse time or intensity with quality.

DECEMBER

Lower Standards

When you get stuck, lower your standards.
—WILLIAM STAFFORD

I often repeat this quote to myself because, as an Al-Anon, it's important that I keep my expectations to a minimum.

I learned early on in recovery that my high standards (read: perfectionism) almost always lead to unfulfilled wishes and resentments. I remember one point in my life, when I had a great job, a wonderful man, and lots of friends, looking around my gorgeous condo and thinking, "What if things aren't as good as they could be?" That's a classic example of how I lived before recovery. I was constantly reassessing my situation, petrified that I might be *settling for less*! My lofty expectations had gotten out of hand.

I consider the fact that people with lower standards generally have better lives. How can you be disappointed when you aren't expecting the moon and the stars? I, for one, am enjoying life much more now that I've lowered my standards.

Having lower standards can actually be pleasant. In fact, I'm having a delightful time writing today's meditation because I'm in complete acceptance that it might not be any good. And because I'm learning to lower my standards, I encourage you to do the same. If only for today.

C'mon, you can do it. Just lower the bar.

In spite of myself:
Let's lower them standards a bit today.

The "the"

Step #12: "Having had a spiritual awakening as the result of these steps, we tried to carry this message to others, and to practice these principles in all our affairs."

This Step states that I *will* have a spiritual awakening as "the result," not "a result," of the Steps. One word: "the." As in, it's going to happen, not: "Sure . . . well, it *could* happen." It's a promise.

This gives me hope that if I do the work, I'll experience a real connection to a Higher Power, and I'll share it with others. The results will be apparent.

In time, I'll come to see that *certain* situations—the ones that used to end in hair pulling and kicking—are fewer and farther between. For instance, instead of being the passive-aggressive grocery clerk who throws a customer's shopping bags into the trunk, loading the heavy cans on top of her bread and eggs, I'll do the opposite. I'll put the heavy items on bottom, and the fragile things on top.

This Step promises me that if I practice these principles in all my affairs and actions, I will feel a connection with my Higher Power, I'll be happy to have a job and eager to be of service, and I'll take things in stride. And when a customer is insolent, I won't even consider ramming her SUV with a shopping cart "by accident."

In spite of myself:

God, help me practice these principles,
especially when I don't feel like it.

Continuation

Today I seriously thought twice about continuing with this meditation book. I mean, who am I to try to inspire anyone or share about Al-Anon recovery? I'm just another knucklehead trudging through life. No one would lose sleep if I didn't complete this book. In fact, at least 7 billion people wouldn't even notice.

"You have the gift of experience, strength, and hope," my Al-Anon friend said. "You're not helping anyone if you don't finish the meditation book. Your job is to complete it, even if only one person reads it. And even if that one person hates it."

I had actually never even considered that the one person who might read this book might hate it.

Despite how I'm feeling today, I have decided to finish the book. I don't know why, but I think the way my friend put things made my efforts seem sort of noble. Plus, it's already December. I might as well just get it done.

Update: I'm feeling much better since I began imagining myself on various talk shows, envisioning my face on buses, and picturing myself winning all types of awards, like "Worldwide Inspirer."

Your turn. Who will you inspire today?

In spite of myself:
Today I will share my experience, strength,
and hope in whatever way I can.

Late Arrivals

My sponsor has worked with one sponsee for *twenty-nine years*. When I heard that, I wept. Not because I was so touched, but because I've never done *anything* in life for twenty-nine years. Unless you include dieting.

It made me sad/depressed/angry/jealous/envious and filled with self-pity because I came so late to the Al-Anon party, and I could have been so much better if I'd arrived earlier.

It takes a special kind of person to be willing to spend thousands of hours listening to another person drone on about their problems without getting any kind of kickback for it. For God's sake, there are times when I want to hang up on myself because I can't imagine being on the other end of the phone line.

But my sponsor listens, treats me with kindness and love, and never gives up on me. She even says movie-script-inspiring things, like, "We don't throw anyone out in Al-Anon," which makes me even more depressed—because there *are* a few people I've been tempted to throw out.

Okay, not throw out. Maybe . . . relocate.

I may have come late to the Al-Anon party, but I'm glad I made it. And I look forward to being the one who might say something movie-script-inspiring one day. But even if I don't, I'm sticking around till the end of the party!

In spite of myself:

I may have arrived late,
but I'm staying till the end of the party.

Temps

Sometimes when I'm overwhelmed and confused by the effect that alcoholism has had on my life, the only thing that helps is to remember that this is all . . . temporary. To put it another way, life is like a temp job in that it will end. Eventually.

When I approach life like it's a temporary assignment, I can cope with things better. When I'm temping, nobody expects me to be extra-smart, and there's less pressure to be "the best." Problems don't seem dire, I don't react as intensely, and the crazy habits of the slackers I have to deal with are much easier to handle. Even when my challenges seem too great, I can trust that my feelings will shift if I turn them over to God.

It's not like I look at disease, loss, or death now and laugh in their faces, but when I remember I'm not the CEO and this is all temporary, it's easier to handle my assignments.

Being an existential "temp" is an alternative for people like me who've been accused of being "too sensitive" or neurotic. And if I totally hate things, I can always ask my Higher Power for another assignment. Which I probably won't get, but that's not the point.

The point is, nothing is permanent, including me. I will show up and do my part, but I'm not the boss anymore. God's running the business, which means I should probably stop taking those extra-long breaks.

In spite of myself:

It's temporary. I don't have to know everything today.

Dangerous Streets

I never gave much thought to that slogan about the "mind being a dangerous neighborhood" when I first came into Al-Anon.

My mind wasn't dangerous. *My* mind was pretty sharp. Yes, it had been both a blessing and a curse, what with my formidable intellect and prodigious mental capacity. But all in all, my mind was rich and sweet, and full of flavor, like a pumpkin spice latte or peppermint mocha ice cream.

And then I found myself curled up in a ball on the floor of my kitchen after having spent a week in total isolation, avoiding friends and meetings, thinking some very dark thoughts about myself and other people. Mostly other people. Finally, I picked up the phone and called a friend in the program.

"Go for a walk or a run, just don't do any more thinking," she said. "Your mind is a dangerous neighborhood right now."

She was right. My mind wasn't just staggeringly unique and exceptional; it was also *dangerous*, inhabited by monsters, an evil grade school math teacher, and a vision of my future decrepit self pushing a shopping cart filled with feral cats.

That frightening neighborhood is uncomfortable, but it also feels very familiar and real, until I call someone who can offer perspective and remind me that when it's good, it's good, but when it's bad, it's *really* bad.

The best thing for me to do when I'm in that kind of neighborhood is to stop thinking and make a run for it.

In spite of myself:

My mind can be a dangerous neighborhood,
so I'll let God push the shopping cart.

Al-Anon Book of the Month

When it comes to love, Al-Anons want it all: intrigue, drama, desire, bad dialogue, and happily ever after. Today, Al-Anon's American Romance Series presents the Book of the Month, *Betting on the Crazy.*

Brie Chastenberry is happy enough with her life, living in the big city, working for a bustling PR firm. After suddenly losing her job with no explanation, Brie escapes to the Carolina countryside in an effort to bond with her estranged sister, Pilaf.

High-powered financier Conoco Phillips knows how to win. Phillips is a self-made man who's worked his way up from the stockyards of Brixton to become one of London's most powerful bankers. He's resolute, gorgeous, generous, and irresistible. Also, an expert bull rider. His clients, the children of Lord Gramercy of London, have sent Conoco to the Carolina countryside to find their newly discovered half-sister, Pilaf.

When Conoco meets Brie and Pilaf, the lines began to blur. Distracted by the gorgeous, bull-riding financier, Brie is torn by her attraction to Conoco and his seeming interest in Pilaf, who, unbeknownst to him, is also his half-sister!

A storm is brewing on the Carolina ranch. For Pilaf, the discovery of a new family, which happens to be one of the world's most powerful dynasties, and for Brie . . . a chance to find true love. For Conoco, the choice between two lovely women who will forever alter his life. Is this the beginning of a passionate whirlwind, or a deadly hurricane of ambition, desire, and reckoning?

In spite of myself:

I will always bet on the crazy.

The Worst

There are times when I receive an e-mail from my boss and I assume it's going to read, "I've decided I made a huge mistake when I hired you. You're vastly overpaid, not that talented, and a bit dim. Anyway, no need to come back in tomorrow."

Even in the program, if I'm doing an excessive amount of thinking, I assume the worst of everything: myself, others, institutions, and especially the government.

The one exception: dogs. I almost always assume the best intentions of dogs. For instance, I never, ever think they're going to bite me, even though a German shepherd bit me when I was a little kid.

Maybe it's a character defect, but it seems that I'm always trying to prepare for the worst.

No one will show up for dinner. He doesn't love me anymore. I have no friends left. It's probably a brain tumor. My life will never get better.

I'm so thankful for Al-Anon, because I get love and understanding from people who care about me and who know what I mean when I say things like, "My life is the worst it has ever been." They've been there, too; it's just that they've chosen not to stay there. At least, not permanently.

In spite of myself:
God, help me remember that it's
rarely the worst it's ever been.

Vents

I used to be a big believer in "venting"—you know, letting it all out. Things would happen, I'd react all over the place, and I'd "let it out." I didn't want to set myself up for a heart attack by holding everything in and just losing it one day.

The problem is, when I would vent, *I* may have gotten it "out" and moved on, but not everyone else moved on with me. Even though I was only venting, and I didn't mean harm, I would get over it, but they wouldn't. I was a walking time bomb, and I was harming other people and leaving messes all over the place.

My vents were usually aimed at totally innocent people whom I didn't even know. "Hey, don't take your frustrations out on me!" they'd say, but I couldn't help myself. I was mad as hell at alcoholism, and was experiencing so much grief that I was constantly exploding.

While I'm no longer overwhelmed by anger, there are times when I need an outlet for my frustrations—throwing ice cubes at a wall, kickboxing classes, therapy, talking to my sponsor, sharing at a meeting—which doesn't include freaking out. If I give myself enough time to let the dust settle, instead of using another person to "let it out" on, I can find healthier outlets.

When I stop to look for the right kind of help, which always involves connecting with my Higher Power, I feel less like a blathering lunatic and more like someone who just needs to talk things through. When I do that, there's never a mess to clean up. There's rarely a mess to clean up. Let's put it this way: Things go better when I lay off of the venting.

In spite of myself:

I'll let the dust settle before venting about anything today.

The End

I liken my Al-Anonism to certain movies I love watching over and over again, even though I know how badly they're going to end. For example, I knew things were not going to end well for our sixteenth president, but I still went to the theater to see *Lincoln*. And every time the movie *Titanic* airs on TV, I'm on the edge of my seat for the entire three and a half hours. Waiting. To see what will happen . . . to a ship I *know is going to go down, killing most of the people on board.*

How is this like Al-Anon? I'm so glad you asked! You see, I've often walked into relationships, or jobs, or partnerships where I thought, *I know where this is headed, and I probably should buy tickets to a different movie.* But I didn't; I went ahead and bought the ticket to a story I knew was going to have a bad ending.

Sometimes, even after hearing horrible reviews, I'll still go see a movie, just because I want to experience the craziness and the drama, even though I know it'll ruin my day. Because of Al-Anon, I'm starting to trust myself, and I'm learning not to buy that ticket or go to that theater, although it's intriguing. That is when I ask my Higher Power for the courage to follow through with my decisions.

I hope you get what I'm saying, because I've run out of movie metaphors to mix. The point is, when I know the plot's bad or depressing, and the ending won't satisfy me, it's probably best if I don't buy the ticket.

In spite of myself:

God, give me the courage not to buy *that* ticket.
You know the one.

Stand Up, Sit Down

I heard the speaker at an open AA meeting say, "Fall seven times. Stand up eight." I rolled it around in my head and made a thoughtful face, like the deep person I wanted to be.

I pondered his words a few more times and I decided to change it up a bit. Here, my friends, is the unrecovered Al-Anon version of that phrase:

Fall seven times. And . . . think about this for a moment. Do you really want to get up? There's a relatively strong possibility that if you get up, you're going to fall down again, like that guy said. So really, what's the point? You could lay, or lie, or just sit here for a bit, like you are resting. You could pretend someone else tripped you, or make a scene by throwing your hands up and yelling, "Help, I've fallen and I can't get up!" Surely no one's heard that one in a while.

And if you did, someone might help you. They might also walk right by and totally ignore you—which is more likely. And that would be a real drag. Uncomfortable . . . humiliating. There's nothing more humiliating than asking for help and being ignored.

It's probably better to stay put until you can pull yourself up on your own, when you're ready. You're an Al-Anon; you don't need anyone else's help. Besides, even if someone else did try to help you, they'd most certainly screw it up.

You're an Al-Anon. You don't need anyone else's help.

In spite of myself:
I may fall down seven times, but I refuse to ask for help up!

Open Letter to Mother Birds

Dear Mother Birds,

It has come to my attention that millions of baby birds are being pushed out of their nests every day. Whether they're ready for it or not. I've heard rumors that these innocent animals are being forced out of perfectly good nests and pushed into premature flight at alarming rates.

What's all the pushing about, Mama? Why so aggressive with the warm-blooded vertebrates who've done you no harm? Do you honestly believe that heaving us, er, them, out of their nest will teach them to survive in a harsh world? Might you consider that some simply need more time to . . . launch?

No one is questioning your parenting methods, but you might want to reconsider your "I know best" and "one-size-fits-all" approach to life. Some of us may need a soft, warm place to land, three square meals a day, and time to chill out a little before being thrust into the cruel world. If you could cool it with all the shoving, we'd much appreciate it.

Far be it from me to tell you how to run your life, but you may want to check out a program called Al-Anon. That's a suggestion, by the way, and by no means a criticism. Anyway, happy foraging, and have a lovely day.

Sincerely,

Anonymous

In spite of myself:

Could it be I don't always know what's best for others?

Miracles

I was celebrating my fourth year in recovery; I was taking a birthday cake (my home group celebrates birthdays by "taking cakes") at an Al-Anon meeting, and I felt great!

After I'd taken my cake and was leaving the meeting, one of the men who knew me from my early days in the program stopped me. "You know, when you first started coming to this meeting, I thought, 'What a mess. This poor woman can't even tie her own shoelaces!'"

He then cited a few examples of how unstable I seemed when he first met me.

At first, I seriously considered clocking him. "Listen, buddy," I wanted to say, "I acted like a mess because I *was a mess*. I wasn't purposefully trying to be a kook. I didn't *know* any better. If I'd known better, I would have done better. Duh!"

He finally stopped and added, "You're so grounded and together now. You're a complete miracle of the program."

Then I felt bad for wanting to clock him, because he was being sincere. And he was right. I am more grounded and capable, but I didn't say that aloud. Instead, I smiled and thanked him.

Recovery has taught me to think twice about speaking my initial thoughts, and also about clocking people. Especially when they've just called me a "miracle." Which is, in itself, a complete miracle.

In spite of myself:

Today I'll thank God for all the miracles, even me.

Sexy Program

Sometimes I get depressed when I think about being a codependent Al-Anon, because it just doesn't sound as sexy or as intense as being an alcoholic or an addict.

Al-Anons aren't traditionally known for being the most exciting group; we're the Anthony Michael Hall character in *Sixteen Candles*—obsessive to a fault, kind of nerdy, and neurotic. We actually *like* rules and crave structure, and few people, other than other Al-Anons or codependents, truly "get" us. Our stories, while they might be peculiar, are rarely as riotous as the stories of people in those "other programs."

I'm not bashing Al-Anons and codependents, because we truly are phenoms—compulsive and nutty—and we don't even need a substance to get that way! For instance, I was once thrown in jail for assaulting a police officer. Not exactly assaulting, but I did serve two hours in jail for smarting off to a cop who pulled me over in downtown L.A., and I wasn't even drunk!

I retract my previous statement about codependents not being intense or sexy enough. We are. The fact that we can get out of control and wreak havoc, without the help of anyone or anything, makes us well kind of . . . extreme . . . badass, and that's . . . pretty sexy!

In spite of myself:

Let's hear it for the sexy program!

Reviews

The only thing exposed in the movie
by this writer/director is a lack of thought.
—HOLLYWOOD REPORTER

The reviews for my film were in. Some were good, some were not so good, and then, there was *that* one. I was devastated. The beginning and ending of my career as The Indie Filmmaker Who Was Going to Make a Difference—the forebear to a movement generating films made about strong, interesting women who weren't afraid to laugh at themselves.

But God had other plans, and that isn't what happened, thanks to the stupid critic who ruined my career.

In reality, my career as a hotshot filmmaker didn't happen because that wasn't my Higher Power's plan for me, and today, I'm fine with that. Because by the time I'd finished the film, my career had become my "Higher Power," and I was *not* happy.

Years have passed since that review, and when I read it now, it doesn't sting at all, because other people's opinions don't mean as much as they used to. Al-Anon has taught me that not everyone will like my work, and it might even get panned, but I can still keep creating and have a good life.

It's not like I'm super spiritual or I'm made of Teflon, but my opinion of myself today is way more important than my critics'. I'm a child of God who is lovable whether or not anyone else agrees. Especially my critics, no matter what form they take.

In spite of myself:

Hey, God, thanks for thinking I'm great,
despite what other people may think.

Big Deal

"I can't show up at that event alone," I said to my friend who was canceling on our plans. "What will everyone think?"

My clever but unreliable friend replied, "They'll probably think, 'Hey, that lady is here by herself.' Then they'll think, 'Does my hair look good parted on the left side? Will I ever find a meaningful relationship that will last?' Most people are not as concerned about you as they are about themselves."

When I get wrapped up in how Big of a Deal I am, when I put myself in the lead role, I always overestimate the amount of time people spend thinking about me. I also spend less time wondering what God thinks of me, and I lose sight of what's important. I'm generally happier when I keep the focus off myself and on my Higher Power.

One of the gifts recovery has given me is the ability to step out of the spotlight and be "one of the crowd," and it never fails to relieve my fears.

"Go, have fun, and forget about what other people think," my flaky friend continued, "because, if you want to know how much others think about you, consider how often you think about them. Then extrapolate."

I think she was just trying to make me feel better because she was canceling. I *know* there are plenty of people who think about *me* more than that.

In spite of myself:
I always feel better when I share the spotlight.

Fandytale

One of the characters from the TV show *Burning Love* said she believed in "fandytales," where fantasy and fairy tales come true. In my fandytale, I'd be a mermaid/supermodel/brain surgeon married to George Clooney.

As the total package femme fatale of the sea—the perfect combination of athletic grace, brains, and beauty—my life would be superb. I'd voyage across oceans, morphing from a mermaid into a supermodel/brain surgeon whenever humans were in peril, someone needed brain surgery, or there was a red carpet event—my doting husband, George, at my side. I'm not sure how the morphing from mermaid into a brain surgeon would work, or what I'd use to keep my skin soft and supple—or, candidly, how poor George would breathe underwater. But particulars aren't important when it comes to fandytales.

What *is* important in fandytales is that I get *everything I want.* No hardships, cellulite, or upset friends. No worries about the future or working deadlines. Just me, the ocean, and George. And his oxygen tank. Because the more I think about it, the more I worry. What if George can't swim?

I suppose that is why fandytales and details don't go together.

In spite of myself:
Do I prefer fandytales to reality?

Distractions

I'd hit bottom. I was sitting in my nephew's red loaner pickup truck, formulating my plan. I would run a garden hose from the exhaust pipe to the front seat, hit the "play" button on my iPod and . . . well, you can fill in the blank. The problem was, I couldn't remember if the truck had a catalytic converter—which is what releases carbon monoxide, according to my uncle. At least, that's what I think he said. Also, since I'd lost my home and no longer had a garage, I was terrified of someone interrupting me or, God forbid, some poor kid discovering my body in a public garage.

Also, I didn't have a garden hose.

So, I drove to Goodwill in search of a hose. And that was when the miracle happened. I noticed a gorgeous silk suit in *exactly* my size, and then I saw an *almost new* Burberry coat. *Burberry? For ten bucks?*

I was at a crossroads: the suit, the coat, or the hose? I couldn't afford them all. If I were dead, I wouldn't have any of them. I sat down on the floor and cried. And then a store clerk came over and took the hose out of my hand. It wasn't for sale. He wiped my tears and whispered, "I'll let you have the suit for a dollar, but that's a Burberry coat, sugar. I can't go lower than ten dollars."

I now know there's a God in heaven who's not finished with me yet because for a moment I had a glimpse of what life could be with that suit and that coat, and in the end, the clothes took precedence over the garden hose. I took myself and my new used clothes straight to an Al-Anon meeting.

In spite of myself:
There's a God, and he's not finished with me yet.

High Anxiety

I was talking to a friend about going to school to get my esthetician's license. I'd been out of work for a long time, and I needed something to do. And, well, I like skin. It seemed logical.

"School is a good idea for people like you," said my friend when I told her my plans, "who tend to be anxious." While I may be someone who tends to be anxious, I have a real problem when other people try to identify me as such. I'm already worried about the fact that I'm fearful. It's not like I want to be, or like I don't think about *not* being anxious. In fact, I think about my anxiety a lot and I wonder if it's another way to self-sabotage. Or, is it just a character defect? Will it go away someday when I'm not looking?

Anxiety is like trying to think of everything all at once and figure it all out, but it's really thinking about nothing—running in circles—and it rarely does me, or anyone else, much good.

Recovery has taught me to laugh about my high-strung ways. A little. I don't find them to be funny ha-ha, but I accept that they're a part of me, for now. I can be anxious about my anxiety, or I can accept that it has served me in some ways—I just can't think of them right now.

Instead of stressing over my stress, I take contrary, non-anxious actions and try not to freak out on insensitive people who infer that I'm "tightly wound." Because I'm not. So much. Anymore.

In spite of myself:
Thanks to recovery, I don't have to harm people who call me "high-strung."

Countdown

Five more shopping days till Christmas.

I'm going to do it differently this year. I'm not waiting until the last minute to get things done—no! This year, I am going to organize a caroling party and write out—by hand—all of my Christmas cards. I'm going to make wassail and sew gold-shellacked angels. I'll hang garlands above my entryway and even bake a gingerbread house from scratch! *Five days. Totally doable. One hundred and twenty hours.*

This year, I'm going the crafty gift route, including homemade organic chocolate bars; sugar-free, sustainable boysenberry jam; and canned pineapple and mango chutney.

I'll be gracious to everyone I meet, even if they step over me to get to the cupcake toppers at the craft store or take the last two spots in the parking lot with their stupid Priuses. I'm going to spread love everywhere I go this season, no matter what other people do. I'm going to act as if my character defects of impatience, annoyance, discontentment, and irritability have all been removed.

Five days. I can do this. God help me.

In spite of myself:
Of course we can do it. We're Al-Anons!

Sunny-Side Up

Holy sunshine, Batman! It's National Look on the Bright Side Day!

Looking on the bright side may be a bit difficult, as it is the winter solstice, which is the shortest day of the year. And since December days tend to be cloudy, it might not be easy to find a ray of light. You may *want* to pull the shades and hide under the covers, but not today! Because, in spite of this grave-sounding, heavy winter-solstice discussion, I have faith that *you will* succeed at being optimistic!

Just the name National Look on the Bright Side Day itself makes you want to look for something positive in what might otherwise be a bad situation. Doesn't it? You see, bad experiences can offer us great wisdom. Yes, it's true that the lessons are seldom apparent. Or, they don't occur to us until after we've forgotten the point, or are at a place in our lives where we don't care anymore.

Isn't life funny? Or, as Alanis Morissette might say, "ironic"?

If you had a bad day yesterday, or you're having one right now, I want you to Look on the Bright Side. Forget bad experiences and ignore the rain, whether it's on the outside or it's inside your soul. Today, find one thing you're optimistic about and think about it all day long, as many times as you can.

Come on, Sunshine, you can do it!

In spite of myself:

No matter how small it is,
I will focus on that ray of light today!

Regifting

Before I came into Al-Anon, I used to take whatever came my way—*especially* when it came to gifts. If someone gave me a present, I told myself I *had* to love it, even if I secretly didn't like it or I could tell it was a regift. I thought it would be uncouth or selfish not to pretend I loved it.

In Al-Anon, I learned that it's *okay* to want what I *really* want. I don't have to like something because it's free—like those monochromatic carbohydrate breakfasts they serve at commuter hotels—or because my cousin got it online for a discount, or because it came in a package of four. I especially don't have to like something because *someone else tells me* I should like it, or because it's supposed to be good for me.

I might not get what I really want, but by golly, because of Al-Anon, at least now I know what I want. Sometimes I'll even ask for it ahead of time, you know, as in, "This year, for my birthday, I'd love to have dinner with you," or, "For Christmas, I'd really love a gift card to Home Depot" (that'll be the day—but you get the point).

I've also come up with a way to deal with people who are bad at regifting. When I get an obvious regift, I thank the person and write their name on what they've given me. That way I know exactly what to give them *next* Christmas.

Not really. I'm way too Al-Anony to do something *that* obvious.

In spite of myself:

I may not get what I want,
but at least I know how to ask for it now!

Cheers!

During the holidays, it's easy to think I'm the only one who's having a hard time. Everyone else looks like the Macy's picture of holiday joy; they all have perfect houses with perfect green lawns, no one's gossiping or fighting, nobody's wearing off-brand labels, and their children are well-behaved.

The truth is, many people struggle with the holidays. And the thing that *always* lifts my spirits without fail is doing something for someone else. So if you are feeling blue, or challenged by the holidays, we're going to do three things that will lift your spirits. And if you *aren't* feeling a little wistful, you might be suffering from something called "denial," but that's for another day.

Set aside the next ten minutes to sit quietly. You don't have to pretend to be all grateful or spiritual, just close your eyes, sit quietly, and breathe. For ten minutes.

So, how'd you feel? Were you happy? Sad? Lonely? Did you notice the feelings just came and went?

Now, you're going to call two people you know and wish them a lovely day. Just a short, friendly call to let them know you're thinking of them.

Next, you're going to do one *small* thing for someone today without letting anyone know you did it.

The purpose of this exercise is getting the focus off of yourself. In the long run, life feels much better when you're helping someone else than when you're thinking about what a bad time you're having. Trust me, it works.

In spite of myself:
If you did this exercise, you're super cool!
If you didn't, try again tomorrow.

Rush

One of the things I remember most about growing up in Crazytown with crazy divorced parents was being rushed around the city during the holidays to see everyone before the day was over. This was, of course, immensely enjoyable for me.

"Are you done with that slice of turkey?" my mother would say, grabbing the plate out of my hand. "You look full. Your father's waiting outside for you!"

As a result, in addition to being an extremely fast eater, I became adept at figuring things out. When someone's pulling turkey dinner out of your hands, you learn to move fast and make decisions. The upside was that I was in business mode before I'd hit third grade, strategizing about college and negotiating deals with teachers and coaches. The downside was that I was plotting my escape while other kids were, I dunno, eating Christmas dinner and having fun.

Recovery was hard for me. I couldn't control it or speed it up. I still can't, and I don't like it. But I'm learning to trust my Higher Power, and that even when everyone else is going nuts, I might need to just take it easy. Sometimes it means sitting quietly and waiting for answers; at other times, it means trusting my gut and taking action.

Even if everyone else is moving at warp speed, I don't have to join in. I can relish the holidays in my way, at my pace, no matter what other people's agendas are. Lord have mercy, though, on *anyone* who tries to take my turkey dinner out of my hands.

In spite of myself:
No rushing required. God is taking care of me today.

Merry, Merry

I recall one holiday season when a family member changed the date and location of our Christmas dinner, but didn't tell me until Christmas Eve that we wouldn't be celebrating Christmas until the day *after* Christmas.

"WHO THE HECK CELEBRATES CHRISTMAS THE DAY AFTER CHRISTMAS?" I screamed at her over the phone.

This family member will adamantly deny that it happened that way and will also claim that I'm too dramatic and I need to "get over it." Yes, I'm dramatic, but I'm not exaggerating when I say I was devastated. The change of plans ruined my holiday. I didn't know where I'd go for Christmas.

Christmas Eve was pretty rough. However, as the day went on, I began to realize that this was a common pattern with my family, and those last-minute changes had always created a ton of anxiety for me. I decided not to let melancholy and depression ruin my Christmas Day. I had some pretty cool friends in recovery to share the holiday with.

Now it's a tradition: I wouldn't think of celebrating Christmas without my Al-Anon friends. They understand me, even when I'm being dramatic. And they never tell me to "get over" my feelings.

Thankfully, I can count on my friends in recovery to celebrate a holiday on the day it was meant to be celebrated. They may show up late, but they'll never pretend it's a Tuesday when it's a Saturday.

In spite of myself:
I'm going to have a wonderful Christmas Day,
even if I have to change my plans.

Swoop and Bash

Kurt Vonnegut once said that there are two types of writers: "swoopers" and "bashers." "Swoopers" throw everything down on a page, then edit and reedit until it becomes a coherent story. "Bashers" work sentence by sentence, only moving on when the story is perfect.

Both work hard, and neither is better. They're just different.

Recovery is a little like writing. There are the "swoopers," the ones who dig in, get a sponsor, and throw themselves into the Step work. The "bashers" take their time, making sure they're ready before they invest in or commit to the next phase of their recovery.

Accepting we're all doing recovery differently allows us to keep going. Whether we're struggling with a page full of hackneyed twists and trite clichés, or trying to manage angry outbursts and tame our impatient nature, there is no "right" way to do it. There will be times when we're really bad at recovery. Until we aren't anymore.

You have all the time you need. There's no judge, no program warden standing by, only a loving Higher Power who thinks you're doing fine. It doesn't matter if you're "swooping" or "bashing" your way to recovery, just as long as you're doing it.

In spite of myself:

Swoopers and bashers take heart! Things are going to be fine.

What Plan?

Before Al-Anon, I was obsessed with having a purpose. That was a reaction to growing up in alcoholism, sort of a "screw you" to the people who had harmed me—or so I thought. I wanted to know my purpose because I wanted to *be someone.*

One of the coolest things I've learned in recovery is that it's okay if I don't know what my purpose is. Maybe my purpose is to write a few things, fail at a bunch of other things, and throw tantrums until I learn not to anymore.

In short, I've given up on knowing what the point is.

I've decided to live as if my Higher Power has a plan and a purpose for me, and I don't have to know what they are to be content. God is guiding me, so I can trust and surrender to him. As long as I stay in connection with my Higher Power, keep clear of resentments, love others and myself, and stay in service, I'll be content. And maybe *that* is the purpose. If there's a bigger one, it'll become clear as I'm doing those other things.

Not having a Grand Plan used to scare the heck out of me, but not so anymore. If I follow the guidelines I've just stated, at the very least, I'll be peaceful. And if that's all I'm here to do, then that's okay with me. Which makes me feel better, because there will be plenty of people who don't like what I'm doing. That's okay. At least for right now, especially because I haven't yet heard from any of them.

In spite of myself:

There's nothing to fear; the plan is already happening.

Obsession or Emotion

Today I was confused. *Am I having an emotion, or am I in obsession?* The truth is, I don't always know the difference.

Both emotions and obsessions are very powerful. They involve intense feelings, from giddiness and elation to tears of pain and joy. They both include vulnerability, passion, embarrassment, anger, and fascination, and they often require binoculars, hidden security cameras, and GPS trackers. . . . You see, the similarities are endless! Emotions and obsessions both require a great deal of time away from work (when I have a job), and they affect my sleep. And when it comes to either of them, you can forget about eating, socializing, or showing up for other people.

The difference between being in obsession and having an emotion has never been totally clear to me. So for today, I have decided not to push myself to "get" the difference between the two.

"All good things in time," as my good friends in Al-Anon like to say. All good things in time.

In spite of myself:

Am I having an emotion or an obsession?

Improvement

Before Al-Anon, I did a lot of self-improvement stuff. I wanted to be better, and I really thought that if I concentrated and worked harder, I could *change myself.*

So I decided to create a performance review of my behavior and ask friends to fill it out anonymously. The plan was to find areas where I was lacking and get their feedback.

After my friends stopped laughing—who creates a performance review of themselves?—they agreed, because they're good people. When I read what they wrote, I figured I would just make a few behavior changes and BOOM! I'd be better. That didn't happen. I tried hard to change, but it never seemed to stick.

When I got into Al-Anon, I found out the reasons why I couldn't change myself. I'm not God. Change is not up to me. I can act better, but it's only through working the Steps that lasting change occurs. It doesn't come from my actions, willpower, or striving.

I can't change my own faults, and, strangely enough, the more I try to change, the less I do, and the less I try to change, the more I do. I can't give this stuff too much thought, or I'll start getting all weird about it again. Change comes when it comes.

In spite of myself:

Change isn't up to me. It comes when it comes.

Two Thoughts at Once

I've often heard that you can't have two thoughts at the same time. And I used to believe it, but that was before I experienced myself thinking two thoughts at once.

I was sharing at my Wednesday night meeting, trying to impart recovery and wisdom to the people in the room when it hit me: I'd forgotten where I'd put the package of cheddar cheese I'd just bought! *I took the cheese out of the bag, but what did I do with it after that?* I started to panic. What was coming out of my mouth was recovery and the gratitude list I had written that morning. *How can I lose a package of cheese? What else have I lost that I don't remember? Is this the first sign of Alzheimer's?* That was what my head was saying.

When the meeting was over, I decided it might be time for a mental health check. So I went online and did some research. According to the online mental health experts—and goodness knows I trust them—I'm not insane. A person can have two thoughts simultaneously.

Although I'm not completely persuaded, it gives me relief to know that I'm not the only one who is confused about having two thoughts at one time. In Google's estimation, three million people have asked that very question.

In spite of myself:

Today, I'll turn all of my thoughts over to my Higher Power.

Ideas

New Year's Eve can be more stressful than fun for Al-Anons, because we have *ideas*. Ideas about how the day should go. And they are not *always* realistic.

Although my New Year's Eve conversations have never gone this way, I still wish for that moment, right before midnight, when someone will whisper words I've so longed to hear, which strangely enough sound a lot like a mix between *When Harry Met Sally* and *Jerry McGuire*: "I love that you talk to the coffeemaker and expect a response. I love that you go to Al-Anon all the time and you still can't stay out of everyone else's business. I love that dimple on your left cheek that shows up in pictures. Speaking of pictures, I think it's cute that your eyes are always red in photos you post online. I love you for all the things you are and all that you're not. And it's not because I'm lonely and it's New Year's Eve; it's because you are the closest thing to perfect I've seen. If I had you, I could die happy, having never experienced another New Year's Eve again."

Easy to see why New Year's Eve might bring on anxiety for me, what with all my unmet expectations.

Instead of hoping for the impossible, I've decided to say the following: "Hey, New Year's Eve, you don't have the power to ruin my life with your outlandish expectations. While I appreciate and even love you, you're just another day, and I will keep you in perspective!"

In spite of myself:

No matter how you feel about today,
I love you for all that you are and all that you're not.

The Twelve Steps of Al-Anon

1. We admitted we were powerless over alcohol—that our lives had become unmanageable.
2. Came to believe that a Power greater than ourselves could restore us to sanity.
3. Made a decision to turn our will and our lives over to the care of God *as we understood Him*.
4. Made a searching and fearless moral inventory of ourselves.
5. Admitted to God, to ourselves, and to another human being the exact nature of our wrongs.
6. Were entirely ready to have God remove all these defects of character.
7. Humbly asked Him to remove our shortcomings.
8. Made a list of all persons we had harmed, and became willing to make amends to them all.
9. Made direct amends to such people wherever possible, except when to do so would injure them or others.
10. Continued to take personal inventory and when we were wrong promptly admitted it.
11. Sought through prayer and meditation to improve our conscious contact with God *as we understood Him*, praying only for knowledge of His will for us and the power to carry that out.
12. Having had a spiritual awakening as the result of these steps, we tried to carry this message to others, and to practice these principles in all our affairs.

The Twelve Steps of
Co-Dependents Anonymous

1. We admitted we were powerless over others—that our lives had become unmanageable.
2. Came to believe that a power greater than ourselves could restore us to sanity.
3. Made a decision to turn our will and lives over to the care of God as we understood God.
4. Made a searching and fearless moral inventory of ourselves.
5. Admitted to God, to ourselves, and to another human being, the exact nature of our wrongs.
6. Were entirely ready to have God remove all these defects of character.
7. Humbly asked God to remove our shortcomings.
8. Made a list of all persons we had harmed and became willing to make amends to them all.
9. Made direct amends to such people wherever possible, except when to do so would injure them or others.
10. Continued to take personal inventory and when we were wrong, promptly admitted it.
11. Sought through prayer and meditation to improve our conscious contact with God as we understood God, praying only for knowledge of God's will for us and the power to carry that out.
12. Having had a spiritual awakening as the result of these steps, we tried to carry this message to other codependents, and to practice these principles in all our affairs.

About the Author

Misti B., a writer, filmmaker, and recovering codependent, writes humorous books about life in recovery, shining some light into normally very dark spaces.

Misti's career in entertainment—producing live events, and writing and directing for stage, TV, and film—combined with her dysfunctional upbringing provide the fodder for her gritty but inspiring recovery stories.

About Hazelden Publishing

As part of the Hazelden Betty Ford Foundation, Hazelden Publishing offers both cutting-edge educational resources and inspirational books. Our print and digital works help guide individuals in treatment and recovery, and their loved ones. Professionals who work to prevent and treat addiction also turn to Hazelden Publishing for evidence-based curricula, digital content solutions, and videos for use in schools, treatment programs, correctional programs, and electronic health records systems. We also offer training for implementation of our curricula.

Through published and digital works, Hazelden Publishing extends the reach of healing and hope to individuals, families, and communities affected by addiction and related issues.

For more information about Hazelden publications,
please call **800-328-9000**
or visit us online at **hazelden.org/bookstore.**

Other Titles You Might Like

Conquering Shame and Codependency:
8 Steps to Freeing the True You
Darlene Lancer

Learn to heal from the destructive hold of shame and codependency by implementing eight steps to empower the real you. Softcover, 248 pp. Order No. 7554, also available as an e-book

Codependent No More:
How to Stop Controlling Others
and Start Caring for Yourself
Melody Beattie

This iconic resource on the topic of codependency—which has sold over five million copies since its release—has taught innumerous people when to say yes, when to say no, when to forgive, and when to let go. Softcover, 276 pp.

Order No. 5014, also available as an e-book

Beyond Codependency:
And Getting Better All the Time
Melody Beattie

Learn to live free from someone else's problems and master the art of self-care. With personal stories, insights, and activities, this book helps you navigate beyond codependency into the realm of self-love and emotional security. Softcover, 264 pp.

Order No. 5064, also available as an e-book

Hazelden books are available at fine bookstores everywhere.
To order directly from Hazelden Publishing, call **800-328-9000**
or visit **hazelden.org/bookstore**.

More Titles You Might Like